The Reason of Job

The Reason of Job

How Job and Other Prophets Give Shape to the
Messiah Motif in the Bible and the Qur'an

Ayyub (Job)

A Christian Perspective

Scott Cherry

Forewords by Wissam Al-Aethawi
And Dr. John Leonard

RESOURCE *Publications* • Eugene, Oregon

THE REASON OF JOB
How Job and Other Prophets Give Shape to the Messiah Motif in the Bible and Qur'an

Copyright © 2022 Scott R. Cherry. All rights reserved. Except for brief quotations in critical publications or reviews, no part of this book may be reproduced in any manner without prior written permission from the publisher. Write: Permissions, Wipf and Stock Publishers, 199 W. 8th Ave., Suite 3, Eugene, OR 97401.

Wipf & Stock
An Imprint of Wipf and Stock Publishers
199 W. 8th Ave., Suite 3
Eugene, OR 97401

www.wipfandstock.com

PAPERBACK ISBN: 978-1-7252-9530-8
HARDCOVER ISBN: 978-1-7252-9529-2
EBOOK ISBN: 978-1-7252-9528-5

All English Bible quotations are taken from the English Standard Version (ESV) unless otherwise noted, and they are in italics. To a lesser extent, English quotations from the Qur'an are taken from the Clear Qur'an (quran.com) unless otherwise noted as some other English translation.

Dedications and Acknowledgements

To my wife JoEllen who has always been fascinated with the *Book of Job* to the extent that I sometimes refer to her as "*Job*-Ellen." Also to our daughter Aubrey, our son Cameron, my father Robert, my mother Sue, my stepmother Louann, and my late grandfather Gerard Vonk.

The story of Job has been philosophical fodder for the so-called 'problem of evil,' or of pain and suffering, or theodicy. Therefore I wish to acknowledge three of my favorite UM-Dearborn philosophy professors whose exceptional instruction have made philosophy enchanting to me, and who have all given at least moderate attention to Job in the courses I have taken with them: Dr. Imran Aijaz, Dr. Michael Rosano, and Dr. Velimir Stojkovski. I also wish to acknowledge the fine professors at Detroit Baptist Theological Seminary who have done for theology and Old/New Testament Studies what the aforementioned did for me in philosophy: Pastor Ben Edwards (Dean), Dr. Ryan Meyer, Dr. Tim Miller, Dr. Bruce Compton, Dr. Mark Snoeberger, Dr. John Aloisi, and Dr. Kyle Dunham, whose PhD dissertation was on the *Book of Job*. To Dr. C.J. Williams, Professor of Old Testament Studies at Reformed Presbyterian Theological Seminary (Pittsburgh) whose own book on Job I discovered during the course of this project: *The Shadow of Christ in the Book of Job.* And to Dr. John Leonard, Pastor at Cresheim Valley Presbyterian Church and retired Professor of Practical Theology at Westminster Theological Seminary who has inspired me in many ways since I first met him in 2000.

To some of my young student friends who have engaged me in numerous conversations in which our mutual expectations of good reason and logic have fueled my thinking on this subject: Elmi Habib, Bilal Assi, and other UM-Dearborn students including Zenon Sommers, John Shaheen, Christian Ledford, Anthony Safa, Abdul, Mehdi, Sajad, Hussein, Ishmael, several Mohammeds. and my dear lifelong friend Dr. Ibrahim Sablaban, graduate of Wayne State University.

To my esteemed board members who continually provide me with encouragement and support. These include our recently 'retired' Chairman Dave Wood and our new Chairman Kim Carlson, plus Marc Bayne, Chris Samuel, Bob Kozal, Wayne Stolt, and Jon Frazier.

To Pastor Dave Bayne of Redford Church whose help and encouragement on my last book has carried over into this one.

And finally, to two of my trusted friends and colleagues who invested significant time into proofing and advising me, and who each provided considerable support and encouragement in their own gifted ways: Adam Simnowitz and Wissam Al-Aethawi who wrote the foreword.

Thank you!

"I've never been able to read that sacred tale [of Job] without tears. And how much that is great, mysterious and unfathomable there is in it!"

Afterwards I heard the words of mockery and blame, proud words, "How could God give up the most loved of His saints for the diversion of the devil, take from him his children, smite him with sore boils so that he cleansed the corruption from his sores with a potsherd—and for no object except to boast to the devil! 'See what My saint can suffer for My sake.'?"

But the greatness of [the *Book of Job*] lies just in the fact that it is a mystery—that the passing earthly show and the eternal verity are brought together in it. In the face of earthly truth, the eternal truth is accomplished. The Creator, just as on the first days of creation He ended each day with praise: "That is good that I have created," looks upon Job and again praises His creation. **And Job, praising the Lord, serves not only Him but all His creation for generations and generations, and for ever and ever,** since for that he was ordained. Good heavens, what a book it is, and what lessons there are in it! What a book the Bible is, what a miracle, what strength is given with it to man! It is like a mold cast of the world and man and human nature, everything is there, and a law for everything for all the ages. And what mysteries are solved and revealed!

…Read to them about Abraham and Sarah, about Isaac and Rebecca, of how Jacob went to Laban and wrestled with the Lord in his dream and said, "This place is holy"— and he will impress the devout mind of the peasant. Let him read, especially to the child- ren, how the brothers sold Joseph, the tender boy, the dreamer and prophet, into bondage, and told their father that a wild beast had devoured him, and showed him his blood-stained clothes. Read to them…of how the brothers afterwards journeyed into Egypt for corn, and Joseph, already a great ruler, unrecognized by them, tormented them, accused them, kept his brother Benjamin, and all through love: "I love you, and loving you I torment you." For he remembered all his life how they had sold him to the merchants in the burning desert by the well, and how, wringing his hands, he had wept and besought his brothers not to sell him as a slave in a strange land. And how, seeing them again after many years, he loved them beyond measure, but he harassed and tormented them in love. He left them at last not able to bear the suffering of his heart, flung himself on his bed and wept. Then, wiping his tears away, he went out to them joyful and told them, "Brothers, I am your brother Joseph!" Read to them further how happy old Jacob was on learning that his darling boy was still alive, and how he went to Egypt leaving his own country, and died in a foreign land, bequeathing his great prophecy that had lain mysteriously hidden in his meek and timid heart all his life, that from his offspring, from Judah, will come the great hope of the world, the Messiah and Saviour.

Try reading to them also the tale…of the fair Esther and the haughty Vashti; or the wondrous legend of the prophet Jonah in the belly of the whale. [And] do not forget…the parables of Our Lord, especially those in the Gospel According to St. Luke.

The Brothers Karamazov
Character, Father Zossima
– Fyodor Dostoevsky

Contents

Forewords	xi
Preface, parts 1 and 2	xv

– Part 1 –

1. The Messiah Concept in Culture	1
2. Job, A Pre-Jewish Motif?	17
3. Motifs in the Torah, Tanakh	41
4. Motifs in the Qur'an?	57
5. Was Job's Redeemer a Messiah? Part 1	83
6. Prophets as Redeemers: Noah and Jonah	97
7. Prophet Moses as Redeemer	115
8. Back to Job—the Book and The Man —Job's Redeemer, Part 2	129
9. Job's Reverse Messiah Complex —Redeemer ⟷ Messiah	149
10. Job's Redemption and His Friends' —The Burnt Offering	161

– Part 2 –

11. Job as True Myth and Motif	175
12. The Descent-to-Ascent Motif in the Tanakh	197

13. Prophet–Messiah Jesus —Ultimate Redeemer Motif	227
14. Joseph and Jonah in the New Testament	253
15. Job in the New Testament	267

Appendix	279
1. The 39 Books of the Bible's Old Testament with their traditional authors (Protestant Christian arrangement)	280
2. The Scriptures™ – the Jewish Arrangement of the Old Testament (Tanakh)	283
3. The Tanakh: Cross-reference Hebrew to English names and order with meanings	288
4. The 39 books of the protestant Christian canon as listed in their Jewish arrangement	289
5. Some of the Hebrew Prophets in the historical eras in which they prophesied	292
6. The Hebrew Kings and Prophets – A chronological timeline of the Israelite kings and prophets	294
7. A Comparative Table of Prophets (Islamic)	297
8. Additional explication of the time-lapse between the reported burial and resurrection of Jesus	298
Bibliography	302

وَإِذْ أَخَذْنَا مِنَ ٱلنَّبِيِّـۧنَ مِيثَٰقَهُمْ وَمِنكَ وَمِن نُّوحٍ وَإِبْرَٰهِيمَ وَمُوسَىٰ وَعِيسَى ٱبْنِ مَرْيَمَ ۖ وَأَخَذْنَا مِنْهُم مِّيثَٰقًا غَلِيظًا ٧

And ⌈remember⌉ when We took a covenant from the prophets, as well as from you ⌈O Prophet⌉, and from Noah, Abraham, Moses, and Jesus, son of Mary. We did take a solemn covenant from ⌈all of⌉ them.

—Allah to Muhammad, *Qur;an*,
Surah Al-Ahzab (33:7)

וַיֹּאמֶר יְהוָה אֶל־הַשָּׂטָן הֲשַׂמְתָּ לִבְּךָ עַל־עַבְדִּי אִיּוֹב כִּי אֵין כָּמֹהוּ בָּאָרֶץ אִישׁ תָּם וְיָשָׁר יְרֵא אֱלֹהִים וְסָר מֵרָע:

"Have you considered My servant Job? There is no one like him on earth, a blameless and upright man who fears God and shuns evil!"

—The LORD to Satan,
Book of Job 1:8, Tanakh

λέγει αὐτῇ ὁ Ἰησοῦς Ἐγώ εἰμι, ὁ λαλῶν σοι.

"I who speak to you am he."

– Jesus to the Samaritan woman at the well of Jacob,
Gospel of John 4:26, New Testament, Bible

Forewords تصدير

I. Wissam Al-Aethawi

يحويها هو ما يتفق الكثيرون على انه اصعب جزء من ذلك الكتاب, الا وهو اسفار الحكمة. عرّفني الكتاب المقدس (وانا لا ازال في عالم يكرز الها متعاليا بعيدا يتعامل مع حياتنا المعقدة بجمود لا يرى معه سوى الاسود والابيض), عرفني باله يشعر بالمصائب التي كثر ما نمر بها بل ويمضي من وقته في مشاركة احزاننا ليسأل معنا "لماذا؟" حينما يكون الجواب هو اخر ما نريده. اتحدث هنا بالتاكيد عن "سفر ايوب" والذي تعرفت من خلاله على اله من القدرة بمكان يراني فيه ككيان ماسكا يدي قائلا لي "اعلم ان الظرف صعب واعدك اني ساكون معك خلال كل هذا."

بعد عقد من الزمان, هاجرت من موطني في العراق ودرست الكتاب المقدس لانضم بعدها للخدمة في مدينة ديربورن.

وجاء حينها (سكوت شيري)—الصديق والواعظ والمعلم الذي يحسن الجوار في تلك المدينة المتعددة الثقافات (وايضا الفيلسوف, الا انه لا يحب ان اناديه ذلك ولذا لن اضايقه بذلك اللقب). يتمتع سكوت بشخصية هادئة تدعو من حوله الى الحوار معه وهذا ما يدفعني فيه الى الجنون, الا ان هذا هو بالضبط ما حدا به وبعماد (صديقه المسلم في الكلية) ان يشاركا بالحوار الذي ابتدأ منذ اربعة عشر قرنا من الزمان واتخذا منعطفات وعرة منذ القرن العشرين. مر حوار سكوت وعماد مرور الكرام بقصة ايوب, وبالذبيحة التي امره الله ان يقدمها كفارة لذنوب معزييه الذين فهموا كلام الله ولم يفهموا تطبيقاته, وتلك الكفارة هي التي دفعت سكوت الواعظ ليؤلف هذا الكتاب.

قد تكون لغة الكتاب (نموذج المسيح) عسرة الهضم على المبتدئين, الا ان الكتاب يوفر كل المعلومات اللازمة لفهم اطروحته. يجادل المؤلف ان قصة ايوب هي نموذج المسيح, وان هذا النموذج يتكرر على طول الكتاب المقدس وعرضه. والنموذج هو نمط متكرر يمكن تمييزه مرئيا او سمعيا او خياليا. وايوب هو نموذج من نوع (النزول للصعود) لانه ينحدر الى وادي الياس ليخرج منه بافضل حال. يتولى سكوت طرح مهمة طرح حجته في رحلة تاخذك للكتب السماوية والادب والثقافات المعاصرة ومحاوراته مع اصدقائه, والكتاب مساهمة ثرية للمكتبة المسيحية وقد يكون بركة شخصية للقارئ.

وسام العيثاوي, الخدمة العربية المسيحية

Translation

One of the first things that attracted me to the Bible, including the God it portrays and the message it conveys, was what many agree to be the most difficult part of it—the Wisdom Literature. Coming from a culture that preached an absolute monarch of a God that is black-and-white on the complicated matrix we are in which we call life, the Bible introduced a God that acknowledges the difficulties we often go through and even takes the time to sit shiva and ask "Why?" when the answer is the last thing we need. Of course, I am specifically talking here about the Book of Job. In it I have met a God who is powerful enough to recognize me as an individual, hold hands with me and say "I know it is difficult, and we will get through all this together."

A decade later, I left my home country of Iraq, went to a Bible school, became a minister, and moved to Dearborn, Michigan. Enter Scott Cherry—the friend, the evangelist, the teacher, the good neighbor in a diverse city (also the philosopher, although he does not like to be called that so I will spare him the unnecessary agony). Scott is of a disposition so engaging and a demeanor so calm it drives me crazy, and yet that is how he and Emad (a Muslim friend he met in college) hopped on to a fourteen-century-old conversation that has been made a little rougher since the twentieth century. The conversations, which took long months, came nonchalantly across the story of Job, and the sacrifices that God ordered him to offer to atone for the sins of his comforters—four men who got the exegesis right and the hermeneutics totally wrong. That atonement triggered the evangelist in Scott to write this book.

The *Reason of Job* may have a vocabulary that is challenging to decode, and yet the book provides all the necessary basics needed to understand its argument. The author argues that "the story of Job is the motif of the Messiah, and this motif runs all through the Bible." A motif is a recognizable and recurring pattern that is visual, auditory or imaginative. Job is a [descent-to-ascent] motif because he goes into the valley of despair and comes out better on the other side.

Scott has assumed the monumental task of building his argument in a journey that takes the reader through scriptures, literature, pop culture as well as real-life conversations with his friends. This book is a rich contribution to the Christian library and can be a real blessing to the reader, Christian, Muslim, or other.

–Wissam Al-Aethawi, Arabic Christian Ministry, Dearborn

....

II. Dr. John Leonard

I met Scott Cherry, the author of this book, 20 years ago and was drawn to him right away because we shared a similar passion – reaching people with the gospel. Over the years I would come to appreciate many other things about him.

Scott has a strong desire to train and mobilize people to take the gospel across cultural barriers. In those years he was part of a group that hosted conferences to motivate, teach, and equip people for sharing their faith cross-culturally. I was invited to speak at two of these and was impressed with the quality of instruction by other people who had years of experience.

Scott is committed to having personal relationships with his immediate neighbors and members of his community, especially those who are college/university students. For the past 20 years he has faithfully reached out to many on the nearby campuses. His persistence and devotion to his calling is admirable, and you will hear those years of personal service shared in the pages of this book.

Scott is a scholar. In this book, *The Reason of Job,* you will discover how his depth of learning and knowledge of this subject will challenge anyone who is serious about studying it.

Lastly, Scott is deeply spiritual. What you will discover as you work through *The Reason of Job* is that this is just not an intellectual exercise but a richly edifying one.

For all these reasons, this book will be a reference you will often return to when you are searching for truth and engaged with others who are as well. Enjoy *The Reason of Job* and work through it thoughtfully with a friend.

Dr John S. Leonard PhD
Pastor, Cresheim Valley Church
Retired Professor of Practical Theology
Westminster Theological Seminary
Philadelphia, PA

Preface

–Part 1–

Meet Emad. He is a Muslim. Until the spring of 2019 we were fellow students at the University of Michigan–Dearborn, albeit in different categories. And I would like to think we were friends. Little did he know that he would be indirectly involved in the conception of this book, and I think he would be pleased.

Emad would tell you plainly that he believes in the Messiah, as all Muslims do. That's because the Qur'an speaks of the Messiah— 11 times in 9 verses to be exact. In those 'ayas' he is either *named* or referred to as the "son of Mary", so it is obvious who he is: *Jesus.* Thus all Muslims believe that *Jesus* was the Messiah, as Christians also believe but for different reasons. We had that in common, among other things. By comparison, most Jews believe in the coming Messiah but not that he was Jesus. They reject him not because he never existed, or that a man named Jesus never died on the cross, however. Rather, many Jews reject him because he did not match the "conquering king" parts of the composite in the Hebrew scriptures, and for other reasons as well.[1] There the Messiah figure appears in hundreds of passages, but he is never named or even referred to as the son of Mary. He is described only, and usually in poetry. That's one reason that a Christian may be unfamiliar with Messiah material if not well-read in the pre-Christian Hebrew scriptures. As it happened, Emad was quite familiar with them, more so than many Jews and Christians. I respected that about him, as well as for his intelligence in general.

Emad and I met when he and his twin brother Assad were freshmen during their first month of the fall semester. They were very curious, and they had an obvious interest in religious discussions, so we had many of them. We even enjoyed some informal Bible studies

---

[1] "They also reject him due to not accepting several passages as messianic that Christians would see in such a way, as well as a host of other factors." Email from Dr. Bryan Murawski, Professor of Old Testament Studies, Cairn University, PA (Westminster Seminary)

together as we were worked through the book of Exodus in the part of the Bible that Muslims call the Tawrat. There the mysterious Messiah figure makes his first appearances in those ancient narratives, but the brothers and I hardly talked about him if I recall correctly. We talked about a lot of other things, but the Messiah was not even on our radar then. Anyway, as time went by they became less interested in interfaith discussions and somewhat more distant, at least with me. Thankfully that was not permanent.

In their third year the brothers took separate paths: Assad transferred to the main campus in Ann Arbor, and I never saw him again except on Facebook. But I was glad to have Emad for another two years. Not only that, for some strange reason he had recaptured his zeal for religious discussions, so I was happily surprised but also intrigued at the same time. *The original Emad was back!* Over the span of his junior year I estimate that we had no less than two dozen conversations about religion. For example, one time Emad sat down with me and we had a totally spontaneous study of a passage from Surah Al-Baqarah[2]—but I don't remember exactly which—and compared it to something in the Injeel.[3] Another time, in the very same booth, we covered progressive revelation and eschatology, or end times. On other occasions we talked about the Islamic doctrine of tawhid (absolute oneness), the divine attribute of love in Islam and Christianity, the early history of Islam and the Jews in Medina,[4] and the essential role of the hadith in understanding the socio-historical settings of revelations in the Qur'an.

Still other examples focused on the Bible. In the first week of Emad's junior year my young friend David was doing open-air easel painting behind the University Center and I was hovering nearby. At

---

[2] "Surah" means chapter. Al Baqarah is the second and longest surah in the Qur'an.

[3] The Qur'anic word for gospel. However, it does not refer to one of the four gospels contained in the Christian New Testament per se. Rather, it refers to a book of revelation given to Jesus. This gospel has never been found, nor is there any historical record of it.

[4] A city in Arabia 272 miles NE of Mecca that is very important in the standard Islamic narrative, according to which the prophet Muhammad fled there from Mecca in 620 AD. There he was widely received as a prophet and established the first Muslim community.

one point Emad approached and drew my protégé David and me into a long discussion about the meaning of the revelation given to the prophet Ezekiel narrated in chapter 18 of that book. That topic was totally his idea; he must have come upon it over the summer. For the first discussion of the semester, that was an intense one! Later that semester he wanted to talk about the philosophy of the trinity, and in the spring of that year we went deep into the question of whether all Muslims go to heaven or which, if any, go to hell (with ample consideration of his understanding of temporary hell, similar to what Catholics would call purgatory.) That discussion included a generous amount of theologizing about the justice of God vs. his mercy. Indeed, every in-depth discussion we ever had included numerous subtopics that became their own focus of study until we circled back to the original one—though it was not always easy to remember and recapture it. And sometimes we got bored or fatigued with it, and let it rest.

More than once Emad and I talked about Job, an important figure in both Islam and Christianity. Job the man, the legend, the priestly prophet, the Old Testament saint, the patient sufferer, the author of the long Hebrew book by his name, the archetype of all who suffer intensely, and whatever else he may have been.[5] But as I recall, it seems we only ever talked about him in passing, as one whose story we both knew as common to our religions, and as one who deserved great respect. A few times we talked about Satan's role in Job's suffering, and God's role in allowing it. And we talked about how Job came through his suffering and received double of all he had lost. But we never talked about the fascinating events just before Job's restoration, including the atoning sacrifices he performed for his dubious friends. In hindsight, it's as though he didn't merit more than a cursory overview. Why is that? I ponder now.

Although many of our discussions took place face-to-face, not all of them were. A lot of them were by Facebook Messenger, which may not be surprising. That way Emad and I could easily keep a

---

[5] As we shall discuss further, Job's prophethood may or may not be a point of agreement between Muslims and Christians. It is speculated that he may have been a king and/or a priest similar to Melchizedek (*Book of Genesis* 14:17-20) and Jethro (*Book of Exodus*. 3:1).

discussion going well into the evening or on weekends or holidays when we were not even within reach. One *really* deep exchange took place over the break between the fall and winter semesters about the theological concept of *atonement*. I don't remember how we got onto this subject, but I could retrieve it exactly because it's all saved. That was the first extended study we had over Messenger, but it would not be the last. In retrospect, we were getting closer to our epic study of the Messiah. When we returned from break we continued to discuss that subject in-person. By the way, Emad is a delightful young man with an engaging personality and sense of humor. Plus, in my opinion he is brilliant in a non-pretentious way. (One paper that he wrote to thoroughly explain his theological views gave evidence to this, which is published in our blog.[6]) I enjoyed every conversation with Emad, and the face-to-face ones included a lot of smiling and even laughter. Not that we were cracking jokes very much, but we often made snarky quips to each other. I mean, our convos usually got pretty intense, but they were not without levity. I would like to think we enjoyed each other's company, even while 'locking horns' with each other as we so often did.

    Thus for me, it was my relationship and interactions with Emad that formed the incubator of this study of Job and other Old Testament figures in relation to the Messiah, and the abundant motifs surrounding him. I call that *authentic*. I will develop this thread in chapter 1 and continue to frame the question.

---

[6] Posted in TaoandTawheed.com under "A Muslim Student's View of Justice And Mercy"

–Part 2–

Words to My Readers

Dear Emad, I hope you will read and enjoy this book. Largely, I wrote it for you. By now you are grad student somewhere, or likely past that. Either way, you have no doubt launched into your career and are building your professional and family life. I believe you will appreciate much of what I have written about Job and the other prophets we both believe in. But as the Muslim that you are, and as you would expect from a book by me, you will not agree with all of it, and a fair bit will rub you the wrong way. No surprise there, right? But if you read this book, you will learn a lot about a Christian understanding of Job and the logic of the whole Bible, or at least mine. And since I also say a lot about Islam, you might even come upon some things you did not know about your own religion.

To Dr. Ibrahim Sablaban: I have also had you in mind as I was writing this book. I believe I've told you that in person. Having met each other in a similar way when you were a freshman at Wayne State University (2006 or 7), you and I have been friends for a lot longer, and we still are. We've had many conversations of this nature over the years, and I know I've offended you at times. Apologies. You are your own person, of course, not Emad or any other Muslim person. But to you I say some of the same things that I said to him. May our friendship endure.

To all other Muslim readers I say similar things. If you are like many other Muslims (and Christians), you probably have not read either the whole Qur'an *or* Bible yet. So why would I expect you to read *this* book by a Christian author? Well, both religious texts can be hard to read cover-to-cover, and sometimes it's easier to read a book *about* them. Plus, there is a lot of scripture material from both books that is woven together in a pretty novel way. The same goes if you happen to be Jewish or a member of any other belief system. Frankly, I think you'll be intrigued.

To my Christian readers: You may or may not have read other books about Job before. Either way, by reading this book I think you will savor the story of Job and the Master Motif of the whole Bible in a refreshing new way. But you will not agree with me on everything, either. That's ok. How often do you agree with *everything* any author says? For me, never. You may not feel that my content on Islam and the Qur'an belongs in a Christian book about Job, for example. I only hope that it provokes you into deeper thinking on the subject.

This book is non-fiction. I view it as a quasi- or semi-scholarly work. I say "quasi/semi" because, like my previous book *The Reason of Reason,* I have intended it for a general, popular audience, not a scholarly one. Despite the 'ordinary' people who did read that, some told me it was over their heads and they "just couldn't do it." Maybe it's because that book was philosophy, which I know is not for everyone. This book is largely theology, not philosophy, but I expect a similar reaction to it. I admit that I am kind of heady and cerebral even when I'm trying not to be, and my writing reflects this for better or worse. At the same time, I would like real scholars to respect this book, which is one reason I have so many academic footnotes and sources from books, theses, and journals.

On the other hand, throughout the book I have included a lot of pop culture material in it that was fun to write and is accessible to everybody. For example, one thing I try to do is to observe the 'messianic' and messiah-complex trends in pop culture, and to celebrate the way the *Job Motif* has permeated Western culture over the millennia even to the present day. For these reasons and others I draw shamelessly upon on the internet for the readily accessible and wide-ranging sources available including scholarly sources found in JSTOR and the like, for example, but also more 'popular' websites, personal and institutional blogs, and yes Wikipedia. I have used it and comparable websites the way any responsible writer should qualify books and journals too, by weighing and gauging the required level of credibility for the purpose against the estimated credibility and accessibility of the source.

Now, allow me now to provide some functional notes to some of the eccentricities of the text of this book.

Technical Notes

1. *The Reason of Job* is kind of a 'hybrid' book. It is intended primarily for a mixed audience of Christians and Muslims—Christians who are interested to learn about Job and other prophets in Islam as well as in Christianity, and Muslims in reverse. Thus, many of the things I have written about, the way I framed them, the verbiage and phraseology I used, and the languages I inserted into the text, are uniquely crafted for this mixed audience.

2. Obviously, its primary language is English, but it contains three other languages as well: Hebrew, Greek, and Arabic. I do not expect to have many readers or scholars who will rely on them. The main reason is for textual flourish, or style. I do not pretend to be proficient in any of them, and I apologize if you are and you find errors.

3. The Hebrew and Greek segments are the respective original languages from which the English Bible is translated in all of its many versions, Hebrew for the Tanakh, or Old Testament, and Greek for the New Testament. The Arabic is inserted for verses from the Qur'an and ahadith. All three are sometimes also used for names, words, and subtitles.

4. Of the three languages there is more Arabic than the other two. This is because I have many verses from the Qur'an and ahadith. If you are a Muslim you know what that is, and I will define it for non-Muslims in the first chapters.

5. In the text of this book, there are a few things I do that you the reader might find eccentric.

   a. I use capital letters intentionally for terms that I think are important, but not in a way that will always seem consistent to the reader unless you know this. For example, I capitalize Messiah and Motif if I'm using it in a 'proper' sense, but not in a generic sense.

   b. As is properly done with book titles, I italicize all specific names of books of the Bible as titles. I realize they are not normally italicized, but I do this to emphasize that they are titles of books that comprise the Bible, either the Tanakh or the New Testament.

6. I call the Hebrew scriptures what Jews call it—the Tanakh. In reference to Christian Bibles containing the two testaments, I sometimes call it the Old Testament interchangeably, but I usually call it the Tanakh.

7. Also for books of the Bible, I have made a deliberate effort not to abbreviate them the way it is common to do in books for Christians only. I almost always spell them out because they are titles. Not only that, but I have often elongated the name of a book for maximum clarity and respect.

   a. Thus the book entitled *Job* is often *The Book of Job* or *Book of Job,* and sometimes simply *Job* so as not to be redundant or awkward.

   b. Gen. is *The Book of Genesis, Book of Genesis*, and sometimes just *Genesis.*

   c. Ex. is *The Book of Exodus, Book of Exodus*, and sometimes just *Exodus.*

d. ...Etc. for all books of the Bible.

8. Prophets and saints (i.e. godly people) of the Tanakh or New Testament may be referred to in ways that are uncharacteristic for the Christian, the Muslim, or the Jew, or all three.

   a. Ones that are definitely considered as prophets by Jews and Christians I often, but not always, refer to as Prophet ____, or the Prophet ____, or the prophet ____. For example, Moses is usually Prophet Moses or the prophet Moses, or even Moses the prophet; but sometimes just Moses. The same goes for John the Baptist in the New Testament.

   b. Ones that *may* be considered as prophets by some Jews and some Christians I sometimes refer to as Prophet ____, or the Prophet ____, or the prophet ____. For example, Job and Jacob are sometimes respectively referred to as Prophet ____, or the Prophet ____, or even ____ the prophet; but sometimes I call them just Job or Jacob.

   c. Ones that are definitely not prophets to Jews or Christians I never call prophets, such as Adam and Lot, etc.

   d. In the New Testament, the Apostles are usually referred to as such. Thus, Matthew will usually appear as (the) Apostle Matthew. The same applies to the Apostles John, Paul, Peter, James, etc.

   e. Jesus is referred to as Jesus, or Jesus Christ which means Jesus the Messiah. Even though he was a prophet at least, Christians never refer to him that way, or even as Messiah Jesus. So I almost never refer to him as Prophet Jesus or a similar form.

9. Muhammad is usually referred to as Muhammed, occasionally as (the) prophet Muhammad, or prophet of Islam, etc. Whether someone was a prophet or not, Christians and Jews do not ordinarily deem it necessary to use the title.

    a. I do not use honorifics for Muhammad such as "peace be upon him" (pbuh) or "alay salam" or any or qur'anic or biblical figure. No doubt this will bother some Muslims who are accustomed to using and seeing them, sorry.

    b. By the same token, I do not use honorifics for God.

10. When speaking of God I use a variety of His names or titles in Christianity, Judaism, and Islam depending on context.

    a. When speaking of God as understood in the Judeo-Christian tradition, I will often use the generic English word "God" that Christians and Muslims often use to converse about him in English. I also use some generic titles such as God Almighty, the Almighty, the Creator, and others that will appeal equally to adherents of all three religions.

    b. In addition, I also use His primary Hebrew name that is usually transliterated as YHWH, or Yahweh when vowels are added, or Yahweh God.

    c. When speaking of God as understood in the Islamic tradition, I often use Allah but I am equally likely to use God or another term in a generic sense.

11. Finally, all English quotations from the Old Testament (Tanakh) or New Testament are taken from the English Standard Version (ESV) unless otherwise noted, in italics. To a lesser extent, translated English quotations from the Qur'an are taken from the Clear

Qur'an (quran.com) unless otherwise noted as some other English translation.

Philosophy on Sources

I have been told by one scholar that scholarly works do not draw on Wikipedia and other internet sources. Perhaps so. That's one reason my book may not be considered 'scholarly' by actual scholars. I'm ok with that, but it seems somewhat snobbish to me. I view the internet in general as the "Bodleian Library" of this age, the world of information at one's fingertips if one knows how to use it well. That's just how the age of knowledge and information is these days, and I don't think it's "cheating." In a world where everyone can do it, good researching is still a challenging exercise, and it doesn't take the skill or art out of good writing. Even someone who has all the 'puzzle pieces' still has to make sense of them and put them together meaningfully, if not beautifully. For the researcher and author, the trick is being able to find what is wanted and validate its credibility at the level that is required. Not every source needs to get the highest possible credibility-rating. Subscription sites such as JSTOR, Scribd, Perlego (all to which I subscribe), and dozens more like them are superb troves of knowledge. And, in my estimation, so too is Wikipedia for the general purposes I use it, and never for the most critical strands of my argument. Plus, it can lead the researcher to a plethora of other resources. So I believe that as long as the estimated credibility of the information matches the demand, it is fair game.

Allow me to give several examples. Using Google as a search engine, when one does a simple search for "Job" only results about jobs come up. In order to find anything about Job the man one must enter something like Job in the Bible, or in Christianity, or in Islam, etc. Using the first, the topmost result is not Wikipedia but an article on Job in Christianity.com. It's solid but also basic. Aside from a link to the Zondervan *Cultural Background Study Bible* there's nothing I can use, and the parts of this study Bible that are available online for free do not include Job. The second thing that comes up is Sparknotes.com. Again, nothing really useful, but there is this interesting paragraph about the rhetoric of Job:

> One of the chief virtues of the poetry in Job is its rhetoric. The book's rhetorical language seeks to produce an effect in the listener rather than communicate a literal idea. God's onslaught of rhetorical questions to Job, asking if Job can perform the same things he can do, overwhelms both Job and the reader with the sense of God's extensive power as well as his pride. Sarcasm is also a frequent rhetorical tool for Job and his friends in their conversation. …The self-deprecating tone and sarcastic response are rare elements in ancient verse. Such irony not only heightens the playfulness of the text but suggests the characters are actively responding to each other, thus connecting their seemingly disparate speeches together. The poetry in Job is a true dialogue, for the characters develop ideas and unique personalities throughout the course of their responses.[7]

This bit is insightful, and I like it, but it's not something I could use. It also briefly states that at the end of the story Job intercedes for his friends and God forgives them, which is a crucial part of my book's argument that requires a lot more attention. I'm glad that at least this piece says that, but otherwise it says nothing about the parts of Job that I plan to focus on.

The next results that show up are Wikipedia articles, one of which is **Job (biblical figure)**, which in my opinion *is exceptional!* To be honest, though, I don't think I paid much attention to it until now, only after I have finished my book. It doesn't seem at all familiar to me, and I didn't cite it anywhere. As an encyclopedia article, it is comprehensive and gives an excellent overview of Job in the three monotheistic religions that venerate him, plus Mormonism and Baha'i. With regard to Judaism, the article contains this fascinating

---

[7] www.sparknotes.com/lit/oldtestament/section11/page/2/

snippet. In this Talmudic view Job was not only alive but actually in Egypt at the time of Moses, working for Pharoah!

> Job was in fact one of three advisors that Pharaoh consulted, prior to taking action against the increasingly multiplying Israelites in the Book of Exodus. As described in the Talmud:[8] Balaam urged Pharaoh to kill the Hebrew newborn boys; Jethro opposed this decree; and Job, though personally opposed to the decree, kept silent and did not protest it. It is for Job's silence that God subsequently punishes him with his bitter afflictions. However, the Book of Job itself contains no indication of this…

Nor do the related chapters of the *Book of Exodus* (1-13) say anything of the sort. I know for sure that I had not read that before! Assuming that the Talmud really says this, where does it get it? You see that if this really mattered to me I would have a new trail to follow.

This article also includes a segment on The Septuagint, the Greek translation of the Hebrew Old Testament to which I refer later. Apparently it contains a verse stating that Job was a grandson of Esau and a ruler of Edom.

> This man is described in the Syriac book as living in the land of Ausis, on the borders of Idumea and Arabia: and his name before was Jobab; and having taken an Arabian wife, he begot a son whose name was Ennon. And he himself was the son of his father Zare, one of the sons of Esau, and of his mother Bosorrha, so that he was the fifth from Abraam.

This also raises the question of sources. How does the Septuagint know all that? I do not know what "the Syriac book" is, and Wikipedia does not say. So if that really mattered to me, which it will if I write a 2nd volume to this book, you see how the former would have given me a lead to follow, but that's it. It would be up to me to do further searches for that to see what I could find.

---

[8] Sotah 11a

Finally, Islam. This article says a lot of interesting stuff, but none of which I used. Remember, I'm only now reading this closely for the first time to illustrate a point. Consider these excerpts:

> In the Qur'an, Job (Arabic: أيّوب, romanized: *Ayyūb*) is considered a prophet in Islam. ...Some Muslim commentators also spoke of Job as being the ancestor of the Romans,[23] but Philip K. Hitti asserted that [Job] was an Arab [in] Northern Arabia.[25] Muslim literature also [says] that he came after Joseph in the prophetic series. ...The Qur'an describes Job as a righteous servant of Allah (God), who was afflicted by suffering for a lengthy period of time. ...The narrative goes on to state that after many years of suffering, God ordered Job to "Strike with thy foot!". At once, Job struck the ground with his foot and God caused a cool spring of water to gush forth from the Earth, from which Job could replenish himself. [28]

That footnote [28] leads to a verse in the Qur'an, Surah 38:41. However, upon reviewing this verse it says no such thing, so it seems to be an error which the skilled researcher is responsible to detect. It could also be a Muslim interpolation from some other Islamic source.

Finally, this Wikipedia article does include a bit on the central passage in my focus of interest—Chapter 19:25-27—again, which I had not noticed until now.

> Job's declaration, "I know *that* my redeemer liveth" (Job 19:25), is considered by some Christians to be a proto-Christian reference to Christ as the Redeemer, and is the basis of several Christian hymns, as well as the opening scene of Part III of Handel's *Messiah*.[9] However, Jewish bible commentators and scholars point out that Job "insists on a divine hearing in his lifetime" (cf. Job 16:19–22).[10]

---

[9] If you are a fan of Handel's *Messiah* like I am, the linked clause about Job in this famous oratorio is to me golden; as many times as I had listened to it, I had forgotten all about this movement. (For that matter, Wikipedia's five articles on said *Messiah* are amazing.)

[10] [19] Cf. "But I know that my *Vindicator* lives; In the end He will testify on earth – this, after my skin will have been peeled off." (Job, 19:25 *Berlin, Adele; Brettler, Marc Zvi*

However, what this article offers is just a snippet, and even if I had noticed it the first time around it would certainly not have been enough even to build on. I had to dig a lot more proverbial holes in to dig way deeper to find what I was looking for.

As for the second Wikipedia article on the **Book of Job,** I judge it to be equally exceptional, but offering much different sorts of information than the first. To this one I gave much more attention, and in Part 2, chapter 11 I quoted extensively from its section on Job's historical pervasiveness in **Music, Art, Literature, and Film.**[11] In my opinion, the content of this section is culturally interesting and impressively assembled, but it has no bearing on the main strand of my argument. I didn't see any reason to disbelieve any 'bytes' of this list of artforms in which Job has appeared, nor to make the effort to confirm any of them. But even if any are incorrect they, or the whole list, can be simply dismissed without any consequence whatsoever.

Prior to that list the same article contains a shorter one of interest to Christians especially:

> Augustine of Hippo recorded that Job had prophesied the coming of Christ, and Pope Gregory I [who wrote six volumes on Job] offered him as a model of right living worthy of respect. The medieval Jewish scholar Maimonides declared his story a parable, and the medieval Christian Thomas Aquinas wrote a detailed commentary declaring it true history. In the Protestant Reformation, Martin Luther explained how Job's confession of sinfulness and worthlessness underlay his saintliness, and John Calvin's interpretation of Job demonstrated the doctrine of the resurrection and the ultimate certainty of divine justice.

Except for Pope Gregory I, these particular scholars' thoughts on Job are ignored in my book. It's hard to include everybody on a

---

(2014). The Jewish Study Bible. [S.l.]: Oxford University Press. p. 1523. ISBN 978-0-19-997846-5. Retrieved 2 January 2017. – Vindicator, Hebrew "go'el", a person, usually a relative, who stood up for his kinsman's rights; also used of God in his relationship with Israel.

[11] wikipedia.org/wiki/Book_of_Job

subject that has been so enormously interesting over the centuries. I am most interested in the Joban Messiah Motif and thinkers that have given attention to it, which is not many. In the *Book of Job*, the Redeemer Motif in chapter 19 and 42 leads to the Job Motif, which in turn leads to the Messiah Motif.

Speaking of which, this outstanding Wikipedia article contains a snippet on our passage of special interest:

> When Christians began interpreting Job 19:23–29…as a prophecy of Christ, the predominant Jewish view became "Job the blasphemer", with some rabbis even saying that he was rightly punished by God because he had stood by while Pharaoh massacred the innocent Jewish infants.

It also contains one brief, passing reference to the lavish burnt offering that God demanded the companions to beseech of Job, which is the second of my two major interests in the book. For an article this comprehensive, that is very strange to me. But this anonymous writer is not unusual. Many exclude this part of the story's resolution or give it minimal attention at best. I intend to give it the attention it deserves.

Chapter 1

The Messiah Concept in Culture

"I think the Messianic concept, which is the Jewish offering to mankind, is a great victory. What does it mean? It means that history has a sense, a meaning, a direction; it goes somewhere, and necessarily in a good direction—the Messiah."

–Elie Wiesel, *Conversations*

What actually *is* a messiah, anyway, and why should it even matter? Also, what does Job have to do with it?

These are the three central questions of this book. Oh, and it might be nice to know his identity too. Who was, or is, or will the Messiah be? We have already seen that Muslims have no quandary about this latter question, nor do Christians but for different reasons. But most Jews do, because for them he was emphatically *not Jesus*. So those who care are still watching and waiting for him.

Elie Wiesel (1928-2016) was a Romanian-born Jew of enormous notoriety and cultural importance in the West. He was a holocaust survivor who became a political activist and author of numerous books and articles. He was a professor of the humanities at Boston University and a sought-after speaker on human rights. In 1986 he won the Nobel Peace Prize, as well as numerous other awards and honorary degrees. Among his 57 books are these two titles that caught my eye: First, *Messengers of God: Biblical Portraits and Legends;* and second, *Jewish, Literary, and Moral Perspectives.* They seem to be consistent with our subject and the quote above. Take a moment to read it again. As an ethnic Jew representing the Jewish 'majority opinion' about Jesus, Wiesel did not agree with Muslims and Christians about the identity of the Messiah.[12] But apparently he *did* believe in the *messiah concept*. This is fascinating to me. First, it suggests that whatever one's religious beliefs, the very *idea* of messiah is important. I agree. Second, it states that Messiah was "the Jewish offering to mankind"[13]. Again, I agree, and there can be little dispute about this. But by that he did not mean *Jesus*, he meant the Messiah of the Hebrew scriptures who *was as yet unidentified* but was nevertheless 'visible' prophetically to its scripture community, the Jews. Therefore, my primary quest will be to explore these propositions and discover the key passages where he appears, whether obvious or obscure; kind of the way archaeologists search for 'living artifacts' and assemble them the way paleontologists try to reassemble bones.

Third, I love this part of the quote: "It means that *history has a sense, a meaning, a direction; it goes somewhere, and necessarily in a good direction*." With this I agree wholeheartedly. To put it another way, there is a 'messiah principle' operative in the world that ensures its purpose, its meaningfulness, and its progression toward an ultimate happy ending. Yes, just as the beginning of the world was good, so also the final chapter of the world will be good.[14] For people that tend to believe this there are various reasons, not to mention a preference, to believe it. But not everyone does. Wiesel is pointing to a happy ending based on what he calls the "messiah concept". Could this be true? I'm 'banking on it', as they say. I and millions of others who subscribe to this concept derive great hope therefrom. It's a huge part of what keeps us going day-by-day and enables us to flourish in this hard life.

However, during the same interview in which Wiesel spoke those optimistic words about the future, he went on to say what seems to me the polar opposite:

---

[12] There is small minority of Messianic Jews that believe in Jesus as Messiah.

[13] See *The Gifts of the Jews*, by Thomas Cahill

[14] The Bible's creation story states that as God was creating the world, five times he saw and declared that "it was good." (*Book of Genesis* 1:4,10,12,18, 31)

...At least we would like to think that history is going in that direction. But I think it's going in the wrong direction. We are heading towards catastrophe. I think the world is going to pieces. I am very pessimistic. Why? Because the world hasn't been punished yet, and the only punishment that could be adequate is the nuclear destruction of the world.

I'm not sure how Wiesel reconciles the two halves of his full statement. Depending on his meaning, we may or may not share his view that the world will get worse before it gets better, *if* it even gets better. The messiah concept does not preclude that, and even assumes it. But let me say very pointedly: This study is primarily one of restoration and fulfillment. The messiah concept is a divine promise that all that is wrong in the world will one day be set right.

....

The "Confidence" Seminar...

During the third year of my relationships with Emad I had begun to think a lot more about this messiah concept. I don't mean Jesus *per se*, I mean the literary 'mold' or relief of him in the Hebrew Scriptures and the mysterious unnamed human figure that was formed by it; one for whom most modern-day Jews are still waiting (in theory anyway). I even conducted an unusual interview on this subject for a cable-tv program called *Eye-opener*. When I got the call from the show's host, Kim Slowinski, she told me I could pick the topic, and I picked *messiah*. It was fascinating to me that all three monotheistic religions have a notion of him, but all different notions. Was Muhammad a messiah-figure? I pondered. Also, what's the difference, if any, between a *prophet* and a *messiah*...and *the* Messiah? What eventually struck me was that if there have been many prophets but only *one* Messiah, there must be a <u>fundamental</u> difference between them. If there is only one of something then it is highly unique, by definition. If there isn't, then it isn't.

In the summer between Emad's junior and senior year my friend Steve and I developed a 4-part seminar which we hosted that July. We called it "Confidence" because its purpose was to bolster the confidence of our attendees in the veracity of the Bible, both its Old and New Testaments. We each had two parts. My first part was on some of the reasons people are skeptical about the New Testament or completely reject it, with special attention to the Muslim perspective. By then Emad had provided me with quite a thorough understanding, in particular why Muslims believe it has been corrupted, or changed. But that is outside the primary scope of this book so we shall not delve very deeply into it. Steve's two parts focused on the credibility of the New Testament, while my second part focused on the Hebrew scriptures, or Tanakh, commonly called the Old Testament by Christians, and sometimes the 'first testament'. Muslims usually refer to this as the Torah, or *Tawrat* in Arabic, but technically this term refers only to the first five books, or Pentateuch—the writings of Moses. In principle, Muslims believe in the *Tawrat* as the "revelations given to Prophet Mousa," or Moses, because the Qur'an affirms them as such[15]. By the same principle they also believe in the *Zaboor* (Psalms), or the revelations given to *Prophet Dawood* (David), and the *Injeel*, the revelations given to *Prophet Isa* whom they equate with Jesus of the New Testament.

I called my second part **"The Messiah Motif"** which focused on the Messiah in the Hebrew scriptures—*Mashiach* in Hebrew, and *Al Masih* in Arabic. The scope of it was to identify and examine passages speaking of the Messiah. These are called *Messianic* passages, shared by Jews and Christians alike (but which are largely unknown to Muslims). My preparation for this lecture was both illuminating and exhilarating to me. I had been reasonably familiar with this subject before, but my in-depth study took me much deeper and soon captivated

---

[15] Qur'an, Surahs 3:45, 4:157, 4:172, 5:17, 5:72-73, 5:75, 9:30-31

me. As I began to identify them, I also compiled a list of the passages, not of all of them but a large number. There are hundreds! Some are short and some are long. Some are obviously messianic, and some are more enigmatic. In most examples its referent is unnamed, but in a few the messiah figure is named with a symbolic name that belonged to deceased great men such as David, Elijah, or Joshua. But even the more cryptic passages can often be identified because of their unique descriptors and appellations that only make sense in reference to a human figure with epic qualities.

The Curse and the Promise

The very first one in the Torah is a good example of this. It appears in the third chapter of the first book of the Bible, the *Book of Genesis* chapter 3:15. It involves the very first two humans and humanity's first crisis episode. In the voice of God it reads…

> *I will put enmity between you and the woman,*
>
> *and between your offspring and her offspring;*
>
> *he shall bruise your head,*
>
> *and you shall bruise his heel.*

Following Adam and Eve's transgression with the forbidden fruit in paradise, or the Garden of Eden, we witness their severe downfall followed by its divine punishment. Before their permanent banishment we have God Almighty speaking with the serpent, who is commonly understood as Satan (al Shaytan), the devil himself.[16] In

---

[16] Some Christians, like my young UM-Dearborn student friend Zenon, question whether the serpent was actually (the) Satan. This is an interesting line of inquiry which merits discussion. Most Christians and Muslims seem to assume it was. In my personal evaluation, either the serpent *was* Satan himself or he was very Satan-like (i.e. a demon) according to all we can know about him from the Old and New Testaments of the Bible. This is all the discussion I will devote to this question.

the second stanza God speaks of a "he" who will "bruise" or "crush" Satan's head, depending on the translation; and whose heel will be bruised or crushed by him. ...So who is *he* exactly? ...And how and when will he bruise, or crush, Satan's head? For that matter, what kind of man can do that? Finally, in what manner will Satan bruise the man's heel? Does this imply that the man will not only deliver a wound to Satan but also incur one from him? It does seem so. That is why many students of the Torah understand this somewhat cryptic passage as referring to a *great and powerful* man of which *the* Messiah seems to be a reasonable candidate. If this were the only passage like this in the Hebrew scriptures perhaps it would not be enough to form a profile of the Messiah. But it's not. It is the first of many. So we could call it the "inaugural" passage—the first brick in the wall, the first stone in the path, or the first piece of the puzzle of the *motif* that will begin to form as we continue this quest, an exploration of both literature and revelation.

Fast-Forwarding...

In the fall semester of Emad's senior, we eventually arrived at the 'front door' of the Messiah himself, as it were. By this I mean that he himself became the actual *focus* of our attention. We approached the subject through the door of the collective *gospel,* the narratives of Jesus with his revelations, i.e. his teachings and his actions. For Muslims this collection is believed to be 'lost' or corrupted. But not for Christians. The New Testament of today's Bible contains four sequential books called *gospels* named *Matthew, Mark, Luke* and *John,* in that order, named after their traditional authors. (In all fairness, their true authorship is contested by some scholars as well as by Muslims who may or may not equate them with the Injeel, as I mentioned; Emad does not, others may.) But that is also outside of scope of this book. I subscribe to their traditional authorship. In any case, these four gospels can be understood as the biographies of the person, the works and the teachings of Jesus as they were revealed their writers through experience.

One day Emad and I launched into the historical question of whether Jesus was crucified, whether he was removed from the cross and placed in a tomb, and whether he rose from the dead, as the gospels all state. First we delved deeply into the details of the gospels' accounts themselves, with a lot of deliberation about Roman practices in first-century Palestine. It was vigorous and very interesting! It took place over the course of several months, and much of it spilled over into Facebook messaging as was our usual custom. (I am temp-ted to paste some of our juicier exchanges, but I will resist.) Eventually the course of our discussion led us back in time to the Old Testament, or Hebrew scriptures, as our query then became focused on some of the messianic passages. After all, Emad and all Muslims universally affirm the Messiah because, as I have said, there are 11 references to the Messiah in the Qur'an. But even though none of them define the notion of *messiah*, it is specific about his identity:

He is Issa—Jesus.

In contrast, the Hebrew scriptures describe and *define* the Messiah abundantly, but never actually *name* him (or them, as the case may be).[17] Isn't that interesting? Of course, part of the reason for that is the Qur'an describes him in the past tense, from the future looking back through six centuries of history; but the Bible speaks of him in the future tense from a time well before he would appear. The multiple Hebrew and non-Hebrew prophets who wrote of him, as far back as Moses and Job, were doing so without any personal knowledge of

---

[17] "The Jews of the Qumranic community saw more than one messiah in the Hebrew Scriptures—one suffering, one reigning, one of Israel, one of David. Not all agree with this dualistic interpretation, but probably the majority do." Contributed via personal email by Dr. Bryan Murawski, Professor of Old Testament, Cairn University, Langhorne, PA. (Westminster Seminary, Philadelphia)

him outside of divine revelation, i.e. *foretelling*. So, from the former we can know *who* the Messiah was but almost nothing else. And from the latter, without the New Testament, we cannot identify him, but we can know a lot about him. From the Tanakh we can form an enormously detailed *composite* of him, or what I am calling a "messiah motif". Simply put, a *motif* is a dominant idea, pattern, or distinctive feature, especially in literature, music, and art, and even in religion and other forms of culture.

Remember this, we'll come back to it *a lot*.

"There can be only one."

Many people see symbols or 'motifs' of the messiah in culture, even pop culture. Take this tagline for example. It comes from a movie I saw a long time ago with my wife and we really enjoyed, called "Highlander" (1986). It was about a class of immortal warrior-heroes that served humanity (except some that were evil) by fighting for goodness and defending the weak. If you have even a nebulous understanding of the biblical Jewish Messiah or 'Messiah concept' then you know it involves this kind of heroism. In the movie, there were multiple such immortals scattered around the world, but there could ultimately "be only one". So, oddly, whenever they encountered one another they were supposed to engage in mortal combat. They each had to try to kill each other by decapitation until eventually only one remained who would receive supreme power. Fortunately, the Highlander eventually won the day, because the alternative would have been pretty dismal for the world. In this sense the immortals resembled some of the Greek gods. But in the sense of singularity the Highlander resembled the Jewish Messiah.

In mainstream Jewish history there were lots of prophets, heroes, and 'messiah figures', but there would be only one final Messiah.[18]

---

[18] Some scholars have held that some Jews believed there would be multiple messiahs, at least the Jews of the Qumran community. For example, the manuscript 1QS 9:14, sometimes

(though certainly not because multiple messiahs had to go around killing each other). In the Hebrew Scriptures we can surmise this from the apparent singularity of messianic passages like Genesis 3:15, and many others. Logically, this would be true for Islam and Christianity too because they share most of the same historical figures. One thing we will see is that they always refer to a singular 'he' or 'I', never a plural 'they' or 'we'. Whomever *the* Messiah would emerge as, he would not only be a single *person*, he would also be singular in role and function. The title alone demonstrates this. If there is only one true Messiah then he must be in a class all his own. He may also belong to other categories that are less unique, such as human being, Jew, and even prophet, but in some respect he must belong to a singular category in which he is absolutely unique, like the king of a country, or the president of the United States, for example. Any given country can only have one, so his office is unique in that country while he occupies it.

But the offices of king and president themselves are hardly unique. There have been many kings over the millennia and to-date there are still 26 kings in 43 countries. The concept of president is a much younger one but there still have been many. In the U.S. alone there have been 46, and there are currently hundreds of presidents in

---

called "The Community Rule" reads in part, "... until there shall come the Prophet and the Messiahs of Aaron and Israel..." (note the plural Messiahs). Also, the Damascus Document XIII supports this idea: "Those who follow these statutes in the age of wickedness until the coming of the Messiahs of Aaron and Israel shall form groups of at least ten men, by *Thousands, Hundreds, Fifties, and Tens* (Exod. xviii, 25). And where the ten are, there shall never be lacking a Priest learned in the Book of Meditation; they shall all be ruled by him." Contributed via personal email by Dr. Bryan Murawski, Professor of Old Testament, Cairn University, Langhorne, PA. (Westminster Seminary, Philadelphia)

But some hold the opposing view. In his article "Did Qumran Expect Two Messiahs?" L.D. Hurst from UC Davis argues the opposite: "It has long been held that the Qumran community expected not one but two Messiahs. This assumption has often been accompanied by the act of translating the Hebrew term māšîaḥ in Qumran literature as "Messiah" (with or without the capital "m") rather than as "anointed." The Qumran texts themselves do not necessarily support this viewpoint. A careful examination of the most important literature reveals that the multiple messiahship of Qumran is a creation of modern scholars, not a fact required by the texts themselves." (Bulletin for Biblical Research, vol. 9, 1999, pp. 157-180. http://www.jstor.org/stable/26422234.)

the world. This is true for many other kinds of heads of state. If there were to be a new one called "Super Master" or something, that might be considered a unique office, but he or she would still be a head of state per se, or perhaps an emperor, which is hardly a unique category. There have been many of these too.

Let's apply this to the category of prophet. If you believe in prophets then you believe there have been many of them throughout history. Jews and Christians believe there have been hundreds but less than 50 that can be named. Muslims believe there have been 124,000, most of which are completely unknown and unknowable. By the same principle, 'prophet' is not a unique category, even though a particular prophet may have been singular in his place and time, e.g. the only one, or one of only a few, the first or the last, or some other distinction. But only if there had been only *one* prophet *ever* would it approximate the category of *messiah*.

In the three monotheistic religions there has only ever been, or will be, one Messiah. The Qur'an has the most easily affirmed position on this because it has the most rudimentary presentation of the Messiah, as we have seen: He was one man seen from the perspective of the past. But through the lens of the Bible's Old Testament, or Tanakh, the question is much more layered and complex. Still, a solid case can be made for his singularity, and I should think the New Testament's testimony is self-evident about him. Therefore, the Messiah is both singular and unique. Although he was also a prophet, his role and function were utterly set apart from that of other prophets. There was no mold for him, nor was there a job description, because there had never been a messiah before. Oh, wait! Yes, there *was* a job description—contained in various parts of the Hebrew scripture. That's what we want to explore, and part of it has been presented already. Another, longer part will be introduced soon. For now, let's explore the psychology of *messiah*, and the sociology of a world that seems desperate to have one, and desperately to need one.

What is a *Messiah Complex?*

Ironically, there is another bit of culture that has been dubbed the "Messiah Complex", when somebody believes it is their job to save the world. A scaled-down version, I suppose, is when they feel a responsibility to rescue, say, the Western world, or their country, their city, or even their family. I just did a quick Google search for "Messiah Complex" and got two interesting hits. One was a 2013 live-streamed comedy act written and performed by comedian and podcaster Russell Brand, at London's Apollo Theater. I did not see it, but I recall the striking promo image. Back in 2013 it must have captured my attention on campus bulletin boards or other places. In retrospect, I think I wondered if it was supposed to be a picture of Jesus, but later I understood that it was Brand himself probably trying to get exactly that kind of reaction from passersby like me.

Here's what the Denver Post had to say about it:

> Again and again [Brand] cleverly ties together his outrageous theories and belief systems, blowing them up with a beautiful smile (and foul language), then going deeper and circling back, making us think while laughing. His seemingly scattershot rant is actually organized around a group of heroes: Malcolm X, Che Guevara, Ghandi and **Jesus Christ.** Not only does Brand skewer society's craving for icons and divine wisdom. He knocks religious institutions in

particular. [Sardonic gasp here.][19]

On one level, it's hardly surprising to see Jesus on the list. Would any list of messiah figures be complete without him? It's true, society *does* crave icons and heroes. And why is that? Brand can mock this craving all he wants, but I doubt he is above it. Could it be that we actually *need* great people and exemplars in the world? Could it be that a kind of hero-recognition code has been 'pre-installed' into our collective psyche that even spawns some of them? I mean, not that it would be unjustified—there are an awful lot of disturbing maladies and crises in the world. Who doesn't (openly or secretly) yearn for a Superman or a Wonder Woman, or a whole team of heroes like the Avengers? And isn't that why the recent Marvel *Avengers* series and other superhero movies have been so wildly successful and seem never stop being popular? The glaring thing, of course, is that the world's problems are too big and too numerous even for them. We are desperate for great Humanitarians and lots of ordinary ones too. We rightly crave them, and we should all want to become one (if only in a small sense). Humanity is in no position to disparage people who want to do great good for the world and have the means to do it. On the other hand, an actualized 'messiah complex' can produce a dangerous kind of person if not tempered by love, humility, and compassion, etc. Not everybody is qualified to be a messiah or even messiah-like. Actually, very few are.

X-Messiah

Speaking of which, let's consider another would-be messiah from the Marvel universe—the fascinating X-Men. As far as I can tell, theirs is a completely different kind of reality in which generally 'good' mutations proliferate humanity and create a parallel subspecies of mutants, some good, which we think of as heroes, like

---

[19] denverpost.com/2014/11/26/russell-brand-messiah-complex-a-crazy-brilliant-comedy-special/. Bolding mine.

Wolverine who was prominent in every film and even had three of his own movies, including the finale, "Logan". But some mutants were villain-like such as Magneto, who like others started out good and became evil. If any of the mutants had a messiah-complex it was Magneto who saw himself as the supreme 'savior' of all mutant-dom. With his enormous powers over all things metal, he saw it as his mission to defend other, weaker mutants against the dominant race of humans who were bent on annihilating them, an ever-present threat. But in doing so he was not opposed to slaughtering humans and other mutants that got in his way. Ultimately, Magneto was defeated by the X-Men and later joined forces with them as the world's mutants were systematically hunted down to near-extinction. So apparently he was *not* actually their savior. But deep in the annals of this X-verse there *would yet be* a mutant messiah!

Now, while I do enjoy the X-Men, and I've seen all the movies, I am hardly a devotee, so I would not have known this on my own. Another simple Google search revealed a so-called 'crossover storyline' called **"X-Men: Messiah Complex"** that was never made into a movie (2007-8). Apparently, during a time when mutants were on the verge of extinction, a mutant child was born who would one-day rescue the future generations of mutants. The X-Men knew that because they detected a 'mutant activation' and then discovered that other groups of mutants had already been fighting for possession of the child. The problem was that they did not know its whereabouts. With their very survival in the balance they launched their frantic search. But the bad guys also knew about the savior-child and were searching for it as well. And why, do you suppose? …to offer him their loyalty? Of course not. They wanted to destroy it. Does that sound familiar? Well, it should. About 2000 years ago there was an ancient near-Eastern people anticipating a messiah-child, who also had evil enemies who wanted to find and kill him. But since they couldn't—for an angel had warned his parents to take him to another country—they killed all the male children in the village two years old and under instead.[20] And so in the X-verse the race was on. Which group could find the X-child first was the epic struggle of this storyline. The world needed a messiah, desperately.

One final set of pop-culture examples comes from my own personal consumption of movies on the streaming services to which I subscribe. The first is a one-season Netflix series simply called "Messiah" that aired in 2020. It starred Mehdi Dehbi as a contemporary Jesus-like, Middle Eastern messiah character who also resembled the Mehdi of Islam.[21] Although not based on true events, this intriguing film centered on a modern-day figure that was so believable to people that he quickly gained a large following among Christians, Muslims, and many others with the proclivity to believe, in America and the Middle East. I thought it was pretty good, but apparently it engendered too much controversy and was discontinued. Then, on Prime I watched a three-season tv series called "Britannia" (2018). Set in 43 AD, this story of historical fantasy centers on the Roman invasion of Britain in the very early stages of conquest. Naturally, the native peoples resisted but were systematically subdued or slaughtered. That part is true. On the fictional side of the story, there was a druid prophecy of a young Briton who was destined to become "the One". This turned out to be a pre-teen girl named Cait (Eleanor Worthington). Trained by a druid mentor, she was eventually to emerge as a messiah, a savior, the one-and-only hope of Britannia.

I weave in these stories because they are contemporary examples of what we have been talking about thus far: There is a human condition that we call a *messiah complex* and some people have it. I assert that there is also a kind of *reverse messiah complex* if you will, in which people recognize their need for heroes and messiah figures, consciously or unconsciously. Such people make space for them in

---

[20] *Gospel of Matthew* 2:16-18, New Testament, Bible

[21] In Islam, the Mehdi is not the "Messiah" per se, but he is messiah-like. According to Islamic literature he will appear in the end times to execute final judgment in the world by purging the wicked and killing all swine. He will be accompanied by Jesus.

their views of reality and may even seek them out. And *there is one*, at least in these stories. But stories do not emerge in a cultural vacuum, they reflect culture and the deepest yearnings of human beings. They are built on real-world archetypes and motifs. With the monumental problems that our world has, and always has had, why should we be surprised to find a near-universal longing for, and celebration of, a messiah-mold, or motif, embedded in humanity's art and literature, history, politics, religion, and pop-culture.

It is exactly what we should expect.

Now, allow me to introduce the figure who is the main character and subject of this book. Well, in one sense anyway. He spoke cryptically but emphatically of the Messiah, I assert, but not by name or even by this particular appellation. He was an ancient Near-Eastern figure whose epic and mythic story has persevered to this day, even in popular culture. By epic I mean a long poem, and by mythic I do not mean fictional, for he was very real. I mean he is idealized, famous, and important.[22] He not only prophesied of the Messiah to come, he was himself a messiah figure, a messianic archetype.

In a word, he was a part of the great *Messiah Motif.*

He was Job—the man, the prophet, the legend.

---

[22] collinsdictionary.com/us/dictionary/english/mythic

Chapter 2
Job, A Pre-Jewish Motif?

"I know that my redeemer lives..."

– Job, *Book of Job*, Tanakh

Ok, you say, so there seems to be a messiah motif in culture, and it can look like an epic mutant superhero with some kind of 'messiah complex.' Big deal, that's only fiction. Can we get back to reality please? I mean, is there a *real* messiah in literature, and if so, where does he show up? And who invented the whole idea?

Great questions. That's what this book is about. But first it's about where his *motif* shows up. So far I have asserted that a general messiah motif can be observed in many of the worlds cultures because it is programmed into the human experience. Now I will pick one particular stream of human experience to focus on—the Hebrew or Jewish, and even pre-Jewish experience as captured in their most ancient collection of literature—the Tanakh. Jews and Christians revere it as the epic library of divine revelation for the Jews, and for the world. The Qur'an calls them "The people of the book." In principle, Muslims also acknowledge its God-given revelation in the books of the Torah, the Zaboor (*Psalms*), and the prophets. Job was one of the prophets. In the same sense, Muslims also recognize the gospel of Jesus the Messiah, and Christians as "people of the gospel." Chapter four will delve deeper into Qur'anic texts.

In this book, I argue that the story of Job is the motif of Messiah, and that this motif runs all through the Judeo-Christian scriptures, or Bible. In every kind of literature we see motifs when multiple themes merge together into a prevailing image that controls less-dominant ones that serve it. In the Tanakh, one of the most prevalent motifs is that of Messiah. Throughout the Tanakh, although always a mystery, the profile of the Messiah, or motif, became well-known in Hebrew culture and religion. When one-day he would appear he would become the Savior of God's people with a full spectrum of contrasting yet complementary attributes. In the *Book of Job*, and in Job the man, this motif is powerfully displayed. Although Job was not a Hebrew himself, the Hebrew canon of scripture features him and multiple other figures who contributed to what I call the *descent-to-ascent* contour of the Messiah motif. These include Noah, Moses, Jonah, Jacob, and Joseph, to name a few, all of which we will survey, and which are important prophets in the Qur'an as well.

The Tanakh's 35+ authors wrote over a span of 1500 years and were largely non-contemporaries, so they couldn't have colluded with each other about the Messiah. Following the Israelites' return from exile, if Ezra or someone else *were* to have served as 'master editor' of the Tanakh, as some Muslims and liberal scholars speculate, he could never have been so brilliant as to have developed the Messiah motif in the numerous places of the books, contexts, and dates where it is found. And if he had, wouldn't he have removed all shadow of doubt from the more disputed messianic texts? Therefore, neither a disparate chain of writers, nor even a single author, could have conceived of the Messiah without divine revelation and inspiration. Even the most talented writer/s could not have constructed so comprehensive a Motif so pervasively into the Tanakh over 1.5 millennia without divine oversight and long-term preservation.

In the *Book of Job*, and from the first book of the Torah (*Genesis* 3:15 and 49:8-10) the at-first cryptic Messiah figure is introduced and repeatedly appears with progressive layers to his profile until the full complexity of his attributes is gloriously displayed. Then, toward the end of the Hebrew library, especially in Prophet Isaiah's oracles, we can marvel at a fully-developed Messiah figure that was both recognizable and anticipated by the Jews into the first century. Whatever is believed of the Messiah himself, this anticipation is evident in the narratives of the Christian New Testament as well.

39 Books of the Protestant Old Testament, or Hebrew Scriptures of the Bible (Tanakh)[23]

1. Genesis
2. Exodus
3. Leviticus — **Torah, 5 Books of Moses** (Pentateuch)
4. Numbers
5. Deuteronomy
6. Joshua
7. Judges
8. Ruth
9. 1 Samuel
10. 2 Samuel
11. 1 Kings
12. 2 Kings
13. 1 Chronicles
14. 2 Chronicles — **Writings (history, wisdom)**
15. Ezra
16. Nehemiah
17. Esther
18. **Job**
19. Psalms
20. Proverbs
21. Ecclesiastes
22. Song of Solomon (or *Song of Songs*)
23. Isaiah
24. Jeremiah
25. Lamentations — **5 Major Prophets**
26. Ezekiel
27. Daniel
28. Hosea
29. Joel
30. Amos
31. Obadiah
32. Jonah
33. Micah
34. Nahum — **12 Minor Prophets**
35. Habakkuk
36. Zephaniah
37. Haggai
38. Zechariah
39. Malachi

---

[23] The Jewish canon contains 22 books because many are combined. Roman Catholic and Orthodox editions of the Bible contain 7 additional books derived from the Septuagint, the Greek translation of the Tanakh. Protestants are in general agreement that these extra books should not have been added to the Hellenized Hebrew canon, or library, as not truly inspired scripture, and they are omitted from protestant Christian Bibles and the Hebrew Tanakh.

As I have mentioned, motifs consist of literary themes of which the Tanakh contains hundreds. Consider just these eight.

Some Old Testament Themes

1. The Sovereignty/Wisdom of God

2. Creation, beauty, and goodness

3. Life, happiness, blessings, and joy

4. Sin, death, and their consequences

5. Redemption and reconciliation

6. A people for God, holy nation

7. Exile and return, restoration

8. Rewards and punishments

Some of these themes converge to form motifs. For now, consider just these three that run throughout the whole Tanakh, or Old Testament, from beginning to end.

Some Messianic Motifs

A. Sacrifice, Offering, Atonement
B. Progressive Messianic Motifs
C. Elaborate Future Prophecies

Here are some scriptural examples of just the first motif.

A. Sacrifice, Offering, Atonement

1. *Book of Genesis* 3:21   Animal Skins for coverings
2. *Genesis* 4:1-4   Cain and Abel's offerings
3. *Genesis* 8:20   Noah's burnt offerings
4. *Genesis* 15:7-21   Abraham's burnt offerings

5. *Genesis* 22   The near sacrifice of Isaac
6. *Exodus* 12   The Passover Sacrifice
7. *Exodus* 24, *Leviticus* 1-7   Laws re: animal sacrifices

Finally, here are numerous examples of the second two motifs.

B. Progressive Messianic Motifs

1. *Book of Genesis* 3:15   Proto-Evangelium
2. *Genesis* 14:17-20   Cameo of Melchizedek
3. *Genesis* 22   The near sacrifice of Isaac
4. *Genesis* 39-50   Joseph as Messianic figure
5. *Genesis* 49:8-12   The blessing upon Judah
6. *Exodus* 1-20+   Moses as Messianic figure
7. *Numbers* 24:15-19   Balaam's Messianic Oracle
8. *Deuteronomy* 18:15-19   The Prophet Like Moses
9. *Job* 19:25-27   The Living Redeemer
10. *Psalm* 2:7-12   Son of God
11. *Psalm* 22:1   Words of Jesus on the Cross
12. *Psalm* 72 (all)   A description of Royal Son
13. *Psalm* 110   Priest, order of Melchizedek
14. *Isaiah* 9:6-7   A child is born; a son given
15. *Isaiah* 11:1-10   The Rod and Root of Jesse
16. *Isaiah* 35:5-6   Messiah's healing ministry
17. *Isaiah* 42:1-3   Role of the Chosen Servant
18. *Isaiah* 52-53   Messiah's full ministry
19. *Isaiah* 55:3-4   Covenant; leader, commander
20. *Isaiah* 59:20   Redeemer to those in Zion
21. *Isaiah* 61:1-4   The Spirit of God upon me
22. *Jeremiah* 23:5-6; 33:15-17   The Righteous Branch

C. Elaborate Prophecy Fulfillment

1. *Book of Genesis* 49:8-12   Blessing upon Judah
2. *Psalm* 16:10   No corruption for holy one

3. *Psalm* 22:1	Words on the Cross
4. *Psalm* 41:8-10	Betrayed by a friend
5. *Psalm* 69:21	Sour wine and gall
6. *Isaiah* 52-53	Full role of Messiah
7. *Micah* 5:2	Birthplace Bethlehem
8. *Jeremiah* 31:15	Slaughter of the Innocents

I realize that a few of these examples appear in both the B and C list because they represent both categories. I am also conscious that there will not be unanimous agreement on all of these, whether among Jews and Jews, Christians and Christians, or Christians and Jews. But I believe there will be significant agreement within each of the three groups, or at least some agreement. A fair amount of agreement is all that is necessary for my argument to stand.

Note example 9 in list B, *Job* 19:25-27. This is one that I and many Christians consider as a messianic passage, and possibly some Jews. It is the driving passage of this book, and one into which I will delve much deeper in chapter 5. In one sense, it is from the primary Hebrew-Jewish stream of scripture with all the rest. But in another sense, it is only half Hebrew. By this I mean that the language of the *Book of Job* is Hebrew, but that's all. It is the testimony of a pre-Jewish man named Job, or Ayoub/Ayyub in Arabic transliteration. Job is the main character of the Hebrew book by his name, which in the Tanakh's table of contents is the third book of the Writings, or Ketuvim, and the sixteenth overall, set between the books of *Proverbs* and *Song of Songs*, or *Song of Solomon*. In the canon of the protestant Christian Old Testament shown on page 27, it is the eighteenth book that falls between *Esther* and *Psalms* where it is considered part of the wisdom literature genre.[24] In both Judaism and Christianity it is recognized as divine poetry. In Islam, this book is absent from the Qur'an and other Islamic literature, but Job the man is regarded as a prophet and his story is fairly well known. So Job is a member of the respective pantheons of all three religions, and his story too. But only

---

[24] In Catholic Bibles it is 22nd, and 26th in Orthodox Bibles. Both share the same 39 books with protestant Bibles. See Appendix 1 for another representation of these 39 books.

Judaism and Christianity possess his book because they share the same Hebrew library.[25]

Both Job the man and the book are unique for multiple reasons, both fascinating and perplexing. The first of them is that some scholars consider it to be the oldest book in the Tanakh, written between 1700 and 1900 BC.[26,27] So if the books of the Tanakh were strictly arranged chronologically by their time of writing, but especially by the age of their events and characters, the *Book of Job* would be first in the table of contents, even before the *Book of Genesis* (aside from its creation account and the fall of Adam and Eve in chapters 1-3). Study this timeline to see what I mean.

OLD TESTAMENT TIMELINE

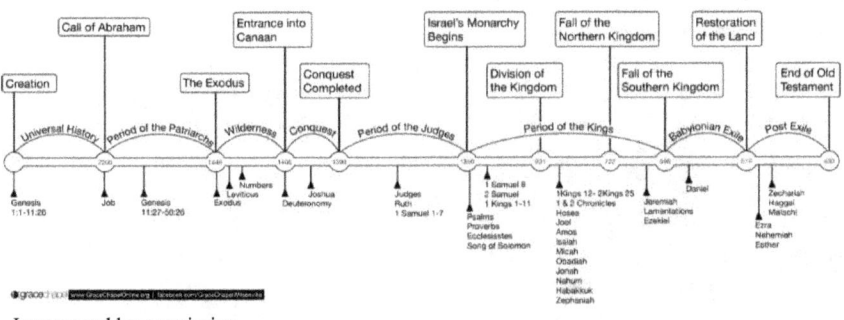

Image used by permission

But regardless of the dating of the book by his name, the man Job lived a very long time ago. There are few clues by which to determine

---

[25] This is true for every book of every prophet in the Tanakh who is mentioned in the Qur'an. The Qur'an contains references to them and statements by them, and even to the entire Tawrat (i.e. Revelation to Moses, Book of the Law, Pentateuch), but it contains none of the whole books of Moses nor the 22 or 39 books attributed to any of the other writers.

[26] These tend to be conservative sources: bible.org/article/introduction-book-job, beliefnet.com/faiths/christianity/what-is-the-oldest-book-in-the-bible.aspx, and icr.org.

[27] However, less conservative sources date it much later (600-400 BC). This is due to a liberal presupposition that much of the Tanakh was written or redacted after the exile by Ezra or one of his contemporaries. wikipedia.org/wiki/Book_of_Job

his specific dates or era, but it was probably between Noah's and Moses's time, late 3rd century to mid-2nd century BC.[28]

Therefore, Job certainly pre-existed the people that later became known as the Jews, or Hebrews, and it is strongly argued by the more conservative scholars that his book did too. Its very first verse starts out, "There was a man in the land of Uz whose name was Job..." Now, if that sounds like the place that Abraham was from, it wasn't. Abraham was from Ur which today is southern Iraq, close to where the Tigris and Euphrates Rivers converge. Uz, on the other hand, is about 1100 miles to the west in what today is southern Jordon or northwestern Saudi Arabia (see on the map on next page). Back then the region in which Uz was probably located was known as Midian, and very close to Edom as the map below shows. Both were part of northern Arabia, the region later to be known as the hijaz along the eastern shore of the Red Sea.

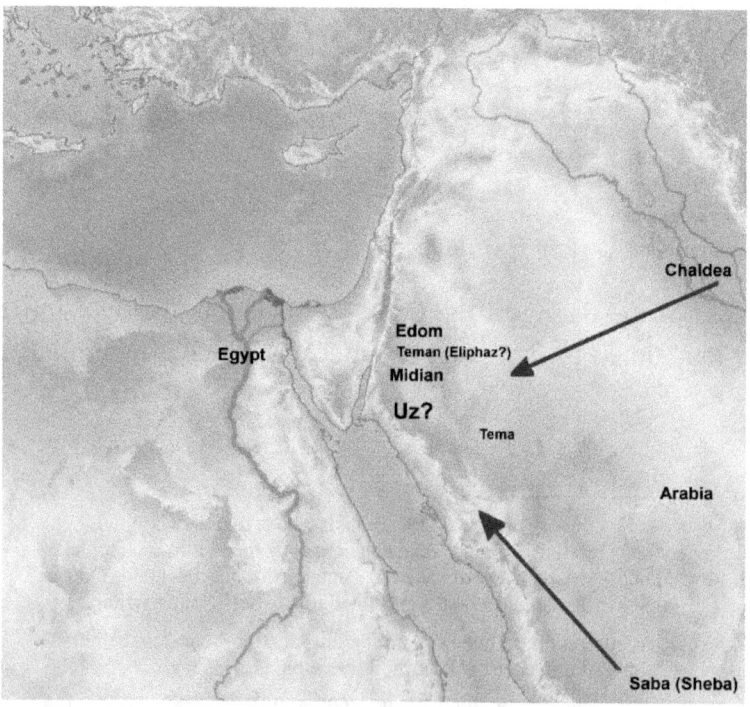

---

[28] apologeticspress.org/apPubPage.aspx?pub=1&issue=603&article=705

Midian was the land to which Moses fled from Egypt, and where he spent the next 40 years. There he married and became son-in-law to Jethro who is also regarded as a prophet in Islam, Prophet Suhaib. It is also a possible location of Mt. Sinai where Moses received the ten commandments and an enormous amount of other revelation recorded in the five books of the Torah.

Job the 'Arab' مهنة

Thus, Job was likely an Arab, i.e. an inhabitant of northern Arabia. If Job lived after the time of Abraham's grandson Esau, that region may have been called Edom depending on the precise latitude of Uz.[29] Esau was the progenitor of the Kingdom of Edom that extended from the southern shore of the Dead Sea in the north to the Gulf of Aqaba in the south.[30] If Job lived before Esau but descended from Abraham, he would either have been an Ishmaelite[31] having descended from Abraham's first son, or a Midianite having descended from Midian, the fourth son of Abraham's second wife Keturah.[32] Midian became the father of the Midianites. Four centuries later, Midian was the land to which Moses fled from Egypt, and where he spent the next 40 years. There he married a Midianite woman and became son-in-law to Jethro, who is also regarded as a prophet in Islam, Prophet Suhaib. This is also a possible location of Mt. Sinai where

---

[29] Early 2nd millennium BC. See this link for a family tree of the patriarchs through the descendants of Esau: wikipedia.org/wiki/Esau

[30] "The Septuagint, an ancient Greek translation of the Hebrew Old Testament, has a revised and updated final verse that claims Job's genealogy, asserting him to be a grandson of Esau and a ruler of Edom." wikipedia.org/wiki/Job_(biblical_figure)

[31] There is a popular theory common among Muslims and some Christians that Muslims are direct descendants of Ishmael, or at least Arabian Muslims. In fact, Muhammad was a major proponent of this idea, claiming to be a descendant of Ishmael according to the Qur'an. There is most likely some truth to this theory. According to missionary and author Kenneth Fleming, "…What we know for certain seems to support the theory that the Ishmaelites are, at the very least, a major element in the Arab genetic line. Old records clearly link the north Arabians with Ishmael's descendants" But it's unlikely that all of those in Arabia are descendants of Ishmael, as the descendants of Keturah and the children of Esau also lived in the Arabian Peninsula. (gotquestions.org/descendants-of-Ishmael)

[32] *Book of Genesis* 25:12-17 and verses 1-4 respectively.

Moses received the ten commandments and an enormous amount of revelation recorded in the Torah's books of *Exodus, Leviticus, Numbers,* and *Deuteronomy.*

Where is this going, you ask? Fair question. We're focusing presently on Job because after God himself (*Genesis* 3:15) Job was quite possibly the first man of God to have spoken revelation about the future messiah, and thus his motif. For this reason Jews and Christians can agree with Muslims that Job was a prophet, or at least prophetic, well before the stream of Hebrew prophets began to form.[33] Indeed, if it was a prophecy of *the* Messiah, then Job gave us some details into the Messianic profile that few of the later prophets give us. But before we get to that a little more literary context is in order. First, since Muslims believe that Job was a prophet, we should expect to find material about him in the Qur'an. We do. There are four passages, or ayas, about Prophet Job as follows:

Job in the Qur'an

Surah 4:163[34]

إِنَّا أَوْحَيْنَا إِلَيْكَ كَمَا أَوْحَيْنَا إِلَى نُوحٍ وَالنَّبِيِّينَ مِن بَعْدِهِ وَأَوْحَيْنَا إِلَى إِبْرَاهِيمَ وَإِسْمَاعِيلَ وَإِسْحَقَ وَيَعْقُوبَ وَالأَسْبَاطِ وَعِيسَى وَأَيُّوبَ وَيُونُسَ وَهَارُونَ وَسُلَيْمَانَ وَآتَيْنَا دَاوُودَ زَبُورًا

Lo! We inspire thee as We inspired Noah and the prophets after him, as We inspired Abraham and Ishmael and Isaac and Jacob and the tribes, and Jesus and Job and Jonah and Aaron and Solomon, and as We imparted unto David the Psalms.

*Allah is speaking to Muhammad.

---

[33] Otherwise, most Jews and Christians generally do not speak of Job as a prophet.

[34] In this chapter, all Qur'anic passages in Arabic and English come from Pickthall's translation: hwww.perseus.tufts.edu/hopper/text?doc=Perseus:text:2002.02.0002

Surah 6:84

وَوَهَبْنَا لَهُ إِسْحَقَ وَيَعْقُوبَ كُلاًّ هَدَيْنَا وَنُوحًا هَدَيْنَا مِن قَبْلُ وَمِن ذُرِّيَّتِهِ دَاوُودَ وَسُلَيْمَانَ وَأَيُّوبَ وَيُوسُفَ وَمُوسَى وَهَارُونَ وَكَذَلِكَ نَجْزِي الْمُحْسِنِينَ

And We bestowed upon him Isaac and Jacob; each of them We guided; and Noah did We guide aforetime; and of his seed (We guided) David and Solomon and Job and Joseph and Moses and Aaron. Thus do We reward the good.

Surah 21:83, 84

وَأَيُّوبَ إِذْ نَادَى رَبَّهُ أَنِّي مَسَّنِيَ الضُّرُّ وَأَنتَ أَرْحَمُ الرَّاحِمِينَ فَاسْتَجَبْنَا لَهُ فَكَشَفْنَا مَا بِهِ مِن ضُرٍّ وَآتَيْنَاهُ أَهْلَهُ وَمِثْلَهُم مَّعَهُمْ رَحْمَةً مِّنْ عِندِنَا وَذِكْرَى لِلْعَابِدِينَ

And Job, when he cried unto his Lord, (saying): Lo! adversity afflicteth me, and Thou art Most Merciful of all who show mercy. Then We heard his prayer and removed that adversity from which he suffered, and We gave him his household (that he had lost) and the like thereof along with them, a mercy from Our store, and a remembrance for the worshippers;

Surah 38:41

وَاذْكُرْ عَبْدَنَا أَيُّوبَ إِذْ نَادَى رَبَّهُ أَنِّي مَسَّنِيَ الشَّيْطَانُ بِنُصْبٍ وَعَذَابٍ

And make mention (O Muhammad) of Our bondman Job, when he cried unto his Lord (saying): Lo! the devil doth afflict me with distress and torment.

Surah 38:42-44

ارْكُضْ بِرِجْلِكَ هَذَا مُغْتَسَلٌ بَارِدٌ وَشَرَابٌ

وَوَهَبْنَا لَهُ أَهْلَهُ وَمِثْلَهُم مَّعَهُمْ رَحْمَةً مِّنَّا وَذِكْرَى لِأُولِي الْأَلْبَابِ

وَخُذْ بِيَدِكَ ضِغْثًا فَاضْرِب بِّهِ وَلَا تَحْنَثْ إِنَّا وَجَدْنَاهُ صَابِرًا

نِعْمَ الْعَبْدُ إِنَّهُ أَوَّابٌ

(And it was said unto him): Strike the ground with thy foot. This (spring) is a cool bath and a refreshing drink.

And We bestowed on him (again) his household and therewith the like thereof, a mercy from Us, and a memorial for men of understanding.

And (it was said unto him): **Take in thine hand a branch and smite therewith and break not thine oath.** Lo! We found him steadfast, how excellent a slave! Lo! he was ever turning in repentance (to his Lord).

That's all for the Qur'an. In other words, that's the sum total that Allah revealed to Muhammad about Prophet Job. But take note of the line I bolded in the final stanza, we shall come back to it.

Job in the Hadith

But his story can also be known from Islamic sources outside the Qur'an in the literature known as *ahadith*, or traditions. This is one of the three major strands of Islamic source literature which inform Muslim beliefs. If you are a Muslim then you know well what this is. If you are not, the hadith are voluminous collections of sayings or reports called narrations about Muhammad and other Islamic and/or biblical figures that are attributed to him, or to his companions, or to other Muslims. Muslim scholars known as Muhaddith such as Al Bukhari (810-870) and Ibn Hibban (884-965) have sifted through as many as 600,000 of the discoverable hadith and rated them from credible (Sahih), to less credible, to not credible at all, forming collections of those deemed 'Sahih' under their names. Thanks to their Herculean effort, a small fraction of that number made the cut (about 2%), and an even smaller fraction are unrepeated narrations.[35] Many hadith are attributed to Muhammad but may instead be attributed to his companions and other Muslim figures of the 7th century. Here is one from Ibn Hibban's (884-965) collection that is attributed to Muhammad:

عَنْ أَنَسِ بْنِ مَالِكٍ أَنَّ رَسُولَ اللَّهِ صَلَّى اللَّهُ عَلَيْهِ وَسَلَّمَ قَالَ إِنَّ أَيُّوبَ نَبِيَّ اللَّهِ صَلَّى اللَّهُ عَلَيْهِ وَسَلَّمَ لَبِثَ فِي بَلَائِهِ ثَمَانَ عَشْرَةَ سَنَةً فَرَفَضَهُ الْقَرِيبُ وَالْبَعِيدُ إِلَّا رَجُلَيْنِ مِنْ إِخْوَانِهِ كَانَا مِنْ أَخَصِّ إِخْوَانِهِ كَانَا يَغْدُوَانِ إِلَيْهِ وَيَرُوحَانِ فَقَالَ أَحَدُهُمَا لِصَاحِبِهِ تَعْلَمُ وَاللَّهِ لَقَدْ أَذْنَبَ أَيُّوبُ ذَنْبًا مَا أَذْنَبَهُ أَحَدٌ مِنَ الْعَالَمِينَ قَالَ لَهُ صَاحِبُهُ وَمَا ذَاكَ قَالَ مُنْذُ ثَمَانَ عَشْرَةَ سَنَةً لَمْ يَرْحَمْهُ اللَّهُ فَيَكْشِفُ مَا بِهِ فَلَمَّا رَاحَ إِلَيْهِ لَمْ يَصْبِرِ الرَّجُلُ حَتَّى ذَكَرَ ذَلِكَ لَهُ فَقَالَ أَيُّوبُ لَا أَدْرِي مَا تَقُولُ غَيْرَ أَنَّ اللَّهَ يَعْلَمُ أَنِّي كُنْتُ أَمُرُّ عَلَى الرَّجُلَيْنِ يَتَنَازَعَانِ فَيَذْكُرَانِ اللَّهَ فَأَرْجِعُ إِلَى بَيْتِي فَأُكَفِّرُ عَنْهُمَا كَرَاهِيَةَ أَنْ يُذْكَرَ اللَّهُ إِلَّا فِي حَقٍّ
صحيح ابن حبان كتاب الجنائز باب ما جاء في الصبر
المحدث الألباني خلاصة حكم المحدث صحيح في السلسلة الصحيحة

Anas ibn Malik reported: The Messenger of Allah, peace and blessings be upon him, said, "Job the Prophet of Allah, peace and blessings be upon him, remained in his trial for eighteen years. He was rejected by relatives and strangers alike, except for two men among his closest brothers. They would visit him in the morning and evening. One of them said to his companion: By Allah, Job must have sinned like no one else before him. His companion said: Why is that?

---

[35] An excellent *Islamic* treatment of *hadith* is found in Wikipedia: wikipedia.org/wiki/hadith. The reader will find that I am not averse to drawing upon Wikipedia articles and similar sites that I consider to be credible, especially material that is non-essential to my claims.

He said: For eighteen years, Allah has not shown him mercy or granted him relief. When his companion went to Job in the evening, he could not help but mention it to him. Job said: I do not know what you speak of, but that Allah knows I would pass by two men who were arguing while mentioning Allah. I would return to my house and perform expiation for both of their sins, as I hate for Allah to be mentioned but in the manner he deserves.

Ṣaḥīḥ Ibn Ḥibbān 2974[36]

One observation I make from this is that apparently Muhammad knew more about Job than what Allah actually revealed to him. It would seem that he had access to other sources of information about Job that were not revealed to him from Allah. Either that or he did not declare everything that was revealed to him. Both are plausible. But if the standard Islamic narrative is to be believed, the former seems probable since in the 7th century there was a large Jewish community in Medina and elsewhere in Arabia to which Muhammad would have had exposure, in addition to his travels with his wife's caravans. Still, what this hadith passage adds to our knowledge of the Islamic Job is not very much more than what we can know from the Qur'an alone.

Sources and Interpretation

According to popular Muslim writer Aisha Stacey, another hadith attributed to Muhammad narrated by Abu Huraira deemed credible (Sahih) by Al-Bukhari (810-870) tells us that one day toward the end of his ordeal Job was taking a shower or bath. Just then Allah showered him with golden grasshoppers, or locusts.[37, 33]

---

[36] abuaminaelias.com/dailyhadithonline/2016/02/04/ayyub-arguments-allah-dislike/.

[37] Sahih Al-Bukhari 279, Book 5, Hadith 31 (sunnah.com/bukhari:279)

وَعَنْ أَبِي هُرَيْرَةَ، عَنِ النَّبِيِّ صلى الله عليه وسلم قَالَ " بَيْنَا أَيُّوبُ يَغْتَسِلُ عُرْيَانًا فَخَرَّ عَلَيْهِ جَرَادٌ مِنْ ذَهَبٍ، فَجَعَلَ أَيُّوبُ يَحْتَثِي فِي ثَوْبِهِ، فَنَادَاهُ رَبُّهُ يَا أَيُّوبُ، أَلَمْ أَكُنْ أَغْنَيْتُكَ عَمَّا تَرَى قَالَ بَلَى وَعِزَّتِكَ وَلَكِنْ لاَ غِنَى بِي عَنْ بَرَكَتِكَ ". وَرَوَاهُ إِبْرَاهِيمُ عَنْ مُوسَى بْنِ عُقْبَةَ عَنْ صَفْوَانَ عَنْ عَطَاءِ بْنِ يَسَارٍ عَنْ أَبِي هُرَيْرَةَ عَنِ النَّبِيِّ صلى الله عليه وسلم قَالَ " بَيْنَا أَيُّوبُ يَغْتَسِلُ عُرْيَانًا

Narrated Abu Huraira:
The Prophet (ﷺ) said, "When the Prophet (ﷺ) Job (Aiyub) was taking a bath naked, golden locusts began to fall on him. Job started collecting them in his clothes. His Lord addressed him, 'O Job! Haven't I given you enough so that you are not in need of them.' Job replied, 'Yes!' By Your Honor (power)! But I cannot dispense with Your Blessings.'"

Nowhere is this to be found in the *Book of Job* itself, nor is it in the Qur'an, so it cannot have been revelation. So where did the Prophet get it? I confess that I do not know. But logically, either it had a source (other than Allah), or the Prophet himself is the source. I also observe that it is qualitatively different from anything in the actual Joban material; to me it has the ring of fable.

But the Qur'an and hadith are not the only sources that Muslims look to. The third stream is the Sirah, or life of Muhammad. These include the biographies of the prophet by two (or three) primary Muslim authors and one French author.[38] Still another trusted Islamic source is called *Stories of the Prophets* by Ibn Kathir. Based on her

---

[38] The first (*Sīratu Rasūli l-Lāh* سيرة رسول الله, *The Life of God's Messenger*) was by Ibn Ishaq (704–767) which did not survive except as it was copied and edited by Ibn Hisham (died 833) in the later decades of that century or the early 9th century (*As-Sīrah an-Nabawiyyah* السيرة النبوية, *The Life of the Prophet*). These are collectively known as *Al-Sirah* for short. Al Tabari (839-923) also incorporated some of Ibn Ishaq's material into his writings. Citing again from Wikipedia, Ibn Hishām omits stories from [Ibn Ishaq] that contain no mention of Muḥammad, certain poems, traditions whose accuracy could not be confirmed, and passages that could offend the reader. Al-Tabari includes controversial episodes of the so-called Satanic verses including an apocryphal story about Muḥammad's attempted suicide. (See wikipedia.org/wiki/Ibn_Hisham and wikipedia.org/wiki/Ibn_Ishaq for full articles and footnotes.) The third 'biography' by Alfred Guillaume (1888-1965) is no more a new one than was Ibn Hisham's. First published in 1955, it is commonly thought of as a translation of Ibn Ishaq (from Arabic into French), which of course would be impossible. According to Dr. Abdul Latif Tibawi, Guillaume's work is actually a translation of his reconstruction of Ibn Ishaq that is based on the edited material of Ibn Hisham's and Al Tabari. (www.icraa.org/ the-life-of-muhammad-a-critique-of-guillaumes-english-translation/)

understanding of his coverage of Job, and probably also from tafsir (Islamic commentary), Stacey also tells us the meaning of the line that I bolded two pages ago in Surah 38:44. She writes…

> Throughout his ordeal, Job remained devoted to God. His lips and tongue remained moist with the remembrance of God and he never despaired or complained. He continued to thank God even for this great calamity that had befallen him. Satan was at a loss, he did not know how to entice Job away from his devotion to God so he decided to harass Job's wife. He came to her in the form of a man and reminded her of the old days and how easy their life had once been. Job's wife burst into tears and confronted Job saying, "ask your Lord to remove this suffering from us". Job was saddened and reminded his wife that God had blessed them with wealth, children and health for 80 years and that this suffering had been upon them for a relatively short period of time. He declared that he was ashamed to call on God to remove the hardship and admonished his wife saying that if he ever regained his health he would beat her with 100 strokes. Job's loving wife was devastated, she turned away and sought shelter elsewhere. Job felt helpless, he turned to God, not to complain but to beg for mercy:
>
> ***"Verily! distress has seized me and You are the Most Merciful of all those who show mercy." So We answered his call, and we removed the distress that was on him, and We restored his family to him (that he had lost), and the like thereof along with them as a mercy from Ourselves and a Reminder for all who worship Us."*** (Surah 21:83-84)
>
> God restored Job's health almost immediately. Job's wife could not bear to be parted from her beloved husband for very long so she returned and was amazed when she saw his recovery. She cried out her thanks to God, and on hearing her words, Job became worried. He had taken an oath to beat his wife but he had no desire to hurt her for he loved her dearly. God wanted to ease the heart of his devoted, patient servant so he advised him to ***"take in your hand a bundle of thin***

grass and strike therewith your wife, and break not your oath". (Surah 38:44)[39]

In her piece Stacey quotes two passages about Job from the Qur'an, which I also quoted some pages ago. My first observation concerns the English translation of the last verse in Surah 38:44:

وَخُذْ بِيَدِكَ ضِغْثًا فَاضْرِب بِّهِ وَلَا تَحْنَثْ ۗ إِنَّا وَجَدْنَاهُ صَابِرًا ۚ نِعْمَ الْعَبْدُ ۖ إِنَّهُ أَوَّابٌ

I am not sure which English translation she used as it does not exactly match any of the 37 that I reviewed, termed "Generally Accepted Translations of the Meaning."[40] It is more similar to some than to others. In specific, Stacey's version of choice contains the phrase **your wife** (without quotation marks) to refer to Job's wife, while most others do not. This phrase, or the single noun, is found only in 9 of the 37 versions. Two others contain the pronoun "her" but 26 omit it entirely. The most obvious reason that omit any reference to Job's wife is that it is not in the Arabic. It is absent. Here's a literal translation of this verse called Word for Word by Dr. Shehnaz Shaikh, et al.

> "And take in your hand a bunch and strike with it and (do) not break (your) oath." Indeed, We [We] found him patient, an excellent slave. Indeed, he repeatedly turned.[34]

For comparison, here's Yusuf Ali's translation:

> "And take in thy hand a little grass, and strike therewith: and break not (thy oath)." Truly we found him full of patience and constancy. How excellent in our service! ever did he turn (to Us).[34]

Notice how both of these versions contain words or phrases in

---

[39] www.islamreligion.com/articles/2721/story-of-prophet-job/#_ftn21221. Bolding mine
[40] See www.islamawakened.com/quran/38/44/ for all of these and many more.

(parentheses). This indicates that they are not in the Arabic. Rather, they are the interpretive insertions of the translators, i.e. the translators believed that the word/s are implied, or that it should be inserted for some other reason based on what he thinks it means. Other ways of inserting words that are absent in the Arabic are by using [brackets], or *italics,* or these ⌜marks⌝. Like the other 24 versions, neither of these contains the word (wife), or ⌜wife⌝, or [your wife], or *her,* but the other nine versions do. Still another way this can be done is to insert the word/s with no symbols at all as if they belonged to the Arabic text and were not inserted by the translator. This is how Stacey's version appears, and one of the two versions that inserts the feminine pronoun **her** (Shakir translation). In this case, the average non-Arabic reader has no indication that words or phrases have been inserted and is led to believe that they are native to the text. But they are not.

In actual fact, Surah 38:44 says nothing about Job's wife. In my analysis, therefore, it is impossible to know that it has anything to do with her at all, much less to arrive at Stacey's interpretation.
So why do Stacey's and these other 11 versions insert it, even though the majority do not? That is the question. The answer seems to be that it comes from the traditions and the Tafsir, or the Islamic commentaries. One example of these can be found in MyIslam.org which proffers an interpretation very similar to Stacey's.[41] But to me the question still remains: Without the force and clarity of divine revelation, which is entirely lacking, how could it be known that this verse refers to Job beating his wife lightly with a bunch of grass to fulfill

---

[41] See myislam.org/surah-sad/ayat-44/#:~:text=(38%3A44)%20(and,turned%20(to%20his%20Lord). This tafsir also allows for another interpretation, i.e. that it refers to a person other than Job's wife. Also, "Some jurists hold the view that this concession was specially meant for the Prophet Job (peace be upon him), and some others think that other people also can take advantage of it. The first view has been cited by Ibn Asakir from Abdullah bin Abbas and by Abu Bakr al-Jassas from Mujahid, and Imam Malik also held the same view. The second view has been adopted by Imam Abu Hanifah, Imam Abu Yusuf, Imam Muhammad, Imam Zufar and Imam Shafei. Several Ahadith show that the Prophet (peace be upon him), in order to inflict the prescribed punishment on a fornicator who was too ill or too weak to receive a hundred stripes, also adopted the method taught in this verse."

an oath to Allah? For that matter, how could it be known that it refers to Job beating anybody? It simply is too obscure to be ascertained with any confidence.

As with the previous example, this bit of the Islamic story of Job is found nowhere in the canonical *Book of Job*. Again, one cannot help but wonder from whence it came.[42]

Whatever its origin, from all these streams we can collectively observe at least fourteen things which I enumerate in the following list. I call them "minimal facts." The ones specifically from the hadith are bolded so we may easily identify them.

Minimal Facts About Job

1. Job existed and was counted among the prophets.
2. He was well-regarded by Allah as 'excellent' and steadfast, and often repentant.
3. **He disapproved of disparaging talk about Allah.**
4. **He made vicarious expiation for some.**
5. He was a memorial to humanity.
6. He was duly inspired by Allah.
7. He was afflicted by the devil.
8. Allah allowed him to suffer.
9. **He was rejected by others.**
10. **He was deemed a sinner.**
11. **He suffered** (for 18 years).
12. He cried out to God.
13. He received mercy.
14. He was restored.

With some exceptions, these fourteen observations from the Islamic literature are largely consistent with what the Tanakh tells us, as far as they go.[43] But there are many more things that they do not

---

[42] Perhaps the apocryphal *Testament of Job*? See wikipedia.org/wiki/Testament_of_Job, and www.scribd.com/document/1251114/Testament-of-Job-Revised-English

[43] Two exceptions are these: 1) The *Book of Job* does not tell us for how long Job suffered, but it would seem to indicate a much shorter period of time, maybe only months or weeks. 2)

tell us. That's because the Tanakh contains the entire *Book of Job,* as we have already noted. It consists of 42 chapters ('surahs'), 1071 verses, and 18098 words about Job and the other seven characters in this saga. As you would suspect, with so much more material there can be that much more context and that many more details. The first chapter of Job's book tells us, for example, that Job was very rich and that he was the "greatest of all the people of the east" with an accounting of exactly how many livestock he possessed. He also had ten children—seven sons and three daughters. And yes, he was "excellent" as Surah 38:44 says, so excellent that, according to the Hebrew text, God said there was "no one like him on the earth" (v. 8), which in verse 1 also says that Job was "blameless and upright" (וְיָשָׁר תָּם). Then verse 5 tells us that he had a practice of offering burnt offerings[44] on behalf of his children in case they had sinned against God in their hearts, and this well before Moses received any such revelation from God. Perhaps this is also what the passage from the hadith means by "expiation".

In chapter 1 the divine narration tells us of the invisible 'wager' between God and Satan that permitted Satan to afflict Job and exactly how: first a raid by the Sabeans that took all the oxen and donkeys; then a "fire from God" that burned up all the sheep; then another raid on the camels by the Chaldeans; then a windstorm that killed all his children at once. Then in chapter 2 we are told that after a second 'wager' between God and Satan, the latter was permitted to harm Job's body and infect him with some kind of disease that produced painful boils on him from head to foot (vv. 1-8). Job's wife was spared from death and presumably from the infection, but obviously she was afflicted by all the other losses. A bit later in this chapter, out of her anguish, she admonished Job to "Curse God and die" for which he rebuked her and gave honor to God. ...Nothing more.

Instead of "Allah" the text of *Job* consistently says that Job spoke of אֱלוֹהַּ ('ĕ•lōʷᵃh), a form of Elohim, or יְהוָה (yᵉh•wāʰ·, LORD). Moreover, from the first mention of Him in verse 6, and 23 times after, the text of Job identifies God as יְהוָה (yᵉh•wāʰ· LORD).

[44] Animal sacrifices that were then burned completely in fire.

וַתֹּאמֶר לוֹ אִשְׁתּוֹ עֹדְךָ מַחֲזִיק בְּתֻמָּתֶךָ בָּרֵךְ אֱלֹהִים וָמֻת: וַיֹּאמֶר אֵלֶיהָ
כְּדַבֵּר אַחַת הַנְּבָלוֹת תְּדַבֵּרִי גַּם אֶת־הַטּוֹב נְקַבֵּל מֵאֵת הָאֱלֹהִים וְאֶת־הָרָע
לֹא נְקַבֵּל בְּכָל־זֹאת לֹא־חָטָא אִיּוֹב בִּשְׂפָתָיו: {פ}

His wife said to him, "You still keep your integrity! Blaspheme [curse, bless] *God and die!" But he said to her, "You talk as any shameless woman might talk! Should we accept only good from God and not accept evil?" For all that, Job said nothing sinful.* (vv. 9-10)[45]

All this horrific drama is written in continuous prose in the first two chapters, at the end of which Job's four friends come on the scene to mourn with him: Eliphaz the Temanite, Bildad the Shuhite, Zophar the Naamathite. And Elihu son of Barachel the Buzite. At first they came to mourn with him (2:11), but after a while they shifted their focus into convincing Job that he deserved what he got. The next thirty-five chapters contain their lengthy discourses in the form of monologues—nine by Job and the rest by each of the four men in-turn (some spanning two or more chapters). Thirty-five chapters! In them Job's friends become increasingly more judgmental and Job more defensive. They all seemed to believe in the same one God but they disagreed about His standards and Job's standing with Him. Then in chapter 38 God himself enters the dialogue for the first time and through chapter 42 proceeds to give Job an attitude adjustment. In a word, Job was guilty of misjudging the Almighty for his suffering, but less guilty than were his four companions for the misguided things they believed and spoke about God, i.e. their bad theology. For this reason God required atonement and instructed them to offer burnt offerings—seven bulls and rams (42:7-9). He received Job's prayer for them and then restored Job's health and wealth both.

That's just a summary. There are hundreds of other details we could mine out from the Hebrew *Book of Job* that we could not know from the Islamic literature, and some from the latter that are

---

[45] JPS translation, Sefaria.org/Job.2.9?lang=bi&with=all&lang2=he

dubious.⁴⁶ So in contrast to the Qur'an, the *Book of Job* gives us the whole story of Job in exquisite detail, not just snippets as we seem to get from the Qur'an and hadith.⁴⁷ Nevertheless, in both traditions the story of Job provides a powerful messiah motif.

In the next two chapters we will explore more deeply the concept of *motif*, first in the Hebrew scriptures (chapter 3), and then in the Qur'an (chapter 4). Then in chapter 5 we will come to a cluster of would-be messianic details in chapter 19 of the *Book of Job*. This chapter contains the sixth monologue by Job, in between one by Bildad in chapter 18 and one by Zophar in 20. This particular passage is the crux of our whole study.

---

⁴⁶ See Aisha Stacey's article at www.islamreligion.com/articles/2721/story-of-prophet-job/#_ftnref21221 This online article, for example, presents the discourse between Satan and God, and Satan's grievance against Job resulting in his calamities. Again, from my analysis, this cannot be known from the Islamic texts apart from the Hebrew text. It also cannot be known what Job's message was or that he made any efforts at all to warn his people, as Stacey claims he did. Finally, if Ibn Kathir relied upon sources other than what I have listed, Aisha Stacey does not cite them.

⁴⁷ It would seem logical, then, that the Tanakh's *Book of Job* should be viewed as the original source for the Islamic literature, and possibly apocryphal Jewish literature as well. Further, if the Qur'an is direct revelation from Allah so as to have had no earthly source, then we could know only two-thirds of those minimal facts by direct revelation. Secondly, if the passage from the hadith is not direct revelation (including any other ahadith about Job), then they must have had a pre-existing source which could only have been the traditions of the Jews themselves, which reasonably came from the *Book of Job*. Add to this the fact that by conservative dating of the book it pre-existed any Islamic literature by some 2600 years, and by liberal dating some 1200 years. Also, if it was written or redacted during the post-exilic period by Ezra, or under his editorial oversight, as the liberal view holds, well and good. Ezra was a great man of God who is highly esteemed by Jews, Christians, and Muslims alike, and deserves much confidence. Muslims regard Ezra as a prophet mentioned (once) in the Qur'an who as such was inerrant as all prophets were. The salient point is that the Tanakh's *Book of Job* is essential to provide the full story of Job for all three religions. Logically, the piecemeal nature of the Islamic material is insufficient on its own.

Chapter 3

Motifs in the Torah, Tanakh

> *The story of Job of Uz...and his three friends is a prime example of the topped triad [motif] that highlights the qualitative superiority of Job over his friends, whom he outranks on any count."* (Job 42:7-8)[48]   –Shemaryahu Talmon

Perhaps you feel the need for elaboration on the concept of *motif* especially in literature, and even more especially in Hebrew scripture. If so, you will appreciate this chapter. But I admit that it's a little dense, and I give you leave to jump right to the next chapter if you prefer. You can always come back to this one later.

What is a Motif?

In the visual arts, a motif a visually recognizable and recurring pattern. In music it is an aural or auditory one. In literature motifs are cognitive and imaginative. They can range from the obscure on one end of the spectrum to the blatant on the other, and from minor to major in terms of their prevalence. They can be fictional and purely symbolic on one hand and literally real on the other, and they can be both at once. The study of narrative and novels especially seems to relish and be saturated with them. In *Moby Dick*, for example, whales are an obvious motif, as are ships, and the very sea itself. That story is fictional, but it is not made fictional by the occurrence of motifs in it. Another narrative book that I enjoyed, *Two Years Before the Mast,* has almost identical motifs and yet it is a true account.[49] Still another

---

[48] Talmon, *Literary Motifs and Patterns in the Hebrew Bible: Collected Studies*, pp. 96-97
[49] Richard Henry Dana, 1840

well-known story has the similar motifs—*The Book of Jonah* that we will consider in chapter 4. I am aware that opinion is mixed on whether it is fiction or non-fiction, as I believe, but either way motifs occur in it. The scriptures of the other Hebrew prophets all do too. Actually, all religious texts have motifs, including the Vedas, the Analects, the Qu'ran, and the Bible as a whole. To admit of symbols, tropes[50], and motifs in them, within the boundaries of good faith and reason, need not compromise their divine origins or disparage them.

A Master of Motif-Studies

Dr. Shemaryahu Talmon[51] (1920–2010) was a recognized authority on this subject. Like Elie Wiesel, he was a Jewish scholar who wrote prolifically on biblical subjects, albeit on a more scholarly level. He had a special interest in motifs in the Hebrew Bible, or Tanakh. Also like Wiesel, Talmon was born in Eastern Europe (Poland), but he grew up in Germany. In 1939 he too was sent to a concentration camp (Buchenwald), but soon escaped and emigrated to Palestine, avoiding the fate of his parents and two sisters in the holocaust. In 1956 he earned his Ph.D. from the Hebrew University of Jerusalem with a thesis on the text and versions of the Tanakh, especially "double meanings" in Biblical texts.[52] He then stayed on to serve in the Bible department of the university between 1957 and 1988, becoming a renowned scholar in Biblical Studies with multiple achievements and honors. In 2013 **Literary Motifs and Patterns in the Hebrew Bible** was published posthumously, a collection of 18 of his studies on biblical motifs, patterns, collocations[53], themes, and other important elements of Jewish scripture. It is possibly one of the only scholarly resources of its kind.

---

[50] a figurative or metaphorical use of a word or expression.

[51] Born Shemaryahu Zelmanowicz. See more at www.sbl-site.org/publications/article.aspx?ArticleId=869

[52] Wikipedia.org/wiki/Shemaryahu Talmon

[53] The habitual juxtaposition of a particular word with another word or words with a frequency greater than chance.

On the first page of the introduction of this seminal work we immediately come upon this definition:

> A **literary motif** is a representative complex theme that recurs within the framework of the Hebrew Bible in variable forms and connections It is rooted in an actual situation of an anthropological or historical nature. In its secondary literary setting, a motif gives expression to ideas and experiences inherent in the original situation and is employed by the author to re-actualize in the audience the reactions of the participants in that original situation. The motif represents the essential meaning of the situation...[54]

For a man of his station and intellect, we should not be surprised that this is dense, and it is a very abstract concept to start with. Allow me to break this down a bit. First, a motif is a real thing in the Hebrew Bible. And Jewish scholars like Talmon are not the only ones who think so. More than a few Christian scholars and thinkers do too.

The Shepherd Motif

In her blog called Xenos, for example, Mary Beth Gladwell has an excellent essay on the *shepherd motif* in the Tanakh:

> The idea of shepherding, and in specific the idea of God acting as the Shepherd of His people, is a motif found throughout the Bible, from beginning to end. In Gen. 48:24, as Jacob, on his deathbed summarized his life, he declared that God had been his *"shepherd all of his life to this day."* ...Why did God choose to include this motif as part of His revelation to man? Scripture itself does not give a direct explanation, so the answer cannot be definitive. However, there would appear to be several good reasons. Shepherding was, and still is to a certain extent, a very common

---

[54] Talmon, *Literary Motifs and Patterns in the Hebrew Bible, Collected Studies*, p. 4, bolding mine.

occupation for those in the Middle East. The Patriarchs were all shepherds, as was Moses and of course David. ...The terrain and geography of the area lend itself to the raising of both sheep and goats, but in particular sheep. There is scarcity of grass and less than abundant sources of water. Sheep are moved from one area to another with relative ease and require less water than other domestic animals. Everyone was familiar with shepherding—to say the people to whom the scriptures were first written had a working knowledge of the concept would indeed be an understatement.

So shepherds and shepherding were a big deal in the culture of ancient Israel. So much so that when the extended family of Jacob entered into ancient Egypt at the invitation of Joseph and the current pharoah, they were given, or confined to, the land of Goshen for that reason. The narrative tells us that "...every shepherd is an abomination to the Egyptians." (*Genesis 46:34b*) In Egypt they were pariahs. But of course Egypt did have her own shepherds, and so also did most other peoples of the Ancient Near East. Gladwell goes on to say...

...However, it may be most noteworthy to realize that leaders and rulers being called shepherds was not exclusive to the Bible or for that matter to the nation of Israel. King Hammurabi of Babylon called himself a shepherd, and Homer regularly styles the Greek chiefs as shepherds of their people. In fact, history has shown, "from ancient antiquity rulers were described as demonstrating their legitimacy to rule by their ability to 'pasture' their people." This makes sense then of verses like those found in Jeremiah 49:19 and 50:44, where God asks, "*who is the shepherd who can stand against me?*" In this connection, the royal staff, or scepter, a common accessory for kings in the Ancient Near East, was itself a form of shepherd's rod. Shepherds commonly used long poles such as these to poke around crevices in caves to scare out scorpions and snakes. It came to be a symbol of protection, power and authority. Even in Egypt, a divine symbol of kingship was the shepherd's crook. It is true that the idea of shepherd as leader was not exclusive to the Bible. However, what we will find is that God as the ultimate shepherd of His people takes this concept to a level not present in other cultures.[55]

Talmon would surely agree. In this case, a biblical motif is a *recurring, complex theme* throughout the Hebrew scripture, like shepherd and shepherding. It is rooted in an actual, historical situation (such as Prophet Job's crisis, or Noah's, or Abraham's). So it has a primary and a secondary setting in both history and scripture. In its secondary setting a motif expresses particular ideas and experiences that originated in its primary setting. In the following eleven chapters, we will see that there is a very prominent *redeemer motif* in the Tanakh, including the *Book of Job*. But it originates with Noah, and even before him with Adam and Eve in the *Book of Genesis*.[56] Talmon goes on to say that the secondary author employs the motif to "re-actualize in the audience the reactions of the participants in that original situation."

It's important to restate here that although there are multiple authors of Hebrew scripture, they are all secondary, and they are all human of course. Only humans write, so <u>everything</u> that ever has been written was penned by human authors. This includes Bible, the Vedas, the Qur'an, and every other holy book. However, according to scripture's own witness, the primary author of all scripture is God himself, both of the earlier and later scriptures in which the motif appears.[57] So when Talmon gives credit to the human author who

---

[55] www.xenos.org/essays/shepherd-motif-old-and-new-testament#_ftn2

[56] *Book of Genesis* 3:21 when God made garments of animal skins for them.

[57] Among multiple forms, the LORD's words are divine revelation and recorded as holy scripture. For example, in the first four chapters of the Bible, or Tanakh, or Torah (*Genesis* 1-4), the phrase "God said" or a derivation thereof appears 26 times in reference to Adam, Eve, the serpent (Satan), Cain, to the angels or other heavenly beings, or to himself. (Yes, God speaks to himself.) Then chapters 6-11 contain 9 more instances of the phrases "God said" or "the LORD (יְהוָה = Yahweh) said" in reference to Noah, or to the angels or the heavenly beings, or to himself. Chapters 12-25 contain "God said" (5) or "the LORD said" (8) to Abraham 13 times, plus 1 in reference to Rebekah, the wife of Isaac, 1 to King Abimelech, and 2 to the angels, or himself, or the heavenly beings. Then the remaining chapters of *Genesis* (25-50) contain 5 instances of "God said" or "the LORD said" in reference to Jacob (*Genesis* 21:12, 31:3, and 35:1, 10 and 11). Finally, in the remainder of the Torah either of these phrases, or a combination of them (e.g. "the LORD your God") occur **85** times in reference to Moses, 3 times to Aaron, and 3 to Balaam the pagan prophet.

employs the motif, I read that as God using the man to write what God wants written. I'm not sure if Talmon would agree with me on that or not. Either way, even when God is the divine author of something, there is always a human author, no exceptions. Talmon goes on to elaborate on this concept:

> A discerning examination of pivotal **motifs**…within the unfolding and changing modes of their employment in diverse strata of the Hebrew Scriptures, can assist us in gauging the intellectual faculties of the biblical authors, as well as the scope of the theological insight, societal comprehension, and historical information that they shared with their audiences. (p. 5)

It's worth it.

This just means that studying biblical motifs is worth it. It can help us understand the minds of the human authors, i.e. their intellect, their theological understanding, and their knowledge of society and history. Afterall, Jews and Christians have always understood that in giving divine revelation to the Hebrew prophets and other writers of

---

Altogether, these add up to **146**. In the historical revelation books of the Tanakh (Joshua – Esther) the phrase "God said" (14) or "the LORD said" (93) or "the LORD spoke" (9) occurs a total of **107** times, including to Joshua, Gideon, and other men who were not "prophets" per se. In the poetic revelation books (Job – Song of Solomon) the LORD spoke 14 times including to Job. Then in the remaining books of the prophets these phrases occur **61** times, plus at least twice when it is said that "the Spirit" spoke to the prophet Ezekiel (2:2 and 3:24). It is also said that the LORD spoke "through" the prophet or man of God such as is recorded in Jeremiah 37:2 and Hosea 1:2, and of course *every* time God told them to say or speak to the people on His behalf, another 41 times. Then there are 73 more times where it is recorded that "the LORD commanded" which is to speak. Yes, the prophets and men of God wrote holy scripture, not only what the LORD said, but also what He did, and the annals of His people. For to record in writing His acts (and theirs) was every bit as much revelation as it was to record his words. Four times the LORD commanded Prophet Moses to "write" down His words and deeds (Ex. 34:27 and Deut. 3, 8, and 31:19). Then once also to Isaiah (30:8), once to Jeremiah (30:2), once to Ezekiel (43:11), and once to Habbakuk (2:2). All this writing, of course, became scripture. But these are only a few of the times that we can read of this. Judging by the volumes of scripture there is in the Tanakh, the prophets and other saints were obviously commanded or inspired by God to write so much more often. Everything was collected and preserved as holy scripture, and according to the great Prophet Jesus, "Scripture cannot be broken." (*Gospel of John* 10:35). If the Torah, the Injeel, and the writings of all the prophets were ever scripture, they can never be corrupted.

the Tanakh, God did not circumvent their minds. Rather, he revealed *through* them.

> Therefore, the investigation of literary motifs and similar conventions in their changing and developing configurations within the overall framework of the biblical literature can be most rewarding in the endeavor to extract from them their conceptual content and intrinsic message. (p. 5)

Again, the study of biblical motifs is worth it. The exercise of motif recognition and comprehension helps us dig deeper into meaning beyond our initial grasp, and unwrapping the motifs themselves offers fuller understanding, not just of an idea in one text of one book of the Tanakh, but of all other texts that contain that motif. I add, therefore, that there are greater and lesser motifs in scripture, the greatest ones qualifying as 'master motifs.' In addition, I also put forth the notions of divine and prophetic motifs. Divine motifs, I assert, are those that God himself installs into the scriptural narratives, especially when they are intertextual. And we know they had different authors, so that it is impossible for any one human author to have engineered any other than those in his own book, if even that.

Job as Motif

'In my view, the whole story of Job is a motif. A divine motif. He is a legendary figure who 'goes down' into the valley of despair and comes out better on the other side. The story of Joseph is one other example, as is Moses, David, and certainly Jonah.

A prophetic motif is one that is also attributable to God. He gave them to his prophets, some of which were human writers of scripture and some which were not. The motif that God gave them was in the form of a prophecy, a foretelling of something future or a forthtelling of something present, or both. In this book, I argue that Job's well-known oracle in chapter 19:25 of his tome is exactly that. He was predicting a *future* redeemer who was as yet anonymous.

Next Talmon offers a methodological tip for the study of biblical motifs. Afterall, he established his scholarly reputation not only for what he discovered but also for the methods of study he developed.

> The analysis should be first conducted intertextually, so as to unravel the textual and literary interaction which can be discerned in the books of the Hebrew Bible, and which confers upon them a palpable unity that transcends their just as tangible disparity. (p. 6)

This means that any good study of biblical motifs should not be confined to just one text, but several texts at least, even many—ideally in all the texts in which that motif can be found. Master motifs, of course, deserve this the most. Ones like shepherd and shepherding, run all through the library of Hebrew scripture, and often into the New Testament, and require the most intertextual study. And that is precisely what I have attempted to do in my study.

Talmon goes on to put forth his three-part thesis as follows:

> 1. The analysis of motifs...is bound to reveal pivotal normative traits in the ancient Israelites' ideonic universe, **relative to their understanding of faith and history,** and their evaluation of the individual's place in society.[58]

> 2. On the other hand, motifs may at times encase sentiments and ideas that diverge from established norms...

> 3. A motif...lends itself to, and even tends to be amalgamated with, other motifs, themes, and literary patterns. ...Because of its complexity...a motif cannot be adequately evaluated in isolation. To gauge its full intrinsic meaning, a motif should be viewed in conjunction with synonymous and against the background of antonymous themes and literary patterns with which it can be linked in variable combinations. (p. 6)

I condensed these three points for brevity and simplicity. Basically Talmon is saying that biblical motifs tell us much about the

---

[58] All bolding on this page and the next mine.

Israelites' "ideonic universe" related to faith and history, or the way they collectively understood God's actions over time. They tend to conform to certain norms, but they can diverge. A motif is complex. It interacts with other literary features and patterns, so it cannot be analyzed in isolation, only in connection with like and unlike elements of the text.

Finally, I return to a point that I skipped over before—the essential recognizability of the motif:

> Like other representative literary tropes, such as metaphors and similes, **motifs are effective only as long as they evoke a clear echo in the listeners' or readers' minds**. Unless an author could expect that his audience would **grasp instantaneously**, or at least without excessive mental effort, the intrinsic signification of a motif or topos[59] which he introduced into his discourse, this convention would lose its very raison d'être. The message contained in it would fall on deaf ears, as it were. **An author must feel assured that his audience would react to the conventions he uses with a déjà vu sensation**, to use Roland Barthes' felicitous term, and would thus be able to integrate itself into his own train of thought. (p. 5)

In most biblical stories there is an immediate and an ultimate audience. Thus in scripture, for the divine and human authors to use it meaningfully, a motif must not escape the attention of either the original hearers or later readers. I assert that they did not. When God made garments of skins for Adam and Eve, that was the first appearance of the redemption motif, and it was understood.[60] The second was Abel's animal offering, his murder, and the birth of Seth as his replacement.[61] The third was the salvation of Noah and his family, the flood, and their safe landing after the flood subsided, and Noah's burnt offerings following. The next series entails multiple events in

---

[59] a traditional theme or formula in literature.

[60] Torah, *Book of Genesis* 3:21

[61] Torah, *Book of Genesis* 4:3-5

the life of Abraham such as the substitution of the ram for the life of his son on the altar of Mt. Moriah.[62] I believe that all of these were understood by those who came later.

The Desert Motif and Others

Talmon doesn't include any of the above in his book, focusing instead on other ones including creation, latter days, the barren wife, the city of Jerusalem, exile and restoration, the "good Israelite," antithetical motifs such as the wilderness (desert) and mountain, the numerical pattern of the topped triad, and historical time vs. motifs. I especially appreciate his treatment of the wilderness (desert) and mountain. In *Literary Motifs and Patterns* he devotes the whole of chapter 4 to this last subject in which he argues that there *is* a wilderness/desert motif in Hebrew scripture with numerous prominent examples. Indeed, almost four fifths of the Torah take place in the wilderness, and the preponderance of later occurrences of the two related words refer back to the wilderness sojourn. But contrary to the views of previous scholars, Talmon argued that the desert as a biblical motif is generally not positive, and that the Israelites should not be viewed as an essentially desert or nomadic people:

> The desert or wilderness is a place of utter desolation: a vast void of parched land…unfit for human habitation (Jeremiah 9:11; 50:40; 51:43; Job 38:26), except for roaming nomads (Jeremiah 3:2 and 9:25). Due to its remoteness from settled areas, the wilderness can become the refuge of outlaws and fugitives, who prefer an off chance of survival in exceedingly adverse circumstances to the calamities which will certainly befall them at the hands of their pursuers.

*Note that he cites the *Book of Job* 38:26.

Talmon also published a separate article on this subject. In it he introduced his discussion a little differently and he challenged what

---

[62] Torah, *Book of Genesis* 22

he believed was an unwarranted "desert ideal" among scholars.

> The study of the "desert motif" in the Bible has played an important role in Biblical research since Budde introduced it into the discussion...as a factor of major importance. Now the desert ideal [has] achieved the proportions of a veritable avalanche. ...[but] R. de Vaux's notes that "our oldest Biblical texts show little admiration for nomadic life..." The desert and the desert period are conceived in the Bible not as intrinsically valuable, but originally and basically as a punishment and a necessary transitory stage in the restoration of Israel to its ideal setting, which is an organized, fully developed society, with a deep appreciation of civilization, settled in the cultivated Land of Israel.
> The "desert motif" that occurs in the Old Testament expresses the idea of an unavoidable transition period in which Israel recurrently is prepared for the ultimate transfer from social and spiritual chaos to an integrated social and spiritual order. [Nevertheless], It appears that this motif is especially well suited for submission to an analysis which will bring out poignant features and characteristics of the "motif" as a literary theme and will illustrate the functions and the developments of a "motif" in a given literary framework. [Although it began with studies of art and music,] in 1897 the term was used in a literary analysis of the Biblical Book of Ruth.[63]

In my research Talmon doesn't appear to delve into motifs in the *Book of Job* as I intend to do. But he believes that the exercise of analyzing any biblical motif can help us in our understanding of others. Still, he does refer to *Job* five times in *Literary Motifs and Patterns*. Here's one in the context of what he calls "topped triads":

The story of Job of Uz, a blameless and upright man (*Job* 1:1), and his three friends is a prime example of the topped triad convention in a narrative framework. In this instance, the names and ethnic origins of the friends are fully spelled out, both at the beginning of the narrative envelope (*Job*

---

[63] Talmon, "The Desert Motif in the Bible and in Qumran Literature."

2:11) and its end (42:9): Eliphaz of Teman, Bildad of Shuah and Zophar of Naamah. These details evince the writer's intent to drape his tale in a seemingly authentic atmosphere of historical realism. However, the paradigmatic nature of the narrative was already recognized by the sages, who opined that Job never existed, but rather was a proverbial figure (b. B.Bat.15a), known as one of a trio of famous just men of bygone days (*Ezekiel* 14:14, 20).70 Modern scholarship has revealed ancient Semitic and folkloristic tales from other cultures, which preserve a similar tradition of "the undeservedly suffering just one) who ultimately is restored to his good fortunes." (Pope, *Job* 1:6-21) The shared theme underpins the definition of the Job narrative as a fable, structured in accord with widely accepted literary conventions. Among these, the topped triad pattern is central to the story. It highlights the qualitative superiority of Job over his friends, whom he outranks on any count (*Job* 42:7-8).[64]

Personally, I cannot agree with the so-called "sages" that the *Book of Job* is a fable and that Job the man was a proverbial figure only. My Muslim readers will probably support me on this. But if you are convinced otherwise, for my purposes one's view on the factual historicity of Job is not critical. Yes, *I* think you should believe that the story of Job was real history, but my thesis is not dependent on it. Even if the *Book of Job* is a fable and Job *was* a mythical character, in context of the whole Tanakh the primary elements of the story are clearly not: God the LORD (YHWH-Yahweh), Satan, the adversarial nature of their relationship, good and evil, suffering, sin, falsehood and error, burnt offering, advocacy, and redemption.

Wiesel on Job

Over the millennia to the present, a great many thinkers have contemplated and written about the lessons to be learned from Job.

---

[64] Talmon, *Literary Motifs and Patterns*, pp. 96-97

Elie Wiesel, whom we met in chapter 1, wrote and spoke much more prolifically about Job than Talmon did, especially in reference to God and unwarranted suffering. For Wiesel the story of Job was centrally about this kind of suffering, and which became for him one of the major lenses of life. In a lecture he delivered on the *Book of Job* he delves deeply into the nature of Job's suffering, the divine wager that allowed it, and God's disposition toward it.[65] He said that even though God did not explain to Job the reason for his gut-wrenching afflictions, He *did* show up for Job in a way that only God could. And he spoke to him in a way that only God would. In that act of speaking alone, argues Wiesel, God showed Job that He was not indifferent toward him, as his family members and members of his community seemed to be. And Job obviously sees that as a very significant fact! But in all that he has to say about Job, Wiesel does not speak of *motifs* as Talmon does, at least not with that word.

Wiesel also wrote **Messengers of God: Biblical Portraits and Legends**, an engaging exposition of several Hebrew prophets and figures, as I also intend to provide.[66] His include Adam, Cain and Abel, Abraham and Isaac, Jacob, Joseph, Moses, and finally Job. In this final, heartfelt portrait, again Wiesel does not speak of "motifs", much less a 'redemption motif' per se that I intend to highlight in this book. More to the point, he seems to have been almost oblivious to the explicit "redeemer" that Job spoke of in chapter 19. But really he was *not* oblivious to the rich motifs in the story of Job and other parts of the Tanakh. Without using the word he sees them in multiple examples, uniting the lessons from Job with those of other such other great patriarchs as Abraham:

> In him [Job] we find the solitary conscience of Abraham…
> He reminds one of Abraham, **for both their tragedies result from seemingly arbitrary ordeals**…But unlike Abraham, he succeeded in maintaining a keen sense of humor. [Really?]
> Four men discovered God on their own—**Abraham,** King

---

[65] youtube.com/watch?v=A2FMIc5HgjA

[66] All bolding on this page mine.

> Ezechias, **Job** and **the Messiah**...The parallel with Abraham seems deliberate; it reappears frequently. Both were kind and charitable men; both suffered. In their quarrels with God, they used almost identical language. Abraham questioned His justice with regard to Sodom and Gomorrah, Job with regard to himself. Abraham pleaded with God for an entire city, Job pleaded for himself. Abraham's purpose was to prevent, Job's was to indict...There exists at least one precedent: What is happening to [Job] has happened before, and to one greater than [Job]: Abraham.[67]

What, then, are the motifs that Wiesel is capturing here? Well, again, he doesn't speak of 'motifs' *per se*, so allow me to offer my suggestions. The first and the most obvious one I think he is getting at is *tragedy and suffering*. In Wiesel's view, both patriarchs experienced it acutely. To him, and to almost anybody, Job's entire story is a tragedy, *essentially*—perhaps even with the happy ending. And Abraham experienced his when he was commanded to sacrifice his beloved son. (Which of their ordeals would have been harder, to lose one's children suddenly to calamity or to endure for three days the knowledge that one must kill one?) For my part, I mostly agree. It's undoubtedly true that many figures of the Tanakh experienced tragedies: Adam and Eve when they fell from the LORD's favor and were banished from paradise, and then when one of their sons was murdered by the other; Noah when the world was destroyed by the flood; Joseph when he was sold into slavery by his brothers and later imprisoned on false charges; Moses when he had to go into exile from Egypt; and David when his son Absalom tried to overthrow his government, to name just a few.

Another motif I see in Wiesel's comparison is 'discovering God.' Another is 'quarreling with God.' Still another, 'justice and the age-old problem of evil'; and finally, intercession. But in contrast to tragedy, many of these figures also experienced redemption, which

---

[67] Wiesel, *Messengers of God: Biblical Portraits and Legends*.

is somewhat the main subject of this book. Abraham, the Torah tells us, did not have to sacrifice his son after all. But he was not just rescued or excused, he was redeemed. The ram was provided by God for that very purpose. Likewise Job, we are told, through all his heart-wrenching suffering, was not only patient or steadfast through it, as the Apostle James says of him.[68] In the end he was redeemed, and became a redeemer. Then he was restored by the God who gave him twice as much as he had before.[69] All these are powerful motifs that appear not only in their immediate texts, but also in numerous others of the Torah and Tanakh, which I will endeavor to show. And some of them are present in the Qur'an as well. In his book *Messengers of God: Biblical Portraits and Legends,* Elie Wiesel wrote the final chapter on Job and called him "A different Messiah, working for the Redemption of the Gentiles." In that segment he said, "One finds nothing but praise and compliments about him in the Midrashic texts [Jewish commentary akin to the Islamic Tafsirs]…A Just Man among the Gentiles, **he was reputed to have tried to save mankind through his suffering.**"[70] Now that is a big idea that deserves our attempt to plumb its depths in the ensuing chapters.

---

[68] *Letter of James* 5:11

[69] A fact with which Wiesel was not altogether satisfied. At the conclusion of his chapter on Job Wiesel wrote: "I was offended by [Job's] surrender in the text. [His] resignation as a man was an insult to man. He should not have given in so easily. He should have continued to protest, to refuse the handouts. Very well, I forgive you… But what about my dead children, do they forgive you?... I demand that justice be done to them, if not to me, and that the trial continue." (p. 234) And with respect to Abraham, he seemed similarly offended that God had such audacity to require him to violate good ethics. "He [Abraham] could have accused him and proved him wrong; he didn't" (p. 93)

[70] p. 218

Chapter 4
Motifs in the Qur'an

"And We showed them signs in which there was a clear test."

– Qur'an, Surah Ad-Dukhan, 44:33

Are there motifs in Islamic literature? Can they be found in the scriptures of its holy book, the Qur'an? And if so, are they a part of Muslims' collective "ideonic universe" as Talmon puts it? In my experience, sources on this question are harder to find than they are in the Judeo-Christian milieu. This suggests to me not that motifs are entirely absent or less prevalent in Qu'ran, but that they may be of less interest to Muslim scholars and writers. But one Muslim scholar who took interest in this subject was Dr. Fazlur Rahman in his book *Major Themes of the Qur'an.*[71] Wait, aren't we examining *motifs?* Yes, themes and motifs can be synonymous or very similar literary concepts. Certainly they overlap and serve some of the same purposes. They are both broad, recurring categories under which many other sub-categories can be subsumed. For the present let's suppose that they are practically identical to get a functional overview of this book, first the author. According to its flyleaf,

> Rahman (1919-88) was born in what is today Pakistan and educated in Islamic schools, [followed by] Punjab University in Lahore (MA, 1942), and Oxford University (PhD, 1949). During his career, Rahman held appointments at Durham University in England, McGill University in Canada, the Central Institute for Islamic Research in Pakistan, and, finally, at the University of Chicago, where he taught

---

[71] University of Chicago Press, 1980, 1989, 2009

from 1969 until his death. In 1983 he received UCLA's Giorgio Levi Della Vida Award for Islamic scholarship, and in 1987 he became the Harold H. Swift Distinguished Service Professor of Islamic Thought at the University of Chicago. Professor Rahman was the author of hundreds of articles and ten books, including *Islam* (1966) and *Islam and Modernity: Transformation of an Intellectual Tradition* (1982).

Another popular source adds:

Fazlur Rahman Malik was a modernist scholar and philosopher of Islam from today's Pakistan. He is renowned as a prominent liberal reformer of Islam, who devoted himself to educational reform and the revival of independent reasoning (*ijtihad*). After teaching in Britain and Canada, he was appointed head of the Central Institute of Islamic Research of Pakistan in 1963. ...Although his works were widely respected by other Islamic reformers, they were also heavily criticized by conservative scholars as being overtly liberal [which] led to his eventual exile in the United States where he taught at the University of California, Los Angeles and the University of Chicago.[72]

More can be read about him in that article, but from this excerpt we can observe that Rahman was not viewed as conservative by other Muslim scholars; perhaps his approach was too novel. Personally, from a broader 'Abrahamic' view of the man, I don't see what they see. Still, let's dig deeper.

Rahman's book, *Major Themes in the Qur'an* is not obscure. I have a hard copy, but it can be readily accessed online.[73] In Goodreads.com there are 276 ratings and 26 popular reviews, and there are 33 in Amazon.com that are generally positive. For example, one Nazmul Hasan wrote:

---

[72] wikipedia.org/wiki/Fazlur_Rahman_Malik

[73] www.geocities.ws/islamic_modernist/Major_Themes_of_the_Quran.pdf

A great thematic overview of the Quran unlike any book written in the English language. Dr. Rahman writes with an astute clarity and a sharp pen, and he assumes the reader can follow along. Each of the ideas are supported by a plethora of verse quotations and annotations. Even in his more controversial opinions Dr. Rahman maintains his scholarly clarity and illuminates his thoughts for the reader. Dr. Fazlur Rahman has produced a supreme achievement in this book for anyone interested in understanding and appreciating the Quranic plea. Not the 'Quranic world' it envisions for man, but the man it envisions for the world God has created: men with a deep awareness of moral and personal responsibility.[74]

Another excellent but more comprehensive review of Rahman's book was produced by E.D. Burns:

> Most Islamic scholarship focuses on verse-by-verse exposition of Qur'anic texts. Some recent works topically arrange Qur'anic texts into helpful indices, but not many scholars attempt to synthesize the major themes of the Qur'an. There are three main areas of Qur'anic study: (1) reconstructions of the Qur'an in chronological order, (2) demonstrations of Jewish and Christian ideas and antecedents to the Qur'an, and (3) descriptions of the content of the Qur'an, either in part or in whole. This third area of study is the least common, and it is this approach that Fazlur Rahman, in his book *Major Themes of the Qur'an*, seeks to employ.
>
> Rahman synthetically outlines the Qur'an's dominant areas of focus in logical order over against chronological order. The following themes are each highlighted in individual chapters: God, Man as Individual, Man in Society, Nature, Prophethood and Revelation, Eschatology, Satan and Evil, and Emergence of the Muslim Community. He organizes these themes based upon his own hermeneutic, or principles of interpretation, which are largely modern.

---

[74] Fazlur, *Major Themes of the Qur'an*

Rahman's work is significant, not necessarily because of his hermeneutical arguments and theological conclusions, but rather, because of the synthetic process by which he unfolds the Qur'an's themes and applies them to Islam's historical and contemporary settings. For the history of Qur'anic interpretation, this is an unusually fresh confluence of modern thought and Qur'an-centeredness.

…Rahman's thematic approach also gives the reader an interpretive grid through which to approach the Qur'an. Knowing the major themes of the Qur'an enables the reader to organize general concepts and to discover minor themes otherwise hidden by the Qur'an's literary complexity. Overall, this book enables access to the Qur'an in a way that few scholars have attempted.[75]

Still other reviews can be found.[76]

My brief critique of this book is limited to the notion of *themes*. Although I said that themes and motifs *can* be synonymous, in this case I don't think they are. All the examples of motifs we have considered thus far—shepherd, desert, barrenness, even triads—have generally been more tangible and visible things, whereas the themes of Rahman's book are intangible and abstract. Take the first one, God (Allah), which he rightly calls the "master theme." Certainly. Is *Allah* also a motif? I don't think so. Why? I would say it's because he is abstract by virtue of the fact that he is invisible, and in other ways 'hidden' as the agnostic complains. Arguably, God is more abstract in Islam than he is in Judaism and Christianity. In the Qur'an, he is also abstract in the sense that he does not enter into the narratives as a character as he does in the Torah/Tanakh, or at least not as often.

In the story of Job, for example, God shows up in a whirlwind to talk with Job directly, but not in the Qur'an. (*Book of Job* 38:1) In

---

[75] Bolding mine. trainingleadersinternational.org/jgc/82/major-themes-of-the-quran

[76] See also https://bit.ly/33x7ZvO, islamresearchetown.wordpress.com/major-themes-of-the-quran-by-fazlur-rahman/, www.academia.edu/35546846/The_Book_Review_Rahman_Fuzlur_Major_Themes_of_the_Qur_a_n, www.jstor.org/ stable/601479? seq=1, www.al-mawrid.org/index.php/articles/view/major-themes-of-the-quran, www.linkedin.com/pulse/quran-major-themes-denis-jonathan-lombardo-ba-hons-/

the epic of Moses God shows up on the mountain to talk to Moses, first in the burning bush (Torah, *Book of Exodus* 3:2-6), and then in some other visible form He called his "glory" (*Book of Exodus 33:18-23*). He is both the 'producer' of the 'play' of revelation and a 'character' in it. But not in the Qur'an. In the Qur'an it seems to me that although Allah is the 'producer' he is not a character in the stories. Moreover, in the Qur'an the otherness and unknowability of God are generally more emphatic (apophatic) qualities than they are in Judaism and Christianity, and in my experience Muslims prize these more than do Jews and Christians (with some exceptions).[77] So God is undoubtedly the 'master theme' in the Qur'an as well as the Torah/Tanakh, but it is probably not quite accurate to call him a *motif* in either scripture. I consider it too obvious.

Rahman's 7 Themes & My Insights

Consider Rahman's seven other major themes in the Qur'an: Man, Nature, Prophethood, Revelation, Eschatology, Satan/Evil, and Emergence of the Muslim Community. Of these, with the exception of nature, I would give similar reasons for why they may not properly qualify as motifs. That said, I believe the Qur'an *does* contain motifs, it's just that Rahman does not capture and call them that in his list of themes the way Talmon does; nor does it seem that he intended to. In addition, one anonymous online writer does provide a short list of what he/she considers as Qur'anic motifs: time, animals, the human body, worship and adoration, and Muhammad as the sacred servant.[78] But that's it. In my search for motifs in the Qur'an or Islam, all other sources that I could discover treat motifs as visual art, not as a feature of literature, much less a feature of the Qur'an itself.

From my own search through the Qur'an, with the assistance of a native Arabic speaker,[79] I personally developed a list of recurring

---

[77] The Sephardic Jewish philosopher Maimonides (1138-1204) was well-known for his apophatic theology of God. wikipedia.org/wiki/Maimonides

[78] gradesaver.com/the-koran/study-guide/symbols-allegory-motifs

[79] Wissam Al-Aethawi from Baghdad, Iraq

words and ideas that to me seem to qualify as significant themes, if not also motifs. I chose them more or less randomly as they came to mind and as each triggered the thought of the next.[80] For starters, the exact phrase "Day and night," and its inverse, occur 19 times, with an additional 25 verses that contain these two words in relation to each other, even if not in that precise couplet. In my estimation, this alone constitutes a motif. Here is one example:

يُقَلِّبُ ٱللَّهُ ٱلَّيْلَ وَٱلنَّهَارَ إِنَّ فِي ذَٰلِكَ لَعِبْرَةً لِّأُوْلِي ٱلْأَبْصَٰرِ ٤٤

Allah alternates the *day* and *night*. Surely in this is a lesson for people of insight.

                                  Surah An-Nur (the Light), 24:44

    Moving on, the word "sky" appears 63 times. Celestial bodies such as the sun (31x), moon (27x), and stars (25x) appear 83 times collectively. (A word that can be translated as "planet" occurs only once in Surah 6:76.) From this I posit that "day and night" + "sky" + the related heavenly orbs constitutes another motif. Then we could add in celestial beings. Besides Allah himself, celestial beings include angels (138x), devils (or demons, 21x), and strange creatures called jinn (38).[81] Thus, Angels alone comprise a number which is certainly significant, let alone the other two, and the sum of all three. So, simply put, we can surmise that the combination of related words and ideas constitutes a major Qur'anic theme, if not also a motif.

    Animals have already been mentioned, but some are more prominent than others. Camel/s and birds each occur 20 times, which seems to qualify them for consideration, while horse/s (6), donkey/s (4), dog (5), and wolf (3) appear less than 10 times each. On the other

---

[80] The reader is asked to allow for a reasonable margin of error on my part, as I do not claim to have conducted exact and perfect searches of these words. Word searches in translations of the original language are sometimes not as simple as they may seem.

[81] In Islamic teachings, beings belonging to a class between angels and demons which are not part of Judeo-Christian cosmology. In the English vernacular they are called "Genies" as in the popular story of Sinbad and Alibaba.

hand, man/men appears in 129 verses, and women/woman in 87.[82] The word "paradise" occurs in 65 verses and "hell" in 110. Law appears in 41 verses, and sin in 107. Transgress is another verb form for to sin, and transgression is the noun form, occurring in a total of 30 verses. The word "revelation" occurs in 156 verses, "faith" in 187, and "prayer" in 104. The "day of judgment" or "judgment day" appear in 106 verses, with many more occurrences of judgment in reference to Allah's final reckoning of all people.

The Qur'an often speaks of the holy books that preceded it. For example, Torah appears 20 times in 18 verses, gospel another 12, and their combination 10. It also speaks of the religious communities that they represent: Jews 22 times, Christians 14, and 13 verses that speak of both. There is another term that the Qur'an uses to refer to them collectively—"people of the book" with two derivations.[83] Collectively these occur 34 times. Prophet/s occurs in 605 verses, which makes it by far the most prominent word/idea in our list, referring to Muhammad and the dozens of other prophets, named and unnamed. But I'm not convinced that this constitutes a motif. Many of these involve the recurring phrase "O Prophet" which always (or usually) refers to Muhammad, while his explicit name occurs 4 times. The prophet Moses appears in 166 verses, Noah in 51, Adam in 26, Solomon in 23, and David in 18. Finally, Jesus, or Issa as he is called in the Qur'an, occurs 25 times by name and another 11 times by his unique title, Messiah. I have also been told that references to Jesus by way of pronouns amount to some 125 times.[84] This should suffice as a brief but fuller survey of Qur'anic themes.

Through the lens of literary, and specifically motif studies, many of these and more could be added to Rahman's plus the anonymous writer's list of themes in the Qur'an, and possibly also as motifs. Sifting through all of the previous examples, I wish to return to the first one and give more attention to the combination of "day and night"

---

[82] Accounting for all occasions when the word occurs twice or more in one verse.

[83] "People of the gospel" and "people of the remembrance".

[84] Quran.com, the Clear Qur'an, Dr. Mustapha Kattab

with the various components of the celestial realm as one compound Qur'anic motif. In a logical sense, it probably fits under Rahman's Nature category, unless by nature he means strictly those natural things that are found on the earth. As a mere sampling, I have selected five verses from the Qur'an to exemplify this motif.

Motif 1: Day & Night, Celestial Things   ليلا ونهارا

أَلَمْ تَرَ أَنَّ ٱللَّهَ يُولِجُ ٱلَّيْلَ فِى ٱلنَّهَارِ وَيُولِجُ ٱلنَّهَارَ فِى ٱلَّيْلِ وَسَخَّرَ ٱلشَّمْسَ وَٱلْقَمَرَ كُلٌّ يَجْرِى إِلَىٰ أَجَلٍ مُّسَمًّى وَأَنَّ ٱللَّهَ بِمَا تَعْمَلُونَ خَبِيرٌ ٢٩

Do you not see that Allah causes the *night* to merge into the *day* and the *day* into the *night*, and has subjected the sun and the moon, each orbiting for an appointed term, and that Allah is All-Aware of what you do?

Surah Luqman (the Wise), 31:29

Notice that this includes the sun and the moon which each has its respective orbit. It seems to say that since Allah had ordered the day and night according to the movements of the sun and moon, he certainly knows everything people do. Here's a similar verse:

وَمِنْ ءَايَٰتِهِ ٱلَّيْلُ وَٱلنَّهَارُ وَٱلشَّمْسُ وَٱلْقَمَرُ لَا تَسْجُدُوا۟ لِلشَّمْسِ وَلَا لِلْقَمَرِ وَٱسْجُدُوا۟ لِلَّهِ ٱلَّذِى خَلَقَهُنَّ إِن كُنتُمْ إِيَّاهُ تَعْبُدُونَ ٣٧

Among His signs are the *day* and the *night*, the sun and the moon. Do not prostrate to the sun or the moon, but prostrate to Allah, Who created them ⌈all⌉, if you ⌈truly⌉ worship Him ⌈alone⌉.

Surah Fussilat (Distinctly explained), 41:37

This one states that these four things serve as signs to those who worship Allah alone, as opposed to those who do not. Similar verbiage is found in Surahs 35:13 (Fatir, Originator) and 39:5 (Az-Zumar, the Troops). Surah Ali 'Imran (Family of Imran) substitutes "those who worship Allah" with "people of reason" (3:190); Surah Yunus (Joseph) substitutes "people who are mindful of him" (10:6) with "people who listen" (10:67); and Surah An-Nahl (the Bee), adds in the stars and "those who understand" (16:12).

وَسَخَّرَ لَكُمُ ٱلَّيْلَ وَٱلنَّهَارَ وَٱلشَّمْسَ وَٱلْقَمَرَّ وَٱلنُّجُومُ مُسَخَّرَٰتُۢ بِأَمْرِهِۦٓ إِنَّ فِى ذَٰلِكَ لَءَايَٰتٍ لِّقَوْمٍ يَعْقِلُونَ ١٢

And He has subjected for your benefit the *day* and the *night*, the sun and the moon. And the stars have been subjected by His command. Surely in this are signs for those who understand.

In the next verse "night" is omitted but "heaven/s" is added.

فَقَضَىٰهُنَّ سَبْعَ سَمَٰوَاتٍ فِى يَوْمَيْنِ وَأَوْحَىٰ فِى كُلِّ سَمَآءٍ أَمْرَهَاۚ وَزَيَّنَّا ٱلسَّمَآءَ ٱلدُّنْيَا بِمَصَٰبِيحَ وَحِفْظًاۚ ذَٰلِكَ تَقْدِيرُ ٱلْعَزِيزِ ٱلْعَلِيمِ ١٢

So He formed the heaven into seven heavens in two *Days*, assigning to each its mandate. And We adorned the lowest heaven with ˹*stars* like˺ lamps ˹for beauty˺ and for protection. That is the design of the Almighty, All-Knowing.

Surah Fussilat (Distinctly explained), 41:12

This final example omits both day and night but includes "heavens and the earth" and the oft-repeated appellation "O Prophet" referring, of course, to Muhammad.

وَلَئِن سَأَلْتَهُم مَّنْ خَلَقَ ٱلسَّمَٰوَٰتِ وَٱلْأَرْضَ وَسَخَّرَ ٱلشَّمْسَ وَٱلْقَمَرَ لَيَقُولُنَّ ٱللَّهُۖ فَأَنَّىٰ يُؤْفَكُونَ ٦١

If you ask them ˹O Prophet˺ who created the heavens and the earth and subjected the *sun* and the *moon* ˹for your benefit˺, they will certainly say, "Allah!" How can they then be deluded ˹from the truth˺?

Surah Al-'Ankabut (the Spider), 29:61

These five examples should suffice to support my suggestion that day and night and celestial things should be considered as a Qur'anic motif. The Qur'an repeatedly presents these compound images. Together they visualizably assert the notion that Allah designed and created all these things as signs of his existence, power, and authority, and he is therefore worthy of worship by all mankind and by celestial beings. If this were a more exhaustive study, many more verses with numerous combinations of related words and ideas could be included to expand our conception of it.

Motif 2: Signs ایات

By way of extension, let's now consider a second motif—sign/s. Notice again that my last paragraph mentions it in relation to the first motif. This word is transliterated as ayat, or ayah in the singular, which are both popular Arabic names for girls in Muslim families. As has been mentioned in a footnote, it is also the word used to refer to verse/s in the Qur'an. To be honest, this only became apparent to me in the hours after I wrote that paragraph: Signs themselves are a Qur'anic motif. According to Hanna E. Kassis' *A Concordance of the Quran,* the word appears 385 times including all verses that contain it twice or three times.[85] Two of the five verses I gave as examples of the first motif also contain the word "signs", and in the other three it is implied. The plain idea is that Allah employs perceivable signs that point to him and to the truths of Islam. Adding to those, let's look at several more. This first one is straightforward and suggests that there are those who would deny them.

وَيُرِيكُمْ ءَايَٰتِهِۦ فَأَىَّ ءَايَٰتِ ٱللَّهِ تُنكِرُونَ ٨١

---

[85] However, according to Qur'an.com there are 228 verses that contain the word sign/s at least once, and sometimes two or three times. This seems to reveal a discrepancy between the two sources for which I do not know the explanation. But I think it is unimportant. The simple fact is that "sign/s" appears in the Qur'an hundreds of times—no less than 228 and up to 385.

And He shows you His *signs*. Now which of Allah's signs will you deny?

                    Surah Ghafir (the Forgiver), 40:81

Not only are signs abundant in the Qur'an, they are also impressively diverse, and ordinary as signs go.

وَمِنْ ءَايَٰتِهِۦٓ أَنْ خَلَقَ لَكُم مِّنْ أَنفُسِكُمْ أَزْوَٰجًا لِّتَسْكُنُوٓا۟ إِلَيْهَا وَجَعَلَ بَيْنَكُم مَّوَدَّةً وَرَحْمَةً إِنَّ فِى ذَٰلِكَ لَءَايَٰتٍ لِّقَوْمٍ يَتَفَكَّرُونَ ٢١

And one of His ***signs***[86] is that He created for you spouses from among yourselves so that you may find comfort in them. And He has placed between you compassion and mercy. Surely in this are *signs* for people who reflect.

                    Surah Ar-Rum (the Romans), 30:21

The conjoining three verses above and below contain "signs" twice each. In the one above, spouses are signs, as are compassion and mercy. The one below echoes the first motif in terms of heavens and earth, as does verse 105 of Surah Yusuf (Joseph). But it also includes the diversity of languages and colors as signs.

وَمِنْ ءَايَٰتِهِۦ خَلْقُ ٱلسَّمَٰوَٰتِ وَٱلْأَرْضِ وَٱخْتِلَٰفُ أَلْسِنَتِكُمْ وَأَلْوَٰنِكُمْ إِنَّ فِى ذَٰلِكَ لَءَايَٰتٍ لِّلْعَٰلِمِينَ ٢٢

And one of His *signs* is the creation of the heavens and the earth, and the diversity of your **languages** and **colors**. Surely in this are *signs* for those of ˹sound˺ knowledge.

                    Surah Ar-Rum, 30:22

In the last verse of the triad the sign is sleep, and apparently the act of seeking Allah's bounty.

وَمِنْ ءَايَٰتِهِۦ مَنَامُكُم بِٱلَّيْلِ وَٱلنَّهَارِ وَٱبْتِغَآؤُكُم مِّن فَضْلِهِۦٓ إِنَّ فِى ذَٰلِكَ لَءَايَٰتٍ لِّقَوْمٍ يَسْمَعُونَ ٢٣

---

[86] All bolding on this page is mine. All italics are from their source.

And one of His *signs* is your **sleep** by night and by day ʿfor restʾ as well as your seeking His **bounty** ʿin bothʾ. Surely in this are *signs* for people who listen.

Surah Ar-Rum, 30:23

One final example is in the *animals* category—the camel, and the female in particular.[87]

وَيَـٰقَوْمِ هَـٰذِهِۦ نَاقَةُ ٱللَّهِ لَكُمْ ءَايَةً فَذَرُوهَا تَأْكُلْ فِىٓ أَرْضِ ٱللَّهِ وَلَا تَمَسُّوهَا بِسُوٓءٍ فَيَأْخُذَكُمْ عَذَابٌ قَرِيبٌ ٦٤

And O my people! This she-*camel* of Allah is a *sign* for you. So leave her to graze ʿfreelyʾ on Allah's earth and do her no harm, or a swift punishment will overtake you!"

Surah Hud (Those who ask forgiveness), 11:64

And this is only scratching the surface of this motif. By comparison, the Judeo-Christian scriptures of the Bible contain signs too, but fewer and more diverse. The Tanakh, which is about four times longer than the Qur'an, only contains 92 references to sign/s, with another 72 in the New Testament (total=164). But in my cursory analysis, there is a qualitative difference between the nature of signs in the Bible compared with those in the Qur'an. In very broad strokes, signs in the Qur'an seem to belong to Allah alone, not to prophets, for example; they are notably commonplace and point largely to the existence of Allah. In the Bible signs are most often given by Yahweh,

---

[87] It is interesting to note that according to another Qur'anic verse about camels in Surah Al Hajj (the Pilgrimage, 22:36), it is permissible in Islam, or halal, to eat camels: "We have made sacrificial *camels* ʿand cattleʾ among the symbols of Allah, in which there is ʿmuchʾ good for you. So pronounce the Name of Allah over them when they are lined up ʿfor sacrificeʾ. Once they have fallen ʿlifelessʾ on their sides, you may eat from their meat, and feed the needy..." While in the Torah the camel is prohibited (unclean) along with the pig, the hare, the rock badger (hyrax), and the horse, etc. (Books of *Leviticus* 11:4 and *Deuteronomy* 14:7). Also see verse 40 in Surah Al A'raf (7, the Heights) which bears a striking resemblance to a saying of Jesus quoted in three parallel verses in the New Testament gospels of *Matthew* (19:24), *Luke* (18:25), and *Mark:* "It is easier for a camel to go through the eye of a needle than for a rich person to enter the kingdom of God." (10:25)

but are also given by his prophets and apostles, by men—the righteous and the wicked—by false prophets and messiahs, and even by demons. Thus there are good signs and bad signs. The good ones seem generally to validate things such as divine promises (e.g. covenants), predictions of future events, the authenticity of true prophets and apostles, and even believers in general. The bad ones are always intended to deceive. Jesus in particular was known as a sign-giver, and to be a sign himself. In the gospels and the *Book of Acts,* approximately 18 references to his signs or his *being* one are ascribed to him. They were also demanded of him by his followers, by the God-fearing in general, and by his opponents. In one instance Jesus even declared himself to be a sign akin to the prophet Jonah (Luke 11:30-32), to which we shall return in later chapters. But again, this is only a passing analysis on my part and beyond the depth of this chapter.

There is still one more prevalent theme in my list that may qualify as a motif but is absent from Rahman's primary list—the **People of the Book**. However, it was later gratifying to discover it in the appendix where he devotes a full six pages to it. Here are some relevant excerpts from this piece:

> That there was messianism among certain Meccan Arab circles at the time Muḥammad (PBUH) appeared has been amply documented. ...After the advent of Muḥammad (PBUH) as God's Messenger, the Qur'ān repeatedly refers to a group of people about whom it says, **"We had already given them the Book [i.e., the Torah and the Gospel]...** It is quite obvious from the Qur'ān that from the beginning to the end of his prophetic career **Muḥammad (PBUH) was absolutely convinced of the divine character of the earlier revealed documents and of the divine messengership of the bearers of these documents.** This is why he recognized without a moment of hesitation that Abraham, Moses, Jesus, and other Old and New Testament religious personalities had been genuine prophets like himself. ...Indeed, the Prophet is made to declare in the Qur'ān that not only does he believe in **the**

Torah and the Gospel but "I believe in whatever Book God may have revealed (42.ash-Shūrā:15)[88]

In these snippets Rahman speaks of "messianism" among some of the Meccan Arabs. He also recognizes the peoples known for their "earlier revealed documents," the Torah and the Gospel. But in speaking of them he does not use the word "motif" as I do, possibly because it wasn't a salient concept for him in 1980, as motif studies was less well developed as a category of study in religion. In any case, I consider this piece to be significant for my following treatment of this subject. Here I compile all the Qur'an's references to it for the purpose of thoughtful analysis.

Motif 3: People of the Book   أهل الكتاب

As I said some pages back, the Qur'an contains 34 references to the "people of the book" (Ahl Al-Kitab) plus the "people of the gospel," and "people of the remembrance." These all refer to the Jews and/or Christians who are collectively spoken of as such in another 23 verses—13 times together, Jews alone 9 times, and Christians alone once. Therefore, they constitute what I think most would consider a very prominent group in the Qur'an. Here is a list of all of the references to the People of the Book, followed by its two derivations, People of the Remembrance, and People of the Gospel. The Book being referred to seems to be a singular way of referring to at least three earlier books of divine revelation—the Torah given to Moses, the Zaboor, or *Psalms* given to David, and the Injeel, or Gospel 'given to' Jesus (not to be equated with the four gospels or the Christian New Testament itself). It may also include a book given to the prophet and patriarch Abraham.[89]

---

[88] www.geocities.ws/islamic_modernist/Major_Themes_of_the_Quran.pdf, p. 112. All bolding on pp. 77-81 mine.

[89] "Indeed, We have sent revelation to you 'O Prophet' as We sent revelation to Noah and the prophets after him. We also sent revelation to Abraham, Ishmael, Isaac, Jacob, and his

All References in the Qur'an[90]
31 occurrences

2:105 (99) Those unbelievers of the **People of the Book**...*
2:109 (103) ...many of the **People of the Book** wish they might restore you as unbelievers...*
3:64 (57) **People of the Book!** Come now to a word common between us and you...*
3:65 (58) **People of the Book!** Why do you dispute concerning Abraham?*
3:69 (62) ...there is a party of the **People of the Book** who yearn to make you go astray...*
*** 3:70** (63) **People of the Book!** Why do you disbelieve in God and his signs?* (Note, another reference to *signs*.)
3:71 (64) **People of the Book!** Why do you confound the truth with vanity?*
3:72 (65) Some of the **People of the Book** say to one another: "Believe in what is revealed to the believers (Muslims) in the morning and deny it in the evening; so that they (the Muslims) may follow suit and abandon their faith. (Malik translation)*
➢ **3:75** (68) There are some among the **People of the Book** who, if entrusted with a stack of gold, will readily return it. Yet there are

---

descendants, ´as well as` Jesus, Job, Jonah, Aaron, and Solomon. And to David We gave the Psalms. (Surah An-Nisa, 4:163) *Notice that Job is in this short list. One might fairly wonder whether a book was given to him too, and if so, what happened to it. ...Thankfully the Tanakh (i.e. Bible) has it.

[90]Hanna E. Kassis, *A Concordance of the Quran*. Forward by Fazlur Rahman. The English text utilized in this work is that of A.J. Arberry, The Koran Interpreted (Oxford, 1964). For alternative definitions the following translations have been consulted: R. Bell, The Qur'an (Edinburgh, 1937), M. M. Pickthall, The Meaning of the Glorious Koran (New York, 1956) and Abdullah Yusuf Ali, The Holy Qur'an (Lahore, 1934). Also, for the purpose of providing more of the immediate context of eight verse fragments that were too short to ascertain their meanings, I first compared their verbiage with five other translations contained in Alim.org, and then replaced the Arberry with the fuller verse from Mustapha Khattab's Clear Qur'an or Malik's translation. These verses are end-noted as such.. The numbers in parentheses refer to an alternate verse numbering system for the Qur'an. Prior to the widespread use of the Yusuf Ali system, this was another system that was in vogue.

others who, if entrusted with a single coin, will not repay it unless you constantly demand it.*
3:98 (93) **People of the Book**, why do you disbelieve…*
3:99 (94) **People of the Book**, why do you bar from God's way the believer…*
3:110 (106) …had the **People of the Book** believed, it were better for them;*
➢ **3:113** (109) …some of the **People of the Book** are a nation upstanding…*
➢ **3:199** (198) …some there are of the **People of the Book** who believe in God…*
4:123 (122) It is not your fancies, nor the fancies of the **People of the Book**…
4:153 (152) The **People of the Book** will ask thee to bring down…
4:159 (157) There is not one of the **People of the Book** but will assuredly believe in him.*
4:171 (169) **People of the Book**, go not beyond the bounds in your religion…*
5:15 (18) **O People of the Book!** Now Our Messenger has come to you, revealing much of what you have hidden of the Scriptures and disregarding much… (Clear Qur'an)*
5:19 (22) **O People of the Book!** Our Messenger has indeed come to you, making things clear to you after an interval between the messengers so you do not say, "There has never come to us a deliverer of good news or a warner." (Clear Qur'an)*
5:59 (64) **O People of the Book!** Do you resent us only because we believe in Allah and what has been revealed to us and what was revealed before—while most of you are rebellious?" (Clear Qur'an)*
5:65 (70) …but had the **People of the Book** believed [but they did not]…*
5:68 (72) Say, 'O Prophet,' "**O People of the Book!** You have nothing to stand on unless you observe the Torah, the Gospel, and what has been revealed to you from your Lord." (Clear Qur'an)*
5:77 (81) **People of the Book**, go not beyond the bounds in your religion…*
➢ **29:46** (45) Dispute not with the **People of the Book**…*

33:26 (26) And He brought down those from the **People of the Book** who supported the enemy alliance from their own strongholds…(Clear Qur'an)*
57:29 (29) ˹This is so˺ that the **People of the Book** ˹who deny the Prophet˺… (Clear Qur'an)*
59:2 (2) …He is the One Who expelled the disbelievers of the **People of the Book** from their homes for ˹their˺ first banishment ˹ever˺. (Clear Qur'an)*
59:11 (11) Have you ˹O Prophet˺ not seen the hypocrites who say to their fellow disbelievers from the **People of the Book**… (Clear Qur'an)*
98:1 (1) The unbelievers of the People of the Book…*
98:6 (5) The unbelievers of the People of the Book…*

People of the Remembrance[91]

2 occurrences

16:43 (45) Question the **People of the Remembrance**…*
21:7 (7) …question the **People of the Remembrance**, if you do not know…*

People of the Gospel[92]

1 occurrence

5:47 (51) …let the **People of the Gospel** judge according to what God has sent down therein…*

It is this last verse and one other that I find especially interesting. But first allow me to make some general observations.

---

[91] Ibid. Thanks to my good friend and scholar Adam Simnowitz for providing me with these search results from Kassis' *A Concordance of the Quran* and linguistic support.
[92] Ibid.

Of course, most of these verses are only partial in this listing, so I realize it may be hard to grasp the full meaning of them without looking up in their contexts, which I have done.[93] I've placed an asterisk after the ones that I think contain most of the thought, or enough to get the gist of it (28). In keeping with first two motifs, I chose this one as a possible motif because of the diversity of themes that are grouped together under its umbrella—*signs* for example. Take Surah 3:70, the sixth from the top of the list. It shows a full thought and also speaks of signs: "People of the Book! Why do you disbelieve in God and his signs?" So, in keeping with the previous sign motif, the people of the book were expected to recognize and believe Allah's signs (thus the connection between the two motifs). They were also expected to believe in Allah's messenger. But some of the people of the book did not recognize Allah's signs and are divinely criticized, in contrast to those who did:

﴿ لَيْسُوا۟ سَوَآءً مِّنْ أَهْلِ ٱلْكِتَٰبِ أُمَّةٌ قَآئِمَةٌ يَتْلُونَ ءَايَٰتِ ٱللَّهِ ءَانَآءَ ٱلَّيْلِ وَهُمْ يَسْجُدُونَ ١١٣

Yet they are not all alike: there are some among the **People of the Book** who are upright, who recite Allah's revelations throughout the night, prostrating ⸢in prayer⸣.

Surah Ali 'Imran (Family of Imran), 3:113

This is obviously the positive half of the distinction, or appraisal, which can be seen in three other verses marked with an arrow: verses 75 and 199 of that surah, the second of which is as follows:

وَإِنَّ مِنْ أَهْلِ ٱلْكِتَٰبِ لَمَن يُؤْمِنُ بِٱللَّهِ وَمَآ أُنزِلَ إِلَيْكُمْ وَمَآ أُنزِلَ إِلَيْهِمْ خَٰشِعِينَ لِلَّهِ لَا يَشْتَرُونَ بِـَٔايَٰتِ ٱللَّهِ ثَمَنًا قَلِيلًا أُو۟لَٰٓئِكَ لَهُمْ أَجْرُهُمْ عِندَ رَبِّهِمْ إِنَّ ٱللَّهَ سَرِيعُ ٱلْحِسَابِ ١٩٩

---

[93] This is easy to do using a searchable, online Qur'an such as Qur'an.com or alim.org.

Indeed, there are some among the *People* of the *Book* who truly believe in Allah and what has been revealed to you ˹believers˺ and what was revealed to them. They humble themselves before Allah—never trading Allah's revelations for a fleeting gain. Their reward is with their Lord. Surely Allah is swift in reckoning.

Surah Ali 'Imran, 3:199

Surah 29:46 may be a third positive example, depending on how one interprets it. That seems to be all of them. But of course there is the negative side too, as can be seen in the other 31 verses. It is glaringly more prominent. So in addition to signs, *distinction* is one of the components of this motif.

On the next page of the list, Surah 4:153 is only shown in part because it is a longer verse. But upon looking it up in full, one sees that this is another one that speaks of both signs and distinctions:

يَسْـَٔلُكَ أَهْلُ ٱلْكِتَـٰبِ أَن تُنَزِّلَ عَلَيْهِمْ كِتَـٰبًا مِّنَ ٱلسَّمَآءِ ۚ فَقَدْ سَأَلُوا۟ مُوسَىٰٓ أَكْبَرَ مِن ذَٰلِكَ فَقَالُوٓا۟ أَرِنَا ٱللَّهَ جَهْرَةً فَأَخَذَتْهُمُ ٱلصَّـٰعِقَةُ بِظُلْمِهِمْ ۚ ثُمَّ ٱتَّخَذُوا۟ ٱلْعِجْلَ مِنۢ بَعْدِ مَا جَآءَتْهُمُ ٱلْبَيِّنَـٰتُ فَعَفَوْنَا عَن ذَٰلِكَ ۚ وَءَاتَيْنَا مُوسَىٰ سُلْطَـٰنًا مُّبِينًا ١٥٣

The People of the Book demand that you ˹O Prophet˺ bring down for them a revelation in writing from heaven. They demanded what is even greater than this from Moses, saying, "Make Allah visible to us!" So a thunderbolt struck them for their wrongdoing. Then they took the calf for worship after receiving clear signs. Still We forgave them for that ˹after their repentance˺ and gave Moses compelling proof.

This one is interesting because it clearly speaks of the Jews. It negatively compares the Jews in Muhammad's time to those in Moses's. In their desert journeys they did indeed receive "clear signs" from God, or Yahweh. In Muhammad's time they apparently had an expectation of written revelation versus oral only. This seems reasonable since they already possessed in writing the complete Torah and Tanakh—containing all of the known prophets, including the *Book of Job*. The Torah's *Book of Exodus* chapter 32 does contain the account of the Israelites' idolatrous worship of the golden calf while Moses was still on the mountain. But it does not contain the Qur'an's charge that they demanded Moses to "make Allah visible to us" and were consequently struck by lightning. If that charge were true, it should be readily apparent to today's readers of it, because it is readily accessible to all the world. But in fact, this is exactly opposite of what the text says actually happened. Rather, the writings of Moses record that for their fear of God, not only did they *not* want to see him, they didn't even want to hear him.

> *...When all the people saw the thunder and the flashes of lightning and the sound of the trumpet and the mountain smoking, the people were afraid and trembled, and they stood far off and said to Moses, "You speak to us, and we will listen; but do not let God speak to us, lest we die.*
>
> *Book of Exodus* 20:18–19[94]

From this example we can see that another component of this motif is *historical precedent*, or rootedness. The Qur'an's claim is that, although not revealed until the 7th-century, its narrative and its message are established upon the long history of the people of the book—including all their prophets and books—which are themselves also components of this motif. This is especially true of the Jews in the pre-Christian era, with all the diversity of themes, events, and images preserved in the ancient books of the Torah and the larger Tanakh, or Old Testament. Islam is actually premised on its affirmation of the Old Testament prophets, most of which were Hebrew, but some, such as Noah, Jonah, and Job, were not.

This brings us back to Surah 5:47.

---

[94] See also the Torah's *Book of Deuteronomy* 5:23-27.

وَلْيَحْكُمْ أَهْلُ ٱلْإِنجِيلِ بِمَآ أَنزَلَ ٱللَّهُ فِيهِ ۚ وَمَن لَّمْ يَحْكُم بِمَآ أَنزَلَ ٱللَّهُ فَأُو۟لَٰٓئِكَ هُمُ ٱلْفَٰسِقُونَ ٤٧

So let the people of the Gospel judge by what Allah has revealed in it. And those who do not judge by what Allah has revealed are ˹truly˺ the rebellious.

In our list, this is the only verse that refers specifically to the "people of the *gospel*," or Christians. It says that they were expected to judge (i.e. believe, understand) by what was revealed in the gospel (of Jesus). This revelation came no less than 500 years before the Qur'an, was written, and was in wide circulation at the time of Muhammad. Moreover, this verse of the Qur'an seems obviously to imply that this gospel was authentic and true in Muhammad's time. Even though, as I said, the Muslim notion of "gospel' is not identical to the Christian one, the only gospel for which there is any manuscript evidence is the Christian New Testament containing the four gospels and the writings of the Apostles. Since they all give account of the same Jesus at the same time, they could and *should* be considered one gospel, or one harmonious narrative of the life and teachings of Jesus. Collectively, they contain the graphic details of Jesus's birth, his adult activities, his miracles, and his words, which are far more abundant than what is contained in the Qur'an about him. It also contains his prolific fulfillments of ancient prophecies, which are entirely absent from the Qur'an.[95]

This seems corroborated by what we read in the next verse:

وَأَنزَلْنَآ إِلَيْكَ ٱلْكِتَٰبَ بِٱلْحَقِّ مُصَدِّقًا لِّمَا بَيْنَ يَدَيْهِ مِنَ ٱلْكِتَٰبِ ...

We have revealed to you ˹O Prophet˺ this Book with the truth, as a **confirmation of previous Scriptures**...[96]

---

[95] Messianic prophecies, which are the overarching theme of this book.
[96] Surah 5:48, bolding mine.

This verse says that the Qur'an was revealed to **confirm** the previous scriptures, including the Torah and the Gospel. Further, as one continues through Surah 5 (Al-Ma'idah), several more verses add to this attestation, including verse 57, 59, and 66 as follows:

وَلَوْ أَنَّهُمْ أَقَامُوا۟ ٱلتَّوْرَىٰةَ وَٱلْإِنجِيلَ وَمَآ أُنزِلَ إِلَيْهِم مِّن رَّبِّهِمْ لَأَكَلُوا۟ مِن فَوْقِهِمْ وَمِن تَحْتِ أَرْجُلِهِم ۚ مِّنْهُمْ أُمَّةٌ مُّقْتَصِدَةٌ ۖ وَكَثِيرٌ مِّنْهُمْ سَآءَ مَا يَعْمَلُونَ ٦٦

And had they observed the Torah, the Gospel, and what has been revealed to them from their Lord, they would have been overwhelmed with provisions from above and below. Some among them are upright, yet many do nothing but evil.[97]

Clearly this verse implies that the people of the book did *not* observe their scriptures, which could certainly be a valid charge, but it validates them nonetheless. The last sentence reinforces the *distinctions* component of this motif. Verse 68 does also, and still more attestation to the validity of the previous scriptures:

قُلْ يَـٰٓأَهْلَ ٱلْكِتَـٰبِ لَسْتُمْ عَلَىٰ شَىْءٍ حَتَّىٰ تُقِيمُوا۟ ٱلتَّوْرَىٰةَ وَٱلْإِنجِيلَ وَمَآ أُنزِلَ إِلَيْكُم مِّن رَّبِّكُمْ ۗ وَلَيَزِيدَنَّ كَثِيرًا مِّنْهُم مَّآ أُنزِلَ إِلَيْكَ مِن رَّبِّكَ طُغْيَـٰنًا وَكُفْرًا ۖ فَلَا تَأْسَ عَلَى ٱلْقَوْمِ ٱلْكَـٰفِرِينَ ٦٨

Say, ⸢O Prophet,⸣ **"O People of the Book! You have nothing to stand on unless you observe the Torah, the Gospel, and what has been revealed to you from your Lord."** And your Lord's revelation to you ⸢O Prophet⸣ will only cause many of them to increase in wickedness and disbelief. So do not grieve for the people who disbelieve.[98]

In light of these multiple attestations to the Jewish and Christian scriptures, then, it is strange that today's Muslims universally charge

---

[97] Surah 5:66, bolding mine.

[98] Surah 5:68, bolding mine.

them with corruption and reject them out of hand. The question can be asked as to when Muslims began to promulgate the assertion of their corruption, but that is beyond the scope of this book.[99]

The simple takeaway here is that, by my analysis, the Qur'an does contain motifs. As with the previous two, People of the Book is one of its significant examples. As to the Qur'an's references to the people of the book, and Surahs 2-5 contain three quarters of them. And, apart from this particular appellation, Surah 5 alone contains much more material related to them.[100]

Upon the completion of this overview, it is my impression that Muslims have given little attention to the consideration of motifs in the Qur'an. In all fairness, motif studies are a somewhat obscure field of study even in the Judeo-Christian milieu, and why should anyone care at all? It's not as though motifs are the gold standard of divine, or even great, literature. But whether they are discovered or not, they are probably there, and they may bring insights to those who discover them. Either way, motif studies in the Islamic world appears to be negligible, or at least the evidence is not readily discoverable. I surmise that the reasons for this are based on the Muslim view of the

---

[99] This is known as the doctrine of tahrif. It seems to be believed by many Muslims that this doctrine stems from the Qur'an itself. But some scholars contend that it arose over 100 years later by Abū 'Uthmān al-Jāḥiz (d. 869). In Chapter 7 of his work "A Gentle Answer" Dr. Gordon Nickel and others assert that "Spanish scholar Ibn Ḥazm (d. 1064) in his work Kitāb al-fiṣal fī l-milal wa l-ahwā' wa l-niḥal, was the first Muslim to develop the accusation of the corruption of the Bible in a substantial and systematic way." Also refer to the bibliography for Abdul Rashied Omar's thesis on the subject, Hava Lazarus-Yafeh's entry on "Taḥrīf" in the *Encyclopaedia of Islam, Second Edition*/BRILL, and Dr. Gordon Nickel's thesis, "Narratives of Tampering in the Earliest Commentaries on the Qur'ān." Chapter 2.

[100] Aside from its attestations to the validity of the Jewish and Christian scriptures at the time of Muhammad, Surah 5 is replete with denunciations of the people of the book. In verse 70 it denounces the Jews for having killed many of their prophets, a charge which is confirmed by the words of Jesus as recorded in the *Gospels of Luke* 11:47-51 and *Matthew* 25:29-35, the *Book of Acts* 7:52, and the *First Letter to the Thessalonians* 2:14b and 15. It especially denounces the bedrock doctrines of the Christians—the divinity of Jesus in verse 72 and 75 (although the latter is strangely worded as "Those who say, '**Allah is the Messiah,** son of Mary,' have certainly fallen into disbelief, as Christians do not assert the divinity of Jesus in this manner): the trinity in verse 73, the divinity of Jesus again in verse 116-117 (again strangely worded as, "And ʾon Judgment Day' Allah will say, "O Jesus, son of Mary! Did you ever ask the people to worship you and your mother as **gods besides Allah?**" He will answer, "Glory be to You! How could I ever say what I had no right to say?", which Christians also do not assert in this convoluted verbiage).

nature of their holy book and of divine revelation. The Qur'an is such that it is believed to be almost all in the voice of Allah as dictated to one man, the prophet Muhammad. As such it is taken by Muslims as 'pure revelation' with no human authors per se. Even Allah, though its source, was not its 'author' in the technical sense of 'writing' or penning it. So first, it cannot be said that Allah 'wrote' or embedded motifs into the Qur'an, but neither did any human writers. Second, it seems to me that in the Islamic view of God, it may be harder to think of Allah as having dictated oral revelation with such 'human' literary features as motifs.

Further, in my personal experience of talking with Muslims, most do not seem to think of the Qur'an as literature. It is divine revelation, which is in a category all its own. Thus, it generally cannot and should not be analyzed as a form of literature. Since motifs are literary features that appear in various kinds of literature, Muslims may see motif studies as beneath the Qur'an.[101] Again, that is not bad. There is no 'rule' that says one *must* look for motifs in one's holy book. And there are probably Christians and Jews that feel that way about the scriptures of the Bible. But students of Hebrew scripture *do* look for them in the Tanakh, as we have already seen, and it seems to be a growing field.

Here is one additional example of this: In his thorough paper entitled, "Moving On With God: Key Motifs in *Exodus* 13-20", Deryck Sheriffs of the London School of Theology sees no less than 19 motifs in four groupings in those eight chapters plus others of the Torah, with allusions to additional books of the Tanakh. These include the **Journey:** leaving to receive, the trail of corpses, road and walk, guidance on the journey; **Testing:** experience and growth, training, father-son relationship, transforming ideal, already/not yet, trial-and-error learning; **Fear of the Lord:** seeing is believing, the paradox of fear, the semantics of fear, new covenant fear; **Covenant Nucleus—Exodus 19:4-6:** I brought you to myself—journey to the

---

[101] Other possible explanations are beyond the scope of this book.

centre, paradox and symbol of presence, paradox of perspective, metaphor and image—**eagle's wings and royal treasure**, and **vocation and nationhood**.[102]

In apparent contrast to the way many Muslims view the Qur'an, the Bible is celebrated as divine *literature*. It is revelation that is revealed by God in multiple literary forms using human authors. Like the Qur'an it was penned by men. Much of it is in the voice of Yahweh and was similar to the 'dictated' verbatim revelation that dominates the Qur'an.

But it is not exactly the same. In the Qur'an the angel Gabriel gets the revelation from Allah and then tells Muhammad what to "say." But in the Jewish and Christian scriptures the Almighty generally skips the angel in favor of a direct connection with the recipient, prophets and non-prophets alike. As we will see He spoke directly to Noah, Moses, Jonah, Job and many other prophets, and in the gospels He spoke directly to Jesus. This is usually indicated by "the LORD said, or spoke to…" as has been noted. In the Tanakh entire sections of scripture spanning as many as ten or more consecutive chapters can be found. Indeed, the amount of this kind of scripture in the Tanakh exceeds that of the Qur'an. But much of the rest is divinely inspired historical narrative and poetry, penned by men, certainly, but inspired by God to employ their own illuminated thinking, reporting, and writing skills. So God was the ultimate Author, but men—prophets and others—were his active instruments. The Qur'an is believed by Muslims to have been delivered through one prophet only, Muhammad.[103] The Tanakh by contrast was delivered by some 35 different men of God over a span of a 1500 years in the pre-

---

[102] Bolding mine. www.thegospelcoalition.org/themelios/article/moving-on-with-god-key-motifs-in-exodus-13-20/

[103] However, most Muslims, including scholars, understand that Muhammad did not pen the Qur'an. Rather, according to accounts in the hadith, verses and passages, even if initially memorized, were transcribed piecemeal by hundreds of the first Muslims who heard the oral recitations of the Qur'an. Then, according to Islamic sources, they were collected, sorted, assembled, and canonized by a central process under the authority of two of the first four Muslim caliphs, especially Uthman (579-656) who distributed 5-10 'authorized' copies to his provinces. Any and all other existing versions were destroyed by fire.

Common/pre-Christian Era. It is one thing to find motifs in the book of a single writer or orator, but it is a much more significant thing to find the same motifs spanning throughout them all. This what we find in the Tanakh, and the writings of Job are an essential part of this. This should be seen, as a divine pattern, I assert, as one strong kind of evidence for the Divine Hand of Authorship and Revelation which I hope to show and develop in the chapters to come.

Chapter 5

Was Job's Redeemer a Messiah? Part 1

> *"In famine he will redeem you from death,*
> *and in war from the power of the sword."*
>
> – Job, *Book of Job* 5:20

> *"Draw near to my soul, redeem me;*
> *ransom me because of my enemies!"*
>
> – David, *Psalm* 69:18 (Zaboor)

In chapter 2 we encountered Job the man, the legend, and the prophet, in the Tanakh and in the Qur'an. In this chapter we will dive deeper into his book to search for important motifs and other features. There are many. Buried among them we shall encounter someone special yet mysterious. He appears only once in the entire tome but his revelation is what I believe qualifies Job as a prophet in the Judeo-Christian sense. He has a very peculiar profile and even seems out of place. I will argue that this person was divinely revealed to Job as a kind of proto-messiah, and even *the* Messiah.

For the sake of consistency with the Arabic passages included earlier I will also give them in Arabic, followed by one translation into English, and then biblical Hebrew.

Book of Job Chapter 19:25-29

أَمَّا أَنَا فَإِنِّي مُوقِنٌ أَنَّ فَادِيَّ حَيٌّ، وَأَنَّهُ لابُدَّ فِي النِّهَايَةِ أَنْ يَقُومَ عَلَى الأَرْضِ. وَبَعْدَ أَنْ يَفْنَى جِلْدِي، فَإِنِّي بِذَاتِي أُعَايِنُ اللهَ. الَّذِي أُشَاهِدُهُ لِنَفْسِي فَتَنْظُرُهُ عَيْنَايَ وَلَيْسَ عَيْنَا آخَرَ، قَدْ فَنِيَتْ كُلْيَتَايَ شَوْقاً فِي

Was Job's Redeemer a Messiah?

دَاخِلِي. وَإِنْ قُلْتُمْ مَاذَا نَعْمَلُ لِنَضْطَهِدَهُ، لِأَنَّ مَصْدَرَ الْمَتَاعِبِ كَامِنٌ فِيهِ؟ فَاخْشَوْا عَلَى أَنْفُسِكُمْ مِنَ السَّيْفِ، لِأَنَّ الْغَيْظَ يَجْلِبُ عِقَابَ السَّيْفِ، وَتَعْلَمُونَ آنَئِذٍ أَنَّ هُنَاكَ قَضَاءً¹⁰⁴

"For I know that my Redeemer lives,
   and at the last he will stand upon the earth.
And after my skin has been thus destroyed,
   yet in my flesh I shall see God,
whom I shall see for myself,
   and my eyes shall behold, and not another.
   My heart faints within me!
If you say, 'How we will pursue him!'
   and, 'The root of the matter is found in him,'
be afraid of the sword,
   for wrath brings the punishment of the sword,
   that you may know there is a judgment."

–Job, *Book of Job* 19:25-27

For our purposes vv. 25-27 are the most salient. Here they are in the biblical Hebrew language from the Masoretic text.[105]

וַאֲנִ֣י יָ֭דַעְתִּי גֹּ֣אֲלִי חָ֑י וְ֝אַחֲר֗וֹן עַל־עָפָ֥ר יָקֽוּם׃
וְאַחַ֣ר ע֭וֹרִֽי נִקְּפוּ־זֹ֑את וּ֝מִבְּשָׂרִ֗י אֶֽחֱזֶ֥ה אֱלֽוֹהַּ׃
אֲשֶׁ֤ר אֲנִ֨י ׀ אֶֽחֱזֶה־לִּ֗י וְעֵינַ֣י רָא֣וּ וְלֹא־זָ֑ר כָּל֖וּ כִלְיֹתַ֣י בְּחֵקִֽי׃

---

[104] Ketab El Hayatt online. www.biblegateway.com/NAV

[105] www.sefaria.org/Job.19.25-27. Besides the Dead Sea Scrolls (DSS), the Masoretic text is the oldest extant Hebrew text of the Tanakh, dating to around 1000 AD/CE. However, the DSS date to around 100 BC and largely match the Masoretic.

Here is another English rendering from the JPS translation:

> *But I know that my Vindicator lives; In the end He will testify on earth— This, after my skin will have been peeled off. But I would behold God while still in my flesh, I myself, not another, would behold Him; Would see with my own eyes: My heart pines within me.*[106]

Note that this translation renders "redeemer" as "vindicator." There are about three other translations that use this word, but in all three instead of "testify" they use "stand." In any case, now that we have this passage before us our task is to interpret, or *exegete* it. To do that I will dissect it, look for definitions, examine each descriptor, consider its narrow and wide context, and any factors that will help us understand its full meaning. First I will confine myself to the text itself in a general sense, then we will mine into the specific details, and then I will refer to commentary on it. I will say up front, my interpretation is not novel in the Christian world, especially among evangelicals. It is said that novelty is overrated in some subject areas. But I hope the way I treat it and arrive at my conclusion will be somewhat fresh to you nevertheless.

Here we have Job speaking to his friends, if that's what they are. But to many interpreters they don't seem very friendly or encouraging. In the previous chapter (18) Job endured a scathing diatribe by Bildad indicting Job of wickedness (v.5) and not knowing God (v. 21). Then with righteous indignation Job retorts, *"How long will you torment me and break me in pieces with words?"* Four verses later he speaks of God when he says, *"Know then that God has put me in the wrong and closed his net about me,"* and proceeds in the next sixteen to bemoan his victimhood. He believes he is an undeserving victim of God, while his friends believe his righteousness is illogical and impossible. God does not visit suffering upon the righteous.

---

[106] Jewish Publication Society, Sefaria.com.

When we come to our passage in vv. 25-29 it seems to be an abrupt shift in both subject and tone. Suddenly Job is speaking of a "redeemer," or someone who redeems (לְגֹּי ga'al); but not just any redeemer, *his* redeemer. This phrase appears in only one other place in the Tanakh, in the *Book of Psalms* (Zaboor) chapter 19:14:

יִהְיוּ לְרָצוֹן ׀ אִמְרֵי־פִי וְהֶגְיוֹן לִבִּי לְפָנֶיךָ יְהֹוָה צוּרִי וְגֹאֲלִי׃

May the words of my mouth and the prayer of my heart be acceptable to You, O LORD, my rock and my redeemer.

Here "redeemer" clearly refers to the LORD God, Yahweh. No inference is necessary. But in *Job* it is not at all obvious. There are no explicit qualifiers, and the ones that are there force us to infer. Who is he? There are many other passages in the Tanakh in which the identity of the redeemer is obviously God himself, including *Psalm* 78:35 and fourteen more—one in the *Book of Jeremiah* and thirteen in the *Book of Isaiah*. <u>Indeed</u>, the prophet *Isaiah* has the most of any other book in the Tanakh's Hebrew library, and every one refers obviously to Yahweh. Remember that because we're heading toward this magnificent book in a later chapter. Here's one example:

כִּי־אַתָּה אָבִינוּ כִּי אַבְרָהָם לֹא יְדָעָנוּ וְיִשְׂרָאֵל לֹא יַכִּירָנוּ אַתָּה יְהֹוָה אָבִינוּ גֹּאֲלֵנוּ מֵעוֹלָם שְׁמֶךָ׃

Surely You are our Father: Though Abraham regard us not, And Israel recognize us not, You, O LORD, are our Father; From of old, Your name is **"Our Redeemer."** [107]

Book of Isaiah 63:16

Job's statement is far more isolated within his book as well as within the early chronology of scripture. And it is the only one quite like it in the whole Tanakh. He states with confidence that "I know

---

[107] Bolding mine

my redeemer lives." This is the only passage in the whole *Book of Job* that speaks of a personal redeemer. Thus, although Job does use the verb redeem once before this (6:23), this word and this oracle are in a category all their own.[108] Also, in the conservative view the *Book of Job* is the oldest book in the Tanakh, even older than the Torah, so in this view this occurrence of the word 'redeemer' would be the very first one. The only time it occurs in the Torah is in *Leviticus*, the third of five books of Moses (25:25).[109] In the more liberal view that it was written much later in the post-exilic period, some of the Torah was written then too. In that scenario, then, at least the setting of the *Job* narrative is pre-Hebrew, so prior to the *Book of Exodus*, and even prior to the last 5 chapters of Genesis in terms of chronology. In that sense as well the usage of the word redeemer in *Job* was the very first in the Tanakh. Then, except for that one reference in *Leviticus* 25:25, the word does not appear again until the *Book of Ruth* where it occurs seven times. The reference in *Leviticus* refers to the redemption, or the buying back of a man's brother's land, and in *Ruth* they all refer to levirate marriage, a sort of 'adoptive marriage' if you will.[110] With that, let's make a short list of the simplest observations we can make from this passage including even the most obvious and redundant:

1. It is a statement of revelation in the first person possessive, so it is personal not impersonal.
2. It is evidently given by the man, the prophet Job.
3. The concept of redeemer *is* present in the *Book of Job*.
4. Job (or the writer) evidently knew the meaning of *redeemer*. What exactly was his understanding?

---

[108] Both Eliphaz and Elihu also use the verb form in one place each: Eliphaz in chapter 5:20, and Elihu in 33:28.

[109] Rabbinic tradition ascribes the Book of Job to Moses as well as the Torah. If this is true, then Moses was very selective about his usage of this word. In Leviticus it clearly refers to a man, but in *Job* that seems less obvious and is part of the inquiry.

[110] Levirate marriage was the Jewish practice of a man whose brother or relative had died marrying the deceased man's widow. That's precisely what the *Book of Ruth* is all about. Indeed, many see the messiah motif as a dominant theme, or type, in it.

5. He apparently believed in a redeemer and believed certain things about him, e.g. that he was currently alive, and that he would stand upon the earth.
6. From the next verse (26), Job believes he will see God.

Now let's ask the central question of this chapter: Is this a 'Messiah appearance' or some kind of motif? The answer is *yes*.

Messiah Appearance or Motif?

Let me pose my question this way: Is *Job* 19:25 an obvious example of a passage in Hebrew scripture that speaks of a messiah, or does it speak of *the* Messiah? If the latter is not obvious, is it a possible candidate? One thing that should be obvious to you is that *I* am aware of this passage, and I have brought it to your attention. So either I think it is a possible messianic passage and I want to show you why, or I am aware that some people think so, but I don't, and I want to show you why I don't.

When we start to analyze this passage, naturally we start with the most obvious problems and move toward the more subtle ones. In my previous book, *The Reason of Reason*, I celebrate the faculty of reason and how we use it to analyze things methodically. We don't suspend reason when dealing with religious questions. We also recognize that everybody starts with it because it is unavoidable. It works exactly the same way when granting assumptions. If you are a Muslim, Christian, or Jew, the only assumption I make about you is that you care about this subject enough to keep following this path with me. For us, I think we assume that there was a prophet named Job who made this statement. But I suppose you don't have to assume that. You could assume that he was just a regular man or even a fictional character of an epic Hebrew myth as it used in the popular sense.[111]

---

[111] In part 2 of this book I will introduce and develop another sense of the word that does not assume fictionality—*true myth*.

But you have to assume at least that, and also that *somebody* wrote this passage. If somebody wrote it, then that person intended to express some meaning to his readers. Nobody writes something coherent without that intention.

Let's go back to bullet points 3-5: The word 'redeemer' appears in this sentence, hence so does the concept. Therefore, Job—or the writer behind his character if you prefer—evidently knows what a redeemer is and believes certain things about it/him (the character at least). For the record, I believe that Job was a real, historical person and that he had a prophetic role, especially with regard to this particular passage. A large percentage of the *Book of Job's* content is the words of Job himself,[112] but this passage appears to be the only prophetic one in the sense that it speaks of the future. And he speaks of a redeemer in both the present and future tenses. But the word is not 'messiah' or even the literal translation of messiah, 'anointed one.' So how could it have anything at all to do with the messiah? Well, that depends on what his role and functions would be. We need to understand this word redeemer better.

What exactly is a *Redeemer*?

Here again is the Hebrew word by itself: גְּאַלִי. The transliteration of it is *ga'al,* to redeem, a verb not a noun. So the literal rendering of the first clause could be, *"I know that my 'person who redeems' lives,,,"* There is no noun form of ga'al, so here and in every other case that is translated as 'redeemer,' it is some form of this verb with qualifiers. But what did it mean 'to redeem' and to be a person who 'redeems'…a redeemer? The trouble with many of the occurrences of this word is that we are not given a definition in most of the passages. So we have to derive the meaning inductively, drawing upon clues

---

[112] In contrast to Tanakh (i.e. the Bible), the Islamic sources contain very little of the words of Job, and nothing 'prophetic' in futuristic terms. Again, without the *Book of Job* nothing of his actual message could be known whatsoever. And even with it, it is arguable that we do not know his message with the exception of our passage in chapter 19.

that they collectively and individually offer. As I celebrated in *The Reason of Reason*, it is a wonderful gift that by the application of reason we can arrive at knowledge this way. It is reason applied to revelation to help us understand even the divine.

Whatever it is, we know already that God can be a redeemer, and a redeemer is a good thing. In the *Book of Isaiah* it is always used as a term of praise and exaltation. However, it can also be used for a human being such as in *Leviticus* 25 which prescribes the practice of the redemption of land (vv. 23-34). In it the LORD installs a system by which a parcel of land that was sold may be recovered for the original family that owned it so it is not lost to them forever. Thus we see that the concept of *redeem* and *redemption* entails *recovery*.

כִּי־יָמוּךְ אָחִיךָ וּמָכַר מֵאֲחֻזָּתוֹ וּבָא גֹאֲלוֹ הַקָּרֹב אֵלָיו וְגָאַל אֵת מִמְכַּר אָחִיו:

If your kinsman is in straits and has to sell part of his holding, his nearest redeemer shall come and redeem what his kinsman has sold.[113]

Book of Leviticus 25:23-34

In the *Book of Ruth* 'redeemer' also refers to human beings, and it is also good. In it God reveals in narrative form what it looks like when redemption is applied to marriage. This book reveals the story of a non-Jewish woman named Ruth[114] whose Jewish husband died and who was later redeemed by another Jewish man named Boaz. Personally, I don't think Boaz married Ruth for love, or at least not for love *only*. Although he was clearly impressed by Ruth's character, He married her to honor God and his family through redemption.

וַתֹּאמַרְנָה הַנָּשִׁים אֶל־נׇעֳמִי בָּרוּךְ יְהֹוָה אֲשֶׁר לֹא הִשְׁבִּית לָךְ גֹּאֵל הַיּוֹם וְיִקָּרֵא שְׁמוֹ בְּיִשְׂרָאֵל:

---

[113] Sefaria.org. All bilingual quotations in this and subsequent chapters are from this source.
[114] Ruth was a Moabite, a descendent of Lot, Abraham's nephew.

And the women said to Naomi, "Blessed be the LORD, who has not withheld a redeemer from you today! May his name be perpetuated in Israel!
Book of Ruth 4:14

This shows that God got the credit for providing a redeemer for Ruth and rescuing both her husband's *and* Boaz's family line. And it so happens that Boaz and Ruth had a son named Obed who was the great grandfather of Prophet-King David. So we see here that *redeem* and *redeemer* again entails the meaning of recovery. But since it is intensely personal and involves a woman who was destitute, it also entails the meaning of *rescue* and *rescuer.*

And that's not all. We still have to factor in all the occasions of the word *redeem* when it is used as a verb rather than a noun. There are a total of 40. Now the search really opens up, and the word appears much more often in the Torah: 4 times in *Exodus,* 11 times in *Leviticus,* and 3 times in *Numbers.* We should also add in the noun 'redemption' which can be found another 26 times throughout the Torah and the wider Tanakh: once in *Exodus,* 5 times each in *Leviticus* and *Numbers,* twice each in the *Psalms* and *Jeremiah,* and a couple more isolated places. However, there are multiple Hebrew words that are translated as *redemption*. There are the words 'peduwth' (פְּדוּת), 'pidyowm' (פִּדְיוֹן), and 'guellah' (גְּאֻלָּה), each with fine distinctions.

But let's keep our focus on *redeem.* Here's one important example in the book of *Exodus* chapter 6; and since there are none in *Genesis,* this is the first one in the whole Torah:

לָכֵן אֱמֹר לִבְנֵי־יִשְׂרָאֵל אֲנִי יְהוָה וְהוֹצֵאתִי אֶתְכֶם מִתַּחַת סִבְלֹת מִצְרַיִם וְהִצַּלְתִּי אֶתְכֶם מֵעֲבֹדָתָם וְגָאַלְתִּי אֶתְכֶם בִּזְרוֹעַ נְטוּיָה וּבִשְׁפָטִים גְּדֹלִים׃

Say, therefore, to the Israelite people: I am the LORD. I will free you from the labors of the Egyptians and deliver you from their bondage. I will **redeem** *you with an outstretched arm and through extraordinary chastisements.*

Unlike our main passage in the *Book of Job*, this one requires no inference. It is explicitly the LORD, Yahweh, speaking in his own first-person voice about himself. He is speaking directly to Moses telling him what to say to the Israelite people in Egypt. He tells them that He will "redeem" them from their bondage of slavery. The meaning of the word here is clearly consistent with the aforementioned. But since it is on such a grand scale it also entails deliverance, liberation, emancipation, and salvation. Also, I think this example serves as a paradigm for all the rest of the passages in the Tanakh that refer to God such as all those in Isaiah. But in *Exodus*, to *redeem* also took on the human dimension, yet it was very distinct from that in *Leviticus* and *Ruth*. Following the first one, the three next occurrences (*Exodus* 13:13, 13:15, and 34:20) refer to the redemption of firstborn animals and humans. So this is not the kind of redeeming that God does, nor is it the kind prescribed in *Leviticus* or exemplified in *Ruth*. It was about ritual animal sacrifice. It was to commemorate the time when God judged the Egyptians by killing all the firstborn, man and animal. For that reason God required the death of an animal in place of every first-born Hebrew male child and every firstborn male animal too—a substitute for the life of the firstborn.

וְכָל־פֶּטֶר חֲמֹר תִּפְדֶּה בְשֶׂה וְאִם־לֹא תִפְדֶּה וַעֲרַפְתּוֹ וְכֹל בְּכוֹר אָדָם בְּבָנֶיךָ תִּפְדֶּה׃

But every firstling ass you shall redeem with a sheep...
And you must redeem every first-born male among your children.

Book of Exodus 13:13

So here, to *redeem* takes on the meaning of *to buy back* or to exchange the value of one thing for another thing, specifically one life for another life. God prescribed that his people could spare their firstborn male child or a firstborn animal by substituting a lamb for it, by killing it in place of the child or the animal. Here *redeem* carries the idea of ransom. This was a very important aspect of the multiform redemption in Jewish theology and practice, one that was expanded and implemented through a comprehensive array of animal sacrifices. We saw that in the story of Job when the narratives tell us that he would sacrifice for his children in case they had sinned against God.

וַיְהִי כִּי הִקִּיפוּ יְמֵי הַמִּשְׁתֶּה וַיִּשְׁלַח אִיּוֹב וַיְקַדְּשֵׁם וְהִשְׁכִּים בַּבֹּקֶר וְהֶעֱלָה עֹלוֹת מִסְפַּר כֻּלָּם כִּי אָמַר אִיּוֹב אוּלַי חָטְאוּ בָנַי וּבֵרֲכוּ אֱלֹהִים בִּלְבָבָם כָּכָה יַעֲשֶׂה אִיּוֹב כָּל־הַיָּמִים: (פ)

When a round of feast days was over, Job would send word to them to sanctify themselves, and, rising early in the morning, he would make burnt offerings, one for each of them; for Job thought, "Perhaps my children have sinned and blasphemed God in their thoughts."

Book of Job 1:5

Exactly how Job knew to do that we do not know; or Abel for that matter (*Book of Genesis* 4:4), or Noah (*Book of Genesis* 8:20), though we are told that God took pleasure in those offerings.[115] Also, in the Garden of Eden it would seem that God himself killed animals with the vicarious intent to make animal-skin clothing for Adam and Eve after they had transgressed his command. "And the LORD God made for Adam and his wife garments of skins and clothed them." (*Book of Genesis* 3:21)[116]

Exodus is the first book of the Torah in which animal sacrifice is revealed by God to Moses and commanded to the Israelite people, in chapters 12 and 29. The first occurrence is the Passover when the people had to slaughter a lamb and apply its blood to

---

[115] Those texts do not say what prompted Abel and Noah to offer animal sacrifices, but logically there was some reason. The best inference, I think, is that either God taught them this practice or they arrived at it on their own. But the former is more logical.

[116] The text does not explicitly say that God killed an animal to obtain the skins but many think it a reasonable if not obvious inference, as do I. How else would He get them?

their doorways to avert the angel of death. Then, in *Leviticus* this practice in its many forms became even more explicit with their overlapping atonement/redemption theologies (chapters 1-7, 8, 12, 14, 16 and 17). Every kind of sacrifice prescribed and every occurrence of a it was for the purpose of redemption—to restore and recover something, something spiritual that was lost, damaged or destroyed. By what? By sin. Sin produces a loss of favor and right standing with a holy and righteous God; redemption restores this. Sin also produces a breach in one's communion with God; redemption heals it. Worse yet, sin incurs the wrath and judgment of God; redemption delivers a person from it.

Chapter 6

Prophets As Redeemers: Noah and Jonah

...[E]ven if these three men, Noah, Daniel, and Job, were in it, they would deliver but their own lives by their righteousness, declares the Lord GOD.

–Book of Ezekiel 14:14

...Out of the belly of Sheol I cried, and you heard my voice.
...But I with the voice of thanksgiving will sacrifice to you.
...Salvation belongs to the LORD!"

–Book of Jonah 2:9
part of Jonah's prayer from
the belly of the great fish

As we have seen, redemption was a big deal for the people of God in the Ancient Near East, and I think it still is. In today's movies and film series it seems common for writers to build it into their scripts, both in concept and in word. I heard it just the other day while watching something on Netflix. Some are even titled "Redemption," like a 2013 feature film I enjoyed starring Jason Statham, and a new tv series starring Paula Malcomson that just came out a few months ago (spring, 2022). It's actually trendy. Throughout the Tanakh there were multiple kinds of redeemer and redemption for as many different but related purposes, demonstrated not only by Jews but also by non-Jews. Animal sacrifice, or burnt offering, was one practiced from the earliest times. We can also see types of redemption in events and persons who had 'starring' roles in those events, such as prophets. In this chapter we'll look at Noah and Jonah, and in the next, Moses.

Prophet Noah נֹחַ نُوحْ

Noah is a prominent example in both the Tanakh and the Qur'an of how God used one man and a huge floating zoo to save, or redeem, all life forms—Noakh in Hebrew transliteration, and Nuh in Arabic transliteration.[117] He saved them and us from the devastating destruction of the worldwide flood as seen in *Genesis* 6-9, the first book of the Torah, and 51 individual verses in the Qur'an.[118]

إِنَّا لَمَّا طَغَى الْمَاءُ حَمَلْنَاكُمْ فِي الْجَارِيَةِ

Indeed, when the floodwater had overflowed, We carried you in the floating Ark ˹with *Noah*˺.

Surah Al-Haqqah (The Reality), 69:11[119]

وَآيَةٌ لَّهُمْ أَنَّا حَمَلْنَا ذُرِّيَّتَهُمْ فِي الْفُلْكِ الْمَشْحُونِ

Another sign for them is that We carried their ancestors with Noah in the fully loaded ark.

Surah Ya-Sin (Be Heaven or Oh Human Being), 36:41

حَتَّىٰ إِذَا جَاءَ أَمْرُنَا وَفَارَ التَّنُّورُ قُلْنَا احْمِلْ فِيهَا مِن كُلٍّ زَوْجَيْنِ اثْنَيْنِ وَأَهْلَكَ إِلَّا مَن سَبَقَ عَلَيْهِ الْقَوْلُ وَمَنْ آمَنَ ۚ وَمَا آمَنَ مَعَهُ إِلَّا قَلِيلٌ

And when Our command came and the oven burst ˹with water˺, We said ˹to *Noah*˺, "Take into the Ark a pair from every

---

[117] The Qur'an has Noah preaching to the people of his day, calling them to the worship of the one God, and warning them of the judgment. The Tanakh has none of that. In chapters 6-9 of the *Book of Genesis* where his story is found, he doesn't even speak. Rather, the narrative gives abundant details about the ark, the flood, the animals, and the covenant.

[118] Instead of one continuous narrative such as the Tanakh has, these are all short verses in almost as many surahs of the Qur'an. There are 6 of these short verses in the Tanakh.

[119] All citations on this page are from Dr. Mustafa Khattab, the Clear Quran, quran.com

species along with your family—except those against whom the decree ʿto drownʾ has already been passed—and those who believe." But none believed with him except for a few.

Surah Hud (Prophet Hud), 11:40

There are also multiple ahadith about Noah. Here is just one:

حَدَّثَنَا مُوسَى بْنُ إِسْمَاعِيلَ، حَدَّثَنَا عَبْدُ الْوَاحِدِ بْنُ زِيَادٍ، حَدَّثَنَا الأَعْمَشُ، عَنْ أَبِي صَالِحٍ، عَنْ أَبِي سَعِيدٍ، قَالَ قَالَ رَسُولُ اللَّهِ صلى الله عليه وسلم " يَجِيءُ نُوحٌ وَأُمَّتُهُ فَيَقُولُ اللَّهُ تَعَالَى هَلْ بَلَّغْتَ فَيَقُولُ نَعَمْ، أَىْ رَبِّ. فَيَقُولُ لأُمَّتِهِ هَلْ بَلَّغَكُمْ فَيَقُولُونَ لاَ، مَا جَاءَنَا مِنْ نَبِيٍّ. فَيَقُولُ لِنُوحٍ مَنْ يَشْهَدُ لَكَ فَيَقُولُ مُحَمَّدٌ صلى الله عليه وسلم وَأُمَّتُهُ، فَنَشْهَدُ أَنَّهُ قَدْ بَلَّغَ، وَهْوَ قَوْلُهُ جَلَّ ذِكْرُهُ {وَكَذَلِكَ جَعَلْنَاكُمْ أُمَّةً وَسَطًا لِتَكُونُوا شُهَدَاءَ عَلَى النَّاسِ} وَالْوَسَطُ الْعَدْلُ ".

Allah's Messenger said, "Noah and his nation will come on the Day of Resurrection and Allah will ask (Noah), "Did you convey (the Message)?' He will reply, 'Yes, O my Lord!' Then Allah will ask Noah's nation, 'Did Noah convey My Message to you?' They will reply, 'No, no prophet came to us.' Then Allah will ask Noah, 'Who will stand a witness for you?' He will reply, 'Muhammad and his followers (will stand witness for me).' So, I and my followers will stand as witnesses for him (that he conveyed Allah's Message)." That is, (the interpretation) of the Statement of Allah: "Thus we have made you a just and the best nation that you might be witnesses Over mankind..."[120]

From this hadith we read that the giving of 'the message' was an essential element of Noah's story, whereas it is entirely absent from the *Genesis* account of the Torah. In it Noah was clearly held accountable for giving the message, and had it not been for Muhammad's witness on his behalf some 2900 years later,[121] apparently Allah would have rejected Prophet Noah's own testimony because the

---

[120] Sunnah.com 3339 : Sahih al-Bukhari 3339 : Book 60, #14 : Vol. 4, Book 55, #555
[121] Based on the possible date of the flood at around 2300-2400 B.C.

people witnessed against him. So for 2900 years after Noah's death he was apparently suspected of lying to Allah who for some reason could not know if he was telling the truth until Muhammad informed him in the 7th century. I have to wonder, where was Noah all that time? In paradise or in hell? Either way, we can be sure that he's in paradise now. He was a great and righteous prophet after all, and he did save people from utter destruction. The number of people Noah saved was very small but *not* insignificant, for through them he saved the entire human race.

Thus Noah was a kind of redeemer. In biblical studies we can call him a *type*. In one sense he redeemed, or rescued, only his family. But in a more important sense he redeemed all of humanity, and all species of animals! If he had not obeyed God in building the ark and trusted God for the outcome, he could not have saved any of them. In the most important sense, of course, the Redeemer was God himself, but in a lesser sense it was Noah. He was the human vessel who was used by Almighty God to redeem his family, humanity, and even the whole animal kingdom.

Millenia later in the Jewish timeline of revelation, the LORD spoke of Noah through the oracles of the prophet Isaiah (54:9) and the prophet-priest Ezekiel (14:14, 20). Centuries after them, Jesus and one of his Apostles, plus two other New Testament writers all spoke of Noah with the great honor due him—and with warnings for their own generations.[122] Jesus said…

> *For as were the days of Noah, so will be the coming of the Son of Man [himself]. For as in those days before the flood they were eating and drinking, marrying and giving in marriage, until the day when Noah entered the ark, and they were unaware until the flood came and swept them all away, so will be the coming of the Son of Man. …Therefore, stay awake, for you do not know on what day your Lord is*

---

[122] Jesus spoke of him once which is recorded in parallel verses in the gospels of *Matthew* (24:37,38) and *Luke* (17:26, 27). The Apostle Peter also spoke of him in his epistles (*1 Peter* 3:20 and *2 Peter* 2:5), as well as the inspired writer of the *Book of Hebrews* (11:7).

coming. ...Therefore you also must be ready, for the Son of Man is coming at an hour you do not expect.

Gospel of Matthew 24:37–44 (excerpts)

Apostle Peter wrote...

For if God...did not spare the ancient world, but preserved Noah, a herald of righteousness, with seven others, when he brought a flood upon the world of the ungodly...[and] *the world that then existed was deluged with water and perished. ...*[For the same reasons] *the heavens and earth that now exist are stored up for fire, being kept until the day of judgment and destruction of the ungodly. But the day of the Lord will come like a thief, and then the heavens will pass away with a roar, and the heavenly bodies will be burned up and dissolved, and the earth and the works that are done on it will be exposed.*

–2nd Epistle of Apostle Peter 2:4, 5, 3:6, 7, 10 (excerpts)

Following the LORD's judgment upon and redemption of humanity, the sins of Noah's time were abated, but they did not go away.

Prophet Jonah   يُونُس, יונה

A second example of a prophet-redeemer is Jonah, or Yonah in Hebrew transliteration, and Younis or Yunus in Arabic transliteration. The Tanakh contains the *Book of Jonah* with four chapters and 48 verses forming a complete narrative of how God sent him to his own people but to a foreign people. Its main character is the man Jonah who is recognized as a prophet in all three religions. In the Hebrew edition it is part of the unit called The Prophets or the Nevi'im. In protestant Christian Bibles it is a standalone book, the

5th among the 12 'minor' prophets and the 32nd of 39 books in total. Jonah and the other 11 are called *minor* not at all because they were less important than other prophets but because their books are comparably shorter and later than those of the major prophets.[123]

But the Qu'ran contains a whole chapter named for Jonah—Surah Yunus which is #10 with 109 ayas (verses). That makes him the only one of the 12 minor prophets to be named in the Qur'an. It's as though to Allah the other 11 and his revelations to them never existed or were insignificant. On another point of comparison, the content of Jonah's book is mostly narrative, with only six verses being in the voice of God himself. In contrast, much of the content of the other 11 prophets' books is in His voice, the only kind of scripture that is considered as true revelation to Muslims. So it seems to me that Allah would not have left out these prophets and so much of his previous revelation from the Qur'an.

Oddly, with only one aya mentioning Yunus (98), Surah 10 is hardly *about* him. Rather, it covers an array of subjects and other prophets and messengers, some named, some unnamed. It contains three ayas about Noah, for example (71-73), and 16 about Moses and Aaron in a longish passage that covers their confrontations with Pharoah (75-90). One may wonder why this surah is named after Yunus and not Moses or Noah. The lone verse on Yunus reads as follows:

فَلَوْلَا كَانَتْ قَرْيَةٌ ءَامَنَتْ فَنَفَعَهَا إِيمَـٰنُهَآ إِلَّا قَوْمَ يُونُسَ لَمَّآ ءَامَنُواْ كَشَفْنَا عَنْهُمْ عَذَابَ ٱلْخِزْىِ فِى ٱلْحَيَوٰةِ ٱلدُّنْيَا وَمَتَّعْنَـٰهُمْ إِلَىٰ حِينٍ ٩٨

If only there had been a society which believed ˹before seeing the torment˺ and, therefore, benefited from its belief, like the people of Jonah.[1] When they believed, We [Allah] lifted from

---

[123] The other minor prophets include Hosea, Joel, Amos, Obadiah, **Jonah,** Micah, Nahum, Habakkuk, Zechariah, Haggai, Zephaniah, Malachi.

them the torment of disgrace in this world and allowed them enjoyment for a while.

The footnote is interesting…

> ¹Initially, the people of Jonah rejected his message. When he was told they would be punished after three days for their defiance, he left his city without Allah's permission before its destruction. Jonah's people became convinced that they were going to be destroyed when he left them and they saw signs of the imminent torment, so they felt remorseful and cried out for forgiveness before the coming of the punishment. Therefore, Allah accepted their repentance and the torment was retracted.[124]

From verse 98, this commentator clearly understood the very opposite of what the Tanakh's *Book of Jonah* says, as we shall see in the next pages. Both the verse and he speak of "the people of Jonah" (Jews?) as the target of his mission, i.e. that he had been sent to his own people, not to the people of Ninevah in Assyria. This verse says nothing about the great fish or 'whale' but another one does:

فَاصْبِرْ لِحُكْمِ رَبِّكَ وَلَا تَكُن كَصَاحِبِ الْحُوتِ إِذْ نَادَىٰ وَهُوَ مَكْظُومٌ

> So be patient with your Lord's decree, and do not be like ʿJonah,ʾ the Man of the Whale, who cried out ʿto Allahʾ in total distress.
>
> Surah Al-Qalam (The Pen), 68:48

A longer passage with more context is Surah 37, which is called in Arabic *As-Saaffat* ("Those who set the Ranks") verses 139-148:

> So also was Jonah among those sent (by Us). When he ran away (like a slave from captivity) to the ship (fully) laden, He (agreed to) cast lots, and he was condemned: Then the big Fish did swallow him, and he had done acts worthy of blame. Had it not been that he (repented and) glorified

---

[124] Clear Qur'an, quran.com/10

Allah, He would certainly have remained inside the Fish till the Day of Resurrection. But We cast him forth on the naked shore in a state of sickness, And We caused to grow, over him, a spreading plant of the gourd kind. And We sent him (on a mission) to a hundred thousand (men) or more. And they believed; so We permitted them to enjoy (their life) for a while.[125]

In the Tanakh the *Book of Jonah* tells the story that God commanded a Jewish prophet named Jonah to go from Israel to Ninevah, the capital of Assur, or Assyria, about 600 miles northeast, situated on the Tigris River in Mesopotamia. By then there had been numerous prophets in Israel, but none had ever been sent there before. In general, Jewish prophets tended to focus on the Jewish people in a much closer and smaller geographical area. The Assyrians were well

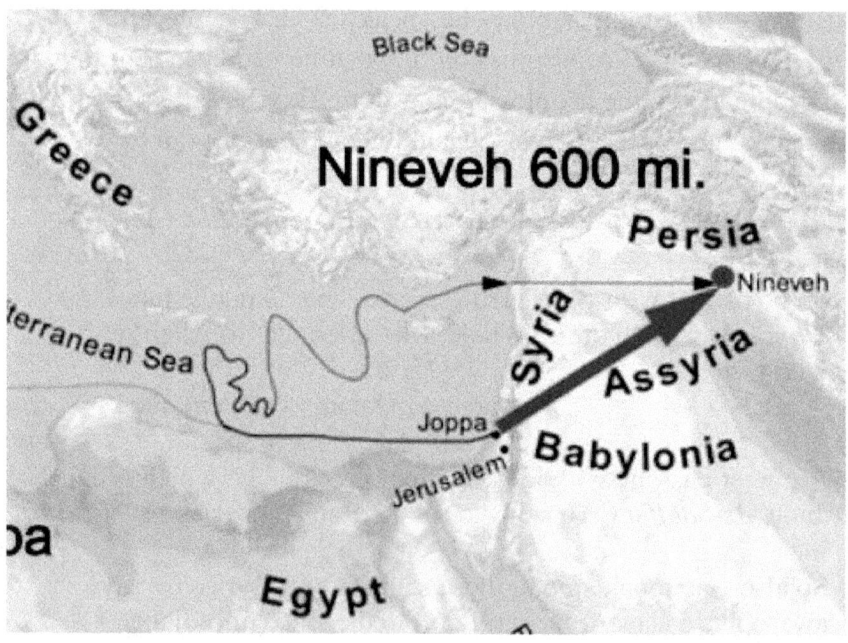

---

[125] Yusuf Ali translation. The Malik translation is similar in its use of the English word "repented." However, some other translations do not use it, e.g. Asad, Mustafa Khattab, and Piktal. See Alim.org for comparison.

outside of it, and they were by no means Jewish. Rather, like all the rest of the world they were pagans, polytheists. They had a pantheon of around 2400 gods of which Ashur became preeminent. And they were known to be very violent, even bloodthirsty. This makes Jonah a 'missionary' in a traditional sense, someone who embraces a special mission from God including its risks, who travels a long distance and crosses ethno-cultural barriers to carry their message to a nation or and/or a people group that is foreign to them.

Until then Jonah prophesied during the peaceful and prosperous time of King Jeroboam II who is chronicled in 2 Kings 14:23-28 of the Tanakh as having ruled in the northern kingdom of Israel from 782 to 753 B.C. Assyria would not be a threat to Israel for another 20 years, and did not conquer them for another 30 (722 BC).[126] This is one reason why chronology matters so much, because by then Jonah would probably not have been able to penetrate Ninevah, much less escape alive. According to the narrative we get in the *Book of Jonah*, the LORD, *Yahweh,* commanded prophet Jonah to go to Ninevah to warn them of God's impending judgment. But he did not want to. He tried to escape this assignment by catching a ship to Tarshish in today's Spain, the most distant city in the Mediterranean world at the time. Soon, the narrative tells us, "The Lord hurled a great wind upon the see, and there was a mighty tempest" that threatened to sink the ship." (1:4) The sailors knew that Jonah was the reason for the storm and reluctantly cast him overboard to save the ship. Then the narrative tells us, *"And the LORD [Yahweh] appointed a great fish to swallow up Jonah...and he was in the belly of the fish three days and three nights."* (1:17) Inside the fish Jonah prayed a desperate prayer for deliverance, so the LORD spoke to the fish which vomited him out onto the beach. (2:10)

We are told that the *LORD* did those things. Then, verse 1 of the next chapter tells us that the LORD again commanded Prophet

---

[126] www.esv.org/resources/esv-global-study-bible/introduction-to-jonah/

Jonah to go to Ninevah "to proclaim to it the message I give you." And Jonah relented. Looking back at Surah 37 again, the *Yusuf Ali* translation and one other tell us that he *repented* (v. 143). Although there are nineteen others that do not use this English word, in thirteen translations the previous aya (142) says that Jonah had done acts "worthy of blame" or was "blameworthy."[127] This obviously implies sin. Jonah sinned.

The notion that Jonah sinned does not bother the Jew or the Christian, but it does bother the Muslim, many of whom have told me directly that prophets are sinless. But it would seem that they are not. The *Book of Jonah* tells us that before he obeyed God, he first did *not*. He tried to run from God, as if that were possible. (It was not that the ship was overloaded.) Verse 3 of chapter 3 says he "obeyed the word of the LORD and went to Ninevah." (NIV) There the prophet did proclaim Yahweh's message, and the entire city repented with what I will call 'emergency fasting'[128] and wearing sackcloth, even the great ruler King Shalmaneser III.[129] In fact, it was he who took Jonah's warning the most seriously and acted the most decisively as the narrative says in chapter 3 verses 6-9, first the Hebrew and then the English.

וַיִּגַּע הַדָּבָר אֶל־מֶלֶךְ נִינְוֵה וַיָּקָם מִכִּסְאוֹ וַיַּעֲבֵר אַדַּרְתּוֹ מֵעָלָיו וַיְכַס שַׂק וַיֵּשֶׁב עַל־הָאֵפֶר:

וַיַּזְעֵק וַיֹּאמֶר בְּנִינְוֵה מִטַּעַם הַמֶּלֶךְ וּגְדֹלָיו לֵאמֹר הָאָדָם וְהַבְּהֵמָה הַבָּקָר וְהַצֹּאן אַל־יִטְעֲמוּ מְאוּמָה אַל־יִרְעוּ וּמַיִם אַל־יִשְׁתּוּ:

---

[127] Alquranenglish.com

[128] Fasting because of an emergency situation. It was a Jewish practice to proclaim a fast in times of impending doom such as this—God was about to destroy the city. But these were not Jews. This is the only example of widescale pagan fasting that the Tanakh offers, so it is impressive for that reason. And it was neither a scheduled fast nor a ritual one.

[129] glasstree.com/shop/catalog/jonah-vs-king-of-nineveh-chronological-historical-and-archaeological-evidence. This journal article also claims that "this unique event is rationally possible" (surviving the ordeal of being swallowed by a large fish, that is). But whether you believe it or not, it isn't essential for the main idea that I am highlighting.

וַיִּתְכַּסּוּ שַׂקִּים הָאָדָם וְהַבְּהֵמָה וַיִּקְרְאוּ אֶל־אֱלֹהִים בְּחָזְקָה וְיָשֻׁבוּ אִישׁ מִדַּרְכּוֹ הָרָעָה וּמִן־הֶחָמָס אֲשֶׁר בְּכַפֵּיהֶם:

מִי־יוֹדֵעַ יָשׁוּב וְנִחַם הָאֱלֹהִים וְשָׁב מֵחֲרוֹן אַפּוֹ וְלֹא נֹאבֵד:[130]

When the news reached the king of Nineveh, he rose from his throne, took off his robe, put on sackcloth, and sat in ashes. And he had the word cried through Nineveh: "By decree of the king and his nobles: No man or beast—of flock or herd— shall taste anything! They shall not graze, and they shall not drink water! They shall be covered with sackcloth—man and beast—and shall cry mightily to God. Let everyone turn back from his evil ways and from the injustice of which he is guilty. Who knows but that God may turn and relent? He may turn back from His wrath, so that we do not perish."

I don't know about you, but to me this degree of city-wide repentance seems both unprecedented and unparalleled! As I think about the entire Tanakh, I can't think of one similar example of such immediate and extensive repentance, especially considering the foreign circumstances. A lone Jew went to a hostile foreign country to warn them of imminent destruction, and they believed him! And he didn't even do miracles. The Egyptians certainly did not respond this way when Moses was sent back to them. This could only have been a special act of Yahweh's Spirit upon their hearts as only He could and would have done.

So, what happened? Did God destroy Nineveh or not? No. Verse 10 tells us that their repentance saved them.

וַיַּרְא הָאֱלֹהִים אֶת־מַעֲשֵׂיהֶם כִּי־שָׁבוּ מִדַּרְכָּם הָרָעָה וַיִּנָּחֶם הָאֱלֹהִים עַל־הָרָעָה אֲשֶׁר־דִּבֶּר לַעֲשׂוֹת־לָהֶם וְלֹא עָשָׂה:[131]

God saw what they did, how they were turning back from their evil ways. And God renounced the punishment He had planned to bring upon them and did not carry it out.

---

[130] Sefaria.org

[131] Ibid.

Repentance μετανοίας

God loves repentance. It stimulates his mercy, and it is essential for forgiveness. In both testaments of the Bible—the Hebrew Tanakh and the Greek New Testament—it is both explicit and implicit that the holy God requires repentance, and all, or most of the prophets preached it. In Jonah's case it is implicit, but in the case of Ezekiel 14:6, for example, it is explicit. But it is far more explicit in the New Testament. From the earliest chapters of all the four gospels it is recorded that John the prophet-baptizer (Yaya) preached repentance, as the following five examples show in their Greek and English translations.[132]

Ἐγένετο Ἰωάννης ὁ βαπτίζων ἐν τῇ ἐρήμῳ καὶ κηρύσσων βάπτισμα μετανοίας εἰς ἄφεσιν ἁμαρτιῶν.

*John appeared, baptizing in the wilderness and proclaiming a baptism of **repentance** for the forgiveness of sins.*

Gospel of Mark 1:4

In his proclamation the prophet John the Baptizer said,

ἐγὼ μὲν ὑμᾶς βαπτίζω ἐν ὕδατι εἰς μετάνοιαν, ὁ δὲ ὀπίσω μου ἐρχόμενος ἰσχυρότερός μου ἐστὶν οὗ οὐκ εἰμὶ ἱκανὸς τὰ ὑποδήματα βαστάσαι· αὐτὸς ὑμᾶς βαπτίσει ἐν πνεύματι ἁγίῳ καὶ πυρί·

*"I baptize you with water for **repentance,** but he who is coming after me is mightier than I, whose sandals I am not*

---

[132] It is widely believed that Jesus and other first-century Jews spoke Aramaic internally due to their 70-year exile in Babylon/Persia. Even if that is true, Hebrew was still retained by the Jews that were left behind in Judah, which was also their religious language. But Greek was the lingua franca of the whole region and was also widely spoken. That's why it makes sense that the all-wise God orchestrated the New Testament to be written in Greek.

worthy to carry. He will baptize you with the Holy Spirit and fire."

Gospel of Matthew 3:11

First he was speaking of himself, of course. But then by "he" the prophet was speaking of Jesus who was his cousin and Messiah. According to the Apostle John's gospel,[133] the next day Jesus appeared at the River Jordan to be baptized—so that he would be revealed to Israel and "to fulfill all righteousness."[134]

Soon after that, following his forty-day fast and confrontation with Satan in the wilderness, Jesus launched into his public ministry of preaching, teaching, and healing. He began by proclaiming a rather Jonah-like message of repentance.

καὶ λέγων· μετανοεῖτε· ἤγγικεν γὰρ ἡ βασιλεία τῶν οὐρανῶν.

"Repent, *for the kingdom of heaven is at hand."*

Gospel of Matthew 3:2[135]

And throughout Jesus's three-year ministry repentance continued to be a very strong element of his message. The inspired writings of Luke, who wrote the third harmonious gospel, report that...

Καὶ ἀποκριθεὶς ὁ Ἰησοῦς εἶπεν πρὸς αὐτούς· οὐ χρείαν ἔχουσιν οἱ ὑγιαίνοντες ἰατροῦ ἀλλὰ οἱ κακῶς ἔχοντες. οὐκ ἐλήλυθα καλέσαι δικαίους ἀλλὰ ἁμαρτωλοὺς εἰς με τάνοιαν.

---

[133] *Gospel of John* 1:29-31; see also verses 32-34. *The Apostle John is not the same as John the Baptizer, the prophet. He was a personal disciple of Jesus. Bolding on this page mine.

[134] See *Gospel of Matthew* 3:15 for this phrase.

[135] See also chapter 4:17 and 11:20, and the *Gospels of Mark* 1:15, *Luke* 13:3 and 5. All bolding on this page mine.

*And Jesus answered them, "Those who are well have no need of a physician, but those who are sick. I have not come to call the righteous but sinners to **repentance**."*

Gospel of Luke 5:31–32

One final example is also found in Luke's gospel in which Jesus declared the absolute primacy of repentance:

Λέγω ὑμῖν ὅτι οὕτως χαρὰ ἐν τῷ οὐρανῷ ἔσται ἐπὶ ἑνὶ ἁμαρτωλῷ μετανοοῦντι ἢ ἐπὶ ἐνενήκοντα ἐννέα δικαίοις οἵτινες οὐ χρείαν ἔχουσιν μετανοίας.

*Just so, I tell you, there will be more joy in heaven over one sinner who repents than over ninety-nine righteous persons who need no **repentance.***

Gospel of Luke 15:7

Thus, some six centuries later Jesus's role was similar to that of Jonah, at least with respect to the proclamation of repentance. In a later chapter we will see that, according to Jesus himself, this was not the only similarity.

In Jonah's case, the Ninevites' mass repentance was what the LORD was after. He wanted to be merciful rather than wrathful, a preference that characterizes him throughout the Tanakh. That should be obvious from the whole story of Jonah. It's impressive like that, and it's the only one quite like it in all of Hebrew scripture. I mean, this great city was on the verge of destruction, but in his mercy God spared them because they repented. Of all the major cities within that general radius of Israel/Judah, why did Yahweh care so much about Ninevah? Why not Tyre and Sidon? Why not Damascus? Why not Inebuhedj (ancient Memphis, former capital of Egypt)? Also, why did they need a foreign prophet, much less a Jewish one? What happened to their own prophet/s? Maybe they had quit, or they were on a long sabbatical. If there had been any on duty, obviously nobody was listening to them. More likely they were part of the problem, teaching the falsehoods of the false gods and probably encouraging the city's rampant corruption. So even if it's true that every people was given its own prophet, apparently the Ninevite prophet was not doing his job.

In any event, Yahweh was obviously not pleased with them, and they were on his 'blacklist.' That could have been game-over for the people of Nineveh, but thanks to Jonah it wasn't, despite his attempted dodge. Still, it's not hard to imagine why Jonah did not want this assignment, and why probably no one would have wanted it. From experience with his own Israelite people and common knowledge, he knew the odds were stacked against him. Why Jonah then? Couldn't the LORD have tapped a more compliant prophet? Yes, certainly. But maybe there was something special about Jonah. Could it be that he had the most well-honed and compelling message? Or the most monotheistic?

Let's explore this a little. At face value, Prophet Jonah's message seems to have been very simple: "Yet forty days, and Nineveh shall be overthrown!" No doubt it's a micro-summary of the fuller message, but it's interesting how Jonah chose to capture it. So if we want to know the content of his fuller message, we cannot. The prophet does not tell us. Neither does the Qur'an tell us much. Other than his prayer in Surah 21:87 there doesn't seem to be any emphasis on monotheism, i.e. believing and worshipping one God only. Now, since Jonah was a Jewish prophet it's safe to assume that when he spoke of God he spoke exclusively of the one and only God. But I also suspect that Jonah's message had a lot to do with ceasing and repenting of their violent conquests, and a spectrum of other atrocities.

But it's obvious that the *Book of Jonah* is really not about his message at all, otherwise the LORD would have given us more information about it. Rather, it's about the character and agenda of Almighty God—His concern for reaching non-Jews as well as Jews and the pagan nations outside of Israel/Judah/Palestine. It's about how a loving God wants to *redeem* people, whole cities, and even whole nations. It's about the way He uses missionaries to accomplish this, and how he calls them to "go." It's about this particular prophet, his stubbornness to care about what God cared about, and how God changed his heart to lead him into obedience. It's about God's judgment and mercy, and how he responds to repentance. And finally, it's about everyone who have ever found themselves in this kind of situation. God knows how to humble people and win their obedience.

But sadly, chapter 4 of this story takes a turn. Although the redemption of an entire city is cause to celebrate by our standards, it wasn't so much for someone who actually *wanted* their destruction. Sadly, this was Jonah. Verses 1-3 reveal this:

וַיֵּרַע אֶל־יוֹנָה רָעָה גְדוֹלָה וַיִּחַר לוֹ וַיִּתְפַּלֵּל אֶל־יְהֹוָה וַיֹּאמַר אָנָּה יְהֹוָה הֲלוֹא־זֶה דְבָרִי עַד־הֱיוֹתִי עַל־אַדְמָתִי עַל־כֵּן קִדַּמְתִּי לִבְרֹחַ תַּרְשִׁישָׁה כִּי יָדַעְתִּי כִּי אַתָּה אֵל־חַנּוּן וְרַחוּם אֶרֶךְ אַפַּיִם וְרַב־חֶסֶד וְנִחָם עַל־הָרָעָה וְעַתָּה יְהֹוָה קַח־נָא אֶת־נַפְשִׁי מִמֶּנִּי כִּי טוֹב מוֹתִי מֵחַיָּי: (ס)

This displeased Jonah greatly, and he was grieved. He prayed to the LORD, saying, "O LORD! Isn't this just what I said when I was still in my own country? That is why I fled beforehand to Tarshish. For I know that You are a compassionate and gracious God, slow to anger, abounding in kindness, renouncing punishment. Please, LORD, take my life, for I would rather die than live.

So it becomes apparent that the main reason Jonah did not want to go to Nineveh was not because of the hardship or that he feared for his safety. Rather, it was because he feared that the LORD would be merciful to them and <u>not</u> destroy them, exactly as it played out. Wow. In my view, that is not impressive. But Jonah certainly got Yahweh's character right—He prefers mercy over judgment. A later Jewish writer put it succinctly when he wrote "Mercy Triumphs over judgment." (Apostle James chapter 2 verse13)

In the very last verse of the book God said...

וַאֲנִי֙ לֹ֣א אָח֔וּס עַל־נִינְוֵ֖ה הָעִ֣יר הַגְּדוֹלָ֑ה אֲשֶׁ֣ר יֶשׁ־בָּ֡הּ הַרְבֵּה֩ מִשְׁתֵּים־עֶשְׂרֵ֨ה רִבּ֜וֹ אָדָ֗ם אֲשֶׁ֤ר לֹֽא־יָדַע֙ בֵּין־יְמִינ֣וֹ לִשְׂמֹאל֔וֹ וּבְהֵמָ֖ה רַבָּֽה׃

> *And should not I care about Nineveh, that great city, in which there are more than a hundred and twenty thousand persons who do not yet know their right hand from their left, and many beasts as well!"*

Jonah's bad attitude toward the people who received God's mercy does not take away from the main points of it—rescue, deliverance, recovery, and restoration—in a word, the short *Book of Jonah* is about *redemption*. But there is a foreign and geographically distant twist that makes this example exceptionally unique in the Tanakh. Still, Jonah is very obscure in the Hebrew canon. Outside of the book by his name he is only mentioned one other time, in 2 Kings 14:25. But to be fair he came very late, so obviously no one before him could have any 'natural' knowledge of him. Other than that one mention, Jesus was the only person in the whole Bible to speak of Jonah, reported eight times in two of the four harmonious gospels, *Luke* and this saying found twice in *Matthew* 12:39, and also 16:4:

> *"An evil and adulterous generation seeks for a sign, but no sign will be given to it except the sign of the prophet Jonah.*

Like Job, Prophet Jonah was a glorious type of redeemer in Jewish and Assyrian history. The LORD was the primary Redeemer, to be sure, but Jonah was a 'junior redeemer' as it were, a messenger of mercy to the Assyrians, despite how unhappy he was about it.

Chapter 7

Prophet Moses as Redeemer

מֹשֶׁה   مُوسَىٰ

> "—This man God sent as both ruler and redeemer by the hand of the angel who appeared to him in the bush."
>
> —Stephen, *Book of Acts* 7:35

> "For if you believed Moses, you would believe me; for he wrote of me."
>
> —Jesus, *Gospel of John* 5:46

750 years before Jonah the renowned Hebrew Prophet Moses (Moshe, Musa, or Moussa) was making his indelible mark on the history of Judaism and the Western world. His example is so much more prominent, enduring, and easier to grasp than Jonah's that our exposition of it need only scratch the surface.

The saga of Moses begins in the *Book of Exodus,* again, the second book of the Torah in the larger Hebrew Tanakh. Recall that it is the first time we see the LORD declaring himself as the Redeemer of the Hebrew people in Egypt. (v. 6:6). We have established that God, Yahweh, is always the primary Redeemer, but He often used humans to achieve his acts of redemption—prophets and non-prophets that I call saints. In the era of Egyptian captivity he used Prophet Moses to achieve probably the most dramatic redemption event called the "exodus," or departure. The fullest sense of the account spans four of the five books of the Torah, from *Exodus* up to the death of Moses recorded in the *Book of Deuteronomy*. But the initial part of the account, the tail-end of the Hebrews' Egyptian slavery up through the crossing of the Red Sea, is captured in-full and revealed to us in continuous narrative in the first 13 chapters of *Exodus*.

My 'micro-summary' of this event is that Yahweh raised up Moses, who was providentially born into the Egyptian royal court, to eventually lead the entire Hebrew people out of Egypt with the force of ten supernatural plagues, then the supernatural parting and crossing of the Red Sea.[136] Another micro-summary comes from the *Book of Psalms* (Zaboor) chapter 77 and verse 21:[137]

נָחִיתָ כַצֹּאן עַמֶּךָ בְּיַד־מֹשֶׁה וְאַהֲרֹן׃

You led Your people like a flock in the care of Moses and Aaron.[138]

A longer but still nicely condensed summary of Prophet Moses's story is found in the New Testament *Book of Acts,* or *Acts of the Apostles*, often called just *Acts* for short. It's a fascinating book reporting the deeds of the Apostles and others in the years immediately after the departure of Jesus and covering up to about the year 60 A.D. It is the fifth book of the New Testament that comes after the four gospels, right after the *Gospel of John* specifically. Chapter 7 of *Acts* contains a long sermon that was preached by a bold Hellenic Jewish man named Stephen just before he was executed by stoning.[139] He

---

[136] The precise dating of the exodus is argued between the conservative and liberal camps but it was generally between 1400 and 1600 BC. Moses's place on the historical timeline came broadly between Joseph, son of Jacob, and Joshua son of Nun.

[137] Verse 20 in most Protestant Christian Bibles.

[138] Aaron was a contemporary, Moses' brother, the prophet Harun in Islam.

[139] Stephen was neither an apostle nor a prophet, yet most casual observers would agree that he had qualities both. Rather, he was a deacon. Chapter 6 of Acts reports that there was an internal conflict within the first year or two of the church between the Hellenistic, or Greek-speaking Jews and the Hebrew-speaking Jews who had become Christians. The former felt that their widows were being neglected in the daily distribution of provisions. So to solve this problem the twelve Apostles instructed the community to choose seven qualified men to address this problem and oversee the distribution–deacons. They were supposed to be men of good reputation and "full of the Holy Spirit and wisdom" (v. 3) As it happened, two of

was a first-generation Christian who had recently been selected as one of seven deacons to serve the burgeoning number of believers in the nascent church community. But he soon showed himself to be as bold as any of the apostles. The text of chapter 6 says...

> Στέφανος δὲ πλήρης χάριτος καὶ δυνάμεως ἐποίει τέρατα καὶ σημεῖα μεγάλα ἐν τῷ λαῷ...καὶ οὐκ ἴσχυον ἀντισ τῆναι τῇ σοφίᾳ καὶ τῷ πνεύματι ᾧ ἐλάλει.

> *And Stephen, full of grace and power, was doing great wonders and signs among the people ...and they could not withstand the wisdom and the Spirit with which he was speaking.* (v. 8, 10)

This greatly angered the Jewish leaders who had been trying to quell this new Christian 'sect.' They dragged Stephen before the council and accused him of almost the same things they accused of Jesus. (v. 11) So on his final opportunity he preached an epic sermon of which chapter 7 is entirely comprised. In it he recounted much of the history of Israel from Prophet Abraham to King Solomon, half of which is about Moses (25 out of 49 verses). Verses 29-36 are focused specifically on the exodus, the spectacular series of events that lead to the Hebrews' miraculous escape from Egypt under the leadership of Moses. Like the whole New Testament, the *Book of Acts* is written in Greek even when it is about Jewish history and culture.

> ἔφυγεν δὲ Μωϋσῆς ἐν τῷ λόγῳ τούτῳ καὶ ἐγένετο πάροικος ἐν γῇ Μαδιάμ, οὗ ἐγέννησεν υἱοὺς δύο. Καὶ πληρωθέντων ἐτῶν τεσσεράκοντα ὤφθη αὐτῷ ἐν τῇ ἐρήμῳ τοῦ ὄρους Σινᾶ ἄγγελος ἐν φλογὶ πυρὸς βάτου. ὁ δὲ Μωϋσῆς ἰδὼν ἐθαύμαζεν τὸ ὅραμα, προσερχομένου δὲ αὐτοῦ κατανοῆσαι

---

these new deacons, Philip and Stephen, also became bold preachers and evangelists. Of Stephen it is said he was "full of grace and power, [and] was doing great wonders and signs among the people. Some "rose up and disputed with Stephen. But they could not withstand the wisdom and the Spirit with which he was speaking." (vv. 9-10) So they seized him and condemned him in a mock trial similar to that forced upon Jesus.

ἐγένετο φωνὴ κυρίου, Ἐγὼ ὁ θεὸς τῶν πατέρων σου, ὁ θεὸς Ἀβραὰμ καὶ Ἰσαὰκ καὶ Ἰακώβ. ἔντρομος δὲ γενόμενος Μωϋσῆς οὐκ ἐτόλμα κατανοῆσαι. εἶπεν δὲ αὐτῷ ὁ κύριος, Λῦσον τὸ ὑπόδημα τῶν ποδῶν σου, ὁ γὰρ τόπος ἐφ᾽ ᾧ ἕστηκας γῆ ἁγία ἐστίν. ἰδὼν εἶδον τὴν κάκωσιν τοῦ λαοῦ μου τοῦ ἐν Αἰγύπτῳ καὶ τοῦ στεναγμοῦ αὐτῶν ἤκουσα, καὶ κατέβην ἐξελέσθαι αὐτούς· καὶ νῦν δεῦρο ἀποστείλω σε εἰς Αἴγυπτον. Τοῦτον τὸν Μωϋσῆν, ὃν ἠρνήσαντο εἰπόντες, Τίς σε κατέστησεν ἄρχοντα καὶ δικαστήν; τοῦτον ὁ θεὸς [καὶ] ἄρχοντα καὶ λυτρωτὴν ἀπέσταλκεν σὺν χειρὶ ἀγγέλου τοῦ ὀφθέντος αὐτῷ ἐν τῇ βάτῳ. οὗτος ἐξήγαγεν αὐτοὺς ποιήσας τέρατα καὶ σημεῖα ἐν γῇ Αἰγύπτῳ καὶ ἐν Ἐρυθρᾷ Θαλάσσῃ καὶ ἐν τῇ ἐρήμῳ ἔτη τεσσεράκοντα.

*...Moses fled [from Egypt] and became an exile in the land of Midian, where he became the father of two sons. "Now when forty years had passed, an angel appeared to him in the wilderness of Mount Sinai, in a flame of fire in a bush. When Moses saw it, he was amazed at the sight, and as he drew near to look, there came the voice of the Lord: 'I am the God of your fathers, the God of Abraham and of Isaac and of Jacob.' And Moses trembled and did not dare to look. Then the Lord said to him, 'Take off the sandals from your feet, for the place where you are standing is holy ground. I have surely seen the affliction of my people who are in Egypt, and have heard their groaning, and I have come down to deliver them. And now come, I will send you to Egypt.' "This Moses, whom they rejected, saying, 'Who made you a ruler and a judge?'—this man God sent as both ruler and **redeemer** by the hand of the angel who appeared to him in the bush. This man led them out, performing wonders and signs in Egypt and at the Red Sea and in the wilderness for forty years. (vv. 29-36)*

There we have it. Stephen called Moses a "redeemer," for that is exactly what he was by the appointment and power of Almighty God, Yahweh. As he would later use Jonah to spare the Ninevites, he used Moses to rescue, deliver, recover, and restore the now millions of descendants of Jacob, the grandson of Abraham. Unlike Jonah, Moses was over-zealous at first, and his brave though premature actions forced him into exile. Forty years later, when Yahweh commanded Moses to return to a hostile Egypt, he was understandably reluctant, if not as reluctant as Jonah.

But Stephen didn't stop there. He went on to say of Moses…

Τοῦτον τὸν Μωϋσῆν ὃν ἠρνήσαντο εἰπόντες· τίς σε κατ έστησεν ἄρχοντα καὶ δικαστήν; τοῦτον ὁ θεὸς ἄρχοντα καὶ λυτρωτὴν ἀπέσταλκεν σὺν χειρὶ ἀγγέλου τοῦ ὀφθέν τος αὐτῷ ἐν τῇ βάτῳ. ³⁶ οὗτος ἐξήγαγεν αὐτοὺς ποιήσα ς τέρατα καὶ σημεῖα ἐν γῇ Αἰγύπτῳ καὶ ἐν ἐρυθρᾷ θαλά σσῃ καὶ ἐν τῇ ἐρήμῳ ἔτη τεσσεράκοντα. ³⁷ οὗτός ἐστιν ὁ Μωϋσῆς ὁ εἴπας τοῖς υἱοῖς Ἰσραήλ· προφήτην ὑμῖν ἀ ναστήσει ὁ θεὸς ἐκ τῶν ἀδελφῶν ὑμῶν ὡς ἐμέ. ³⁸ οὗτός ἐστιν ὁ γενόμενος ἐν τῇ ἐκκλησίᾳ ἐν τῇ ἐρήμῳ μετὰ το ῦ ἀγγέλου τοῦ λαλοῦντος αὐτῷ ἐν τῷ ὄρει Σινᾶ καὶ τῶν πατέρων ἡμῶν ὃς ἐδέξατο λόγια ζῶντα δοῦναι ἡμῖν·

This is the Moses who said to the Israelites, 'God will raise up for you a prophet like me from your brothers.' This is the one who was in the congregation in the wilderness with the angel who spoke to him at Mount Sinai, and with our fathers. He received living oracles to give to us. (vv, 35-38)

Strangely, Stephen quoted Prophet Moses from the last of his five books that comprise the Torah—*Deuteronomy*. These words are found in chapter 18 and verse 15. They clearly speak of some other, later prophet who, paradoxically, "was in the congregation in the wilderness," past tense (v. 38). But how could he be a future prophet to come and also be one who was already there? Could Stephen have intended this as a referent to the Messiah whom Moses seemed to exemplify yet in his time was visibly nowhere on the scene? The main takeaway from this section is that Moses was certainly a **"redeemer,"** and for obvious reasons, probably the most paradigmatic redeemer figure of all.

Islam also regards Moses as a great prophet and deliverer. The Qur'an contains a whopping 234 verses with his name scattered throughout many of its 114 surahs, though it does not use the word "redeemer" referring to him. Here is one:

وَلَقَدْ آتَيْنَا مُوسَى الْكِتَابَ وَجَعَلْنَا مَعَهُ أَخَاهُ هَارُونَ وَزِيرًا

And surely We gave **Moses** the Scripture and appointed his brother Aaron as an assistant...

Surah Al-Furqan, 25:35[140]

Another translation renders "scripture" as "book."[141] Muslims understand Moses as having received from Allah a book of revelation akin to that received by Muhammad in the 7th century. Similarly, Muslims believe such a book was given to Abraham (Ibrahim), David (Daoud – the Zaboor, or *Psalms*), and Jesus (Issa – the Injeel). They believe all of them carried the selfsame message of "Tawhid" or one God, but that all of their books have since been lost or corrupted. On this account, many Muslims will say that they believe in the Bible, by which they mean that they believe in the 'original' Bible, the now lost books given to these four prophets, but not the one that we have today. Recall from chapter five that the Qur'an confirms the previous scriptures of the Torah as having been true at the time of Muhammad, as well as those of the Injil, or Gospel, the Christian scriptures. For example, Surah 3:3 says...

نَزَّلَ عَلَيْكَ الْكِتَابَ بِالْحَقِّ مُصَدِّقًا لِمَا بَيْنَ يَدَيْهِ وَأَنزَلَ التَّوْرَاةَ وَالْإِنجِيلَ

He has revealed to you 'O Prophet' [Muhammad] the Book in truth, confirming what came before it, as He revealed the **Torah** and the **Gospel**.[142]

---

[140] Fadel Soliman, Bridges' translation, quran.com

[141] Dr. Mustafa Khattab, The Clear Quran, quran.com

[142] Surah Ali 'Imran, bolding mine. Ibid. See more examples in Surahs 2:41, 101; 3:3, 48-50, 93; 5:43-44, 46, 66, 68, 6:91; 7:171; 9:111; 10: 94; 11:110, 28:43; 29:47; 41:45; and 62:5.

Conversely, it is difficult to find verses of the Qur'an that plainly and explicitly assert that the original scriptures of the Bible—the Torah, Psalms, and Gospel, have been lost or corrupted.[143]

The Arabic verb/s translated as 'redeem' in one form or another appear eight times in the Qur'an, though there seems to be no noun form; none of them is in reference to Moses such as we find in *Acts 7:35*. More significantly, none of them is in reference to any person as a type of redeemer, not even a prophet. Rather, they seem generally to refer to the redeeming of a captive (90:13) or to persons who want to redeem themselves (5:36, 13:18, 70:11 and 14, 39:47 i.e. from the terrible punishment or eternal torment on judgment day). Once it expresses the idea that a man cannot redeem another man by his own merit (35:18), and once it refers to Allah who states, **"And We redeemed him with a great sacrifice."** (37:107[144])

وَفَدَيْنَاهُ بِذِبْحٍ عَظِيمٍ

The Great Sacrifice

What exactly was that sacrifice? It is not specified in the Qur'an, but it is in the Torah as we have it still today, the original narration by Moses contained in *Genesis 22*. It is the account of when Yahweh commanded Abraham to sacrifice his son, but then rescued him. The angel of the LORD appeared and told Abraham, *"Do not lay your hand on the boy or do anything to him."* Instead, the narration tells us that Abraham turned his eyes to see a ram caught by its horns in a nearby thicket, and he sacrificed that instead. It does not explicitly

---

[143] Some verses of the Qur'an and hadith that seem to suggest that the existing scriptures were being exploited for gain and twisted at least in speech and/or interpretation. The question is whether they were in any way altered in their written form. They are ambiguous. However, a close analysis of these few verses reveals the former, not the latter.

[144] Fadel Soliman, Bridges' translation, quran.com. Bolding mine. Another translation of that Arabic word is "ransomed" (Dr. Mustafa Khattab, the Clear Quran). See also the brief note on this verse in www.islamicstudies.info/tafheem.php?sura=37&verse=99&to=113

say that the LORD either expected or accepted this substitution, but all the details of the scene seem to make it obvious that He did. It's even apparent that it was the LORD's idea. If it was a lesson, the idea of *redemption* seemed to be the primary objective even though the word is not present, or at least one of them. In this particular case it's not the Torah but the Qur'an that uses it explicitly. Again, **"We redeemed him** [Ismael][145] **with a great sacrifice** [the ram]." Note that this little verse also uses the word *sacrifice*, which seems to me to link the two notions together. In the Tanakh, a sacrifice is a redemption, or at least this kind of sacrifice is—an animal sacrifice, a blood sacrifice. On this occasion, God accepted the death of another living thing as a substitute for the boy, and even provided for it. Indeed He required it, for He did not release him without it.

There is an annual Muslim holiday based on this story called Eid Al-Adha, the Feast, or Festival of the Sacrifice. It happens at the culmination of the rites of Hajj when millions of Muslims visit Mecca. It is a three-day celebration during which Muslim families slaughter a lamb or sheep to commemorate the ram that was sacrificed in place of the boy. I have discussed this profound passage with my Muslim friends many times. In my experience, they focus on Abraham's obedience, which was impressive. But they almost never say anything about the "adha" in the story, the sacrifice, the redemption that took place. I almost always have to bring it up, and I have found myself wondering why. I have even asked them if they are familiar with that part of the story. ..."The ram, you mean?" Yes, that. So they know about it, but it's apparently not very important.

Another Qur'anic verse speaking of Moses is this:

وَلَقَدْ ءَاتَيْنَا مُوسَىٰ تِسْعَ ءَايَٰتٍۭ بَيِّنَٰتٍ ۖ فَسْـَٔلْ بَنِىٓ إِسْرَٰٓءِيلَ إِذْ جَآءَهُمْ فَقَالَ لَهُۥ فِرْعَوْنُ إِنِّى لَأَظُنُّكَ يَٰمُوسَىٰ مَسْحُورًا

---

[145] Muslims universally believe that the son in this story was Ishmael, or Ismael, even though no name is stated in this or any passage of the Qur'an. Once I had a deep conversation with a Muslim student named Yusef at the University of Michigan in Dearborn. He took me through an elaborate series of inferences from the Qur'an and Islamic history as to why the boy had to be Ismael. If I recall correctly it was based on the belief that Ismael was with his father Ibrahim when he built the Ka'aba in Mecca.

> And We had certainly given Moses nine evident signs, so ask the Children of Israel [about] when he came to them and Pharaoh said to him, "Indeed I think, O Moses, that you are affected by magic.
>
> Surah Al-Isra (The Night Journey), 17:101[146]

This evidently refers to the account of *Exodus* 5:1-2 and the nine subsequent times when Moses confronted the Pharaoh to demand that he let the Hebrew people go. This happened before each of ten plagues that are described in great detail in chapters 7-12 of the *Exodus* narrative. Concerning this chain of events, the Qur'anic narrative is largely similar to the biblical one, though it mentions only nine signs, not the ten, and does not describe them in much detail.

A third and final example is a much longer one captured in Surah 7 verses 103 through 155. This passage contains the narrative when, having led the Israelites out of Egypt, Moses ascended Mt. Sinai to meet with the LORD, the same place where He first appeared to him in the burning bush about one year prior. It corresponds roughly to the long narrative in the *Book of Exodus* beginning in chapter 19 and culminating in chapter 32 with the scandal of the golden calf. That's 14 chapters with 447 verses. A large percentage of those verses are in the voice of the LORD himself, Yahweh, which is the only kind of scripture that Muslims view as revelation.[147] Twelve of these fourteen chapters start with, "The Lord said to Moses" or continue in His voice from the previous chapter, which is approximately 85% of the whole section. The corresponding passage in Surah Al-A'raf (7, The Heights) is also in the voice of Allah, which most of the Qur'an is.[148]

---

[146] Sahih International, muflihun.com/17/101-102

[147] Jews and Christians view all the contents of the Torah and Tanakh as divine revelation, not only the parts that are in the voice of God. Thus it is a much more comprehensive understanding of revelation, including all of what God wanted to inform and teach his readers.

[148] This surah seems to have a similar purpose as Acts 7 in that it compiles the stories of five other prophets including Noah (again) in vv. 59-64, Lot in vv. 80-84, and Shu'aib (Shu'ayb, Jethro of Midian) in vv. 85-92. Islam considers the latter two as prophets, whereas Judaism and Christianity do not. (Also including Ad and Thamud.)

It contains 53 verses and is probably the longest passage concerning Moses in the Qur'an. Verses 142-154 contain the episode when Moses spent 40 days on the mountain with God. When he came down the first time with the stone tablets, he broke them in righteous anger because the people had been worshiping the golden calf in his absence, which was facilitated by his brother and co-prophet Aaron.

Verse 154 captures the tail-end of the narrative when Moses' anger was finally spent, and of course the LORD's.

وَلَمَّا سَكَتَ عَن مُّوسَى ٱلْغَضَبُ أَخَذَ ٱلْأَلْوَاحَ ۖ وَفِى نُسْخَتِهَا هُدًى وَرَحْمَةٌ لِّلَّذِينَ هُمْ لِرَبِّهِمْ يَرْهَبُونَ

When Moses' anger subsided, he took up the Tablets whose text contained guidance and mercy for those who stand in awe of their Lord.[149]

In this particular narrative at least, the Qur'an doesn't say that Moses first broke the tablets, and more significantly, it does not reveal what was written on them verbatim, as the Torah does. In the Torah, the ten commandments are revealed in their entirety in two places: First in *Exodus* chapter 20 verses 1-17, and again in the *Book of Deuteronomy* chapter 5 verses 6-21. I and many other Jews and Christians regard them as the very bedrock of moral laws, fundamental and essential. So I don't get why Allah, as he was revealing this account, would not have also revealed the actual commandments to Muhammad as he did to Moses. Could he have considered it redundant because he had already revealed them to an earlier prophet who recorded them in the Torah, a book of revelation that was attested to and confirmed by the Qur'an? That seems logical. From the verses we have already listed, the Qur'an 'knew' that the Torah already contained them, and that the authentic Torah was extant and in circulation since well before the advent of Islam.

---

[149] Quran.com, Dr. Mustafa Khattab, the Clear Quran

As Muslims know and others might expect by now, there are multiple ahadith about Moses as well. This one has him engaged in kind of an adversarial conversation with the first man, Adam:

حَدَّثَنَا الصَّلْتُ بْنُ مُحَمَّدٍ، حَدَّثَنَا مَهْدِيُّ بْنُ مَيْمُونٍ، حَدَّثَنَا مُحَمَّدُ بْنُ سِيرِينَ، " الْتَقَى آدَمُ عَنْ أَبِي هُرَيْرَةَ، عَنْ رَسُولِ اللَّهِ صلى الله عليه وسلم قَالَ وَمُوسَى، فَقَالَ مُوسَى لآدَمَ أَنْتَ الَّذِي أَشْقَيْتَ النَّاسَ وَأَخْرَجْتَهُمْ مِنَ الْجَنَّةِ قَالَ لَهُ آدَمُ أَنْتَ الَّذِي اصْطَفَاكَ اللَّهُ بِرِسَالَتِهِ، وَاصْطَفَاكَ لِنَفْسِهِ وَأَنْزَلَ عَلَيْكَ التَّوْرَاةَ قَالَ نَعَمْ. قَالَ فَوَجَدْتَهَا كُتِبَ عَلَىَّ قَبْلَ أَنْ يَخْلُقَنِي قَالَ نَعَمْ. فَحَجَّ آدَمُ مُوسَى ". الْيَمُّ الْبَحْرُ.

> Allah's Messenger (ﷺ) said, "Adam and Moses met, and Moses said to Adam "You are the one who made people miserable and turned them out of Paradise." Adam said to him, "You are the one whom Allah selected for His message and whom He selected for Himself and upon whom He revealed the Torah." Moses said, 'Yes.' Adam said, "Did you find that written in my fate before my creation?' Moses said, 'Yes.' So Adam overcame Moses with this argument."[150]

Since Adam and Moses were around 2500 years apart, and no similar story is found in either the Qur'an or the Tanakh, this raises several interesting questions. One is, does this conversation take place after the death of Moses so that they were both dead? Or was it something more like when King Saul went to the witch (medium) of Endor to bring up the prophet Samuel from the dead? (*Book of 1 Samuel* 28:8-19) Another is about the nature of Islamic revelation. Did the first person to report this do so as a direct revelation from Allah, or did he see this with his own eyes? If he saw it with his own eyes, did he see both prophets in the flesh, or was one of them a ghost of the kind that King Saul must have seen? Or, did the observer see them in paradise after they were both dead but he was still alive? Or, did he die and go to paradise where he saw them both? Whichever the case, all of the logical options are perplexing.

---

[150] Sahih al-Buqari 4736, Book 65, Hadith 258

Finally, chapter 14 of the *Book of Exodus* records the Israelites' miraculous passing through the Red Sea while the Egyptian army was drowned in pursuit of them.[151] Can you imagine the drama of that? These days we don't have to imagine it, because it has been visually captured fantastically in movies as far back as 1956 when Charlton Heston starred as Moses in "The Ten Commandments." Also, in my view, the 2014 film "Patterns of Evidence: Exodus – The Red Sea Miracle" is exemplary for its documentary qualities.

Here's a thought: Since Moses was present for the whole event, he didn't really need God to 'reveal' it to him, did he? He saw it with his own eyes. Indeed he was present for all of the plagues before it and everything in the desert after it too. Except for what God said to Moses privately, every ordinary Israelite saw exactly what Moses saw, which would have been understood as divine revelation to them all! And during the plagues (e.g. blood, frogs, lice, gnats, boils, hail, locusts, etc.) every ordinary Egyptian saw those in addition to the Israelites. These also should be understood as having been divine revelation, to them and everyone since. So in terms of events and actions, in what sense did God *reveal* them to Moses in any kind of verbal way? And why would He have needed to?

The last two verses of chapter 14 state the following:

Thus the LORD saved Israel that day from the hand of the Egyptians, and Israel saw the Egyptians dead on the seashore. Israel saw the great power that the LORD used against the Egyptians, so the people feared the LORD, **and they believed in the LORD and in his servant Moses.**[152]

After their spectacular escape from Egypt, the Israelite people believed in the LORD *and in Moses*. It is simply uncontestable that

---

[151] I am aware that today's mainstream scholarship rejects a literal understanding of the exodus. It doesn't matter for my purposes. Hardly any scholars reject that there was an exodus event or that Moses was an historical figure who had an active role in the deliverance of the Israelites from Egypt.
[152] *Book of Exodus* 14:30, 31, Bolding mine.

Moses played a dramatic role in all of this. He was, with his brother Aaron, the LORD's human vessel of deliverance, or redemption. Thus we can see and understand that the prophet Moses was a redeemer in the most literal sense. By the power of Almighty God he led an entire nation of slaves into freedom.

The prophet Moses's place in Jewish history is monumental. His name appears in the five books of the Torah a staggering 595 times. Following the Torah his name appears another 115 times by most of the prophets and other canonical writers of the Tanakh, and 79 times in the New Testament, including about 18 times by Jesus with great reverence. Indeed, no one after the pharaoh ever spoke of Moses in a negative light. He the man, with the incredible events he narrated, and the laws God gave him, were considered by the Jews the 'gold standard' of divine revelation thereafter.

There are some senses in which Moses was like Job, and Job like Moses. Great men of God have things in common, and possibly these two more than others. Like Job before him, Moses had had everything and lost it. Job, even though he remained in his own place, in a sense was 'exiled' from his good life by the calamities that affected his social status. And so was Moses, as he describes in chapter 2 of the Book of Exodus. (vv. 11-22) In fear for his life, Moses fled to the land of Job or at least its vicinity. There, having taken refuge among the Midianites, he married into the family of Jethro, or Prophet Suhaib as he is known in Islam. It is easy for me to imagine that Moses learned the story of Job from Jethro, and that he took consolation from his story. I can even imagine that Moses learned more deeply about Job's Almighty God, Yahweh. Could that have been part of the reason that He arranged that sojourn for him?

Chapter 8

Back to Job—The Book *and* the Man

Job's Redeemer, Part 2

> *How intriguing it is that Job, even while his tragic circumstances have induced in him a fresh fear of God, never exhibits the least fear of God's judgment.*
>
> Mike Mason,
The Gospel According to Job[153]

This brings us full-circle back to our main passage of examination, the oracle of Prophet Job in chapter 19 of his book (vv. 25-27). In case you've forgotten it, here it is again:

For I know that my Redeemer lives,
    and at the last he will stand upon the earth.
And after my skin has been thus destroyed,
    yet in my flesh I shall see God,
whom I shall see for myself,
    and my eyes shall behold, and not another.
    My heart faints within me!

Remember, the big mystery is that we don't know who Job believed his redeemer was, or would be, as the case may be. But now we know more about what it means to redeem and to *be* a redeemer, so we should be able to continue our exegesis of the passage. Based on the immediate context of our passage there seem to be no

---

[153] p. 220

contextual clues to indicate the identity of Job's redeemer, either in the wording of the passage's immediate context or in context of the wider book. Yes, we know Job felt desperate and yearned for deliverance from his suffering—and even death. But there is no other talk of a redeemer (ga'al or go'el) anywhere else in the *Book of Job*, as noted before. We have also noted that some translations render ga'al as one of various other synonyms e.g. "ransomer" or "avenger."

וַאֲנִי יָדַעְתִּי גֹּאֲלִי חָי וְאַחֲרוֹן עַל־עָפָר יָקוּם:
וְאַחַר עוֹרִי נִקְּפוּ־זֹאת וּמִבְּשָׂרִי אֶחֱזֶה אֱלוֹהַּ:
אֲשֶׁר אֲנִי ׀ אֶחֱזֶה־לִּי וְעֵינַי רָאוּ וְלֹא־זָר כָּלוּ כִלְיֹתַי בְּחֵקִי:

This Jewish translation renders it as "Vindicator."

> *But I know that my **Vindicator** lives; In the end He will **testify** on earth— This, after my skin will have been peeled off. But I would behold God while still in my flesh, I myself, not another, would behold Him; Would see with my own eyes: My heart pines within me.*[154]

Notice that this one also renders the Hebrew verb qum (קוּם) as "testify" rather than "stand." Interesting. Although there are multiple options for this verb in Hebrew lexicons, I have not seen this in any of them. Another Jewish translation goes like this:[155]

> *I know that my **Redeemer** lives [(and He will **requite** you for this)] and He will **endure** after all [men] upon the earth. [(But they pay no heed to my Redeemer, but)] after [the afflictions of] my skin, they have thus tormented [me], and from my flesh I see **Judgment**. What I am aware of within me, and [what] my eyes have seen and not [those of] a stranger is that my kidneys have become consumed in my innards.*

---

[154] Tanakh: The Holy Scriptures, a New Translation, JPS, Sefaria.org

[155] Sefaria.org/Job.19.26?ven=The_Rashi_Ketuvim_by_Rabbi_Shraga_Silverstein&vhe =Tanach_with_Ta%27amei_Hamikra&lang=en

Here "Redeemer" gets re-inserted, but so also do several whole parenthetical phrases and words. "Testify" gets replaced with "endure", and "see God" gets replaced with "see judgment." Indeed, all the references to God have been removed, plus other obvious variations. This translation strikes me as one that tests the boundaries of what is reasonable in translation. There are limits. Also, it reminds me of many verses of the various English translations of the Qur'an with multiple insertions using parentheses and brackets.

Finally, the same Jewish translation renders verse 26 thusly:

And when after my skin this is destroyed, Then without my flesh shall I see God.[156]

It substitutes "in" or "with" for "without." So, among other interpretive challenges there are translation questions. We will return to some of them a bit later but without, I hope, getting too 'lost in the weeds', as it were. Indeed, some scholars have done their entire research project on this passage alone.[157] In any case, the majority of English translations render our passage in a very similar way.[158] They all express the general main idea that Job had hope for a redeemer figure who cared for him and deserved his confidence that he would

---

[156] Ibid.

[157] See Silvy Nasrat, **"Job As His Own Go'-el: Interpreting Job 19:25"** and Emke Jelmer Kuelen, **"God-talk in the Book of Job:** A biblical theological and systematic theological study into the Book of Job and its relevance for the Issue of Theodicy." University of Groningen, 2007.

[158] 21st Century King James Version (KJ21), American Standard Version (ASV), Christian Standard Bible (CSB), Common English Bible (CEB), **Complete Jewish Bible (CJB)**, Contemporary English Version (CEV), Darby Translation (DARBY), **Douay-Rheims 1899 American Edition (DRA)**, English Standard Version (ESV), English Standard Version Anglicised (ESVUK), 1599 Geneva Bible (GNV), Good News Translation (GNT), Holman Christian Standard Bible (HCSB), International Standard Version (ISV), **Jubilee Bible 2000 (JUB)**, King James Version (KJV), Authorized (King James) Version (AKJV), Lexham English Bible (LEB), New American Standard Bible (NASB), New American Standard Bible 1995 (NASB1995), New Century Version (NCV), New English Translation (NET), New International Version (NIV), New King James Version (NKJV), New Revised Standard Version (NRSV), New Testament for Everyone (NTE), Orthodox Jewish Bible (OJB), Revised Standard Version (RSV), **Wycliffe Bible (WYC)**, **Young's Literal Translation (YLT)**.
*Bolding indicates divergent translations.

somehow vindicate and/or deliver Job from his sufferings and/or the shame of his sufferings.

Although there are also a number of interesting intertextual connections to be made between this passage and others in the *Book of Job,* in general this is a stand-alone passage in my opinion, not especially bound by them or by the immediate context of chapter 19.

Now let's dissect the passage itself. What does it tell us about this redeemer? What can we know, and who might it be? First, there is an epistemological claim: Job believes **he knows** something about him, so he has a sense of confidence.

Second, **he lives**. All translations say this. Surely that is essential, but does it really tell us anything useful? Yes. Obviously, it tells us that the redeemer cannot be someone from the past who has died such as Adam or Enoch or Noah; well, not unless he has returned from the dead. He also cannot be someone strictly from the future who doesn't exist yet. Does this alone determine whether the redeemer is human or divine? Perhaps not, except in the sense that it may be superfluous to speak of a divine being who is alive. Isn't a divine being always alive? Actually, no. Many of the Greek gods had a birth and thus a beginning.

Third, **he will stand (or rise) on the earth (or the dust)**. This verse is either metaphorical or it seems to indicate humanness. If you are a Muslim you will affirm that emphatically.[159] To many Muslims, Christians and Jews, if the redeemer is said to "stand" on the earth or the dust—or if he *stands* anywhere at all—he is a man; or it is figurative language. *The* God does not stand. This is also consistent with a platonic point of view in which spiritual beings can never have material bodies. There are many apparent anthropomorphisms of God in the Tanakh, and no doubt many of them really are anthropomorphisms.[160] But they are not all *necessarily* such. Who can actually

---

[159] However, in his book, *The Incoherence of the Philosophers,* the great Muslim philosopher Al-Ghazali (1058–1111) taught that since the Qur'an speaks of God's eyes and hands, etc., we cannot say that he does not have such features.

[160] Apparent anthropomorphisms are when human-like features are ascribed to God in Hebrew scripture, either by Himself or by others.

insist, with perfect knowledge, that God cannot stand? In the Tanakh we find some apparent counterexamples. In the Torah, the *Book of Exodus* 17:6 it is recorded that the LORD said to Moses with his own voice, *"Behold, I will stand before you there on the rock at Horeb."* And again, toward the end of the Tanakh, in the *Book of the Prophet Zechariah,* we are told that "On that day his [the LORD's, YHWH's] feet will stand on the Mount of Olives…" (14:4) These both say that the LORD will *stand* somewhere in seemingly plain terms. Even supposing the latter to be figurative, the former seems quite literal to me. So in my view, this does not disqualify God Almighty as the possible redeemer. I agree with Al-Ghazali on this point, that we should interpret scripture in the plainest possible terms (see note 58). It is therefore apparent from these and other examples that the LORD can materialize at will and stand in the material dimension. That does not prove that the redeemer *was* God, only that it *could have* been, and the language of the most dominant translations lend themselves to this interpretation. Moreover, I do not agree with Silvy Nasrat who argued that Job viewed God as his enemy, and therefore He should be ruled out as a candidate for Redeemer.[161] There are multiple verses showing that Job retained his respect for God's ultimate, sovereign wisdom, and by extension, his benevolence (1:21; 2:10b; 12:13,16; 28:23, 28).

Even setting aside the great prophets Noah, Jonah, and Moses, we have already seen that the Mosaic laws of the Torah provided for human redeemers and redemption. But any such laws would not have been implemented in Job's geo-historical context and would not have been helpful to him even if they had been. Besides that, no such human redeemer is identifiable anywhere in the *Book of Job*. And it would seem to many commentators that Job's friends turned out to be his unyielding critics.[162] In any case, which of them—and what sort of human being at all—could have delivered or rescued him from

---

[161] Silvy, "Job As His Own Go'-el: Interpreting Job 19:25"

[162] Dr. Kyle Dunham, one of my esteemed professors of Old Testament at Detroit Baptist Theological Seminary in Allen Park, MI, in his book *The Pious Sage in Job: Eliphaz in the Context of Wisdom Theodicy*, argues that Eliphaz, at least, was not Job's critic.

the extent of his losses, afflictions, and the shame they brought upon Job and his wife?

...Not one.

On the other hand, I think of the Greek pantheon of gods. All of them could take physical form, walk the earth among normal humans, and do the full range of other human activities, good and bad. And they could all masquerade as mere mortals, and oh did they have vices! Even Zeus, a full-fledged 'god', was no less petulant than the rest, and was believed to have taken on human form. Indeed, several of the demigods were the progeny of Zeus and human women, such as Achilles and Hercules—half god and half human. But it is interesting to observe that their human qualities—and vices—seemed the most prominent. In the pop culture world of DC Comics, Wonder Woman was also a demigoddess, the progeny of Zeus and Hippolyta. All three of them were messiah figures with their own unique 'messiah complexes,' and they were 'redeemer-types.' So could Job have been thinking of a sort of demi-god when he said that his anticipated redeemer will "stand on the earth?" I think not. This is partly because of what we can glean about Job's theology in general, but also from this passage in specific.

In all 42 chapters of his book there is no hint that Job was anything but a strict monotheist, nor his four companions. Their entire discussion revolves around the person of one God alone, the Almighty One, the sole Creator of universe. The two names used for God in the *Book of Job* are Elohim (אֱלֹהִים)[163] used 41 times,

---

[163] However, Elohim is a plural noun, the singular being Eloah. It can also refer to the gods, the godhead, or the divine council. But when it is used it usually employs a singular verb, and other elements of the context usually indicate that it is referring to a singular God, as in the Supreme Ruler over the other heavenly beings such as angels. This is especially obvious when it occurs in conjunction with YHWH which it often does, or alternates with it. In Genesis chapter 1 Elohim is the only named for God used (25 times), and the first three times in chapter 2. But the context makes it obvious that the Deity, or Divine Being spoken about was revealing himself with a singular identity, purpose, and will, as in verse 3 when the texts says, "And God said...", and in verse 22 when the text says, "And God blessed them...". Then, beginning in verse 4 of chapter 2, all the rest of the occurrences are to the "LORD God", or Yahweh Elohim (11 times). In chapter 3

and YHWH (יהוה) transliterated as Yahweh or Jehovah, used 24 times. The former is a name for God that appears exclusively in the very first chapter of the Torah, *Genesis* 1, and 2346 other times throughout the Tanakh. This word translated in-context renders as "the gods" (elohim אֱלֹהִים), but it is usually used as singular with a singular verb. Rather than a proper name, it is a generic name for the one, Supreme Being who rules over all the other celestial beings He created. These include multiple kinds of angels such as cherubim and seraphim, and other heavenly creatures that belong in another category altogether such as "living creatures" and "elders" (Rev. 5:6). The latter appears 6510 times, such as when God first appeared to Moses in *Exodus* chapter 3. Verse 7 says, *"When the LORD (יהוה) saw that he* [Moses] *turned aside to see..."* Then eight verses later we read that the God told Moses his proper name, YHWH, or Yəhōwā, or Yahweh.

וַיֹּאמֶר עוֹד אֱלֹהִים אֶל־מֹשֶׁה כֹּה־תֹאמַר אֶל־בְּנֵי יִשְׂרָאֵל יְהֹוָה אֱלֹהֵי אֲבֹתֵיכֶם אֱלֹהֵי אַבְרָהָם אֱלֹהֵי יִצְחָק וֵאלֹהֵי יַעֲקֹב שְׁלָחַנִי אֲלֵיכֶם זֶה־שְּׁמִי לְעֹלָם וְזֶה זִכְרִי לְדֹר דֹּר׃

*And God said further to Moses, "Thus shall you speak to the Israelites: The **LORD**, the God of your fathers, the God of Abraham, the God of Isaac, and the God of Jacob, has sent me to you: **This shall be My name forever, My appellation** [name] **for all eternity**.*[164]

Book of Exodus 3:15

His name means "He Who Makes That Which Has Been Made" or "He Brings into Existence Whatever Exists." This example is special because it's the first time God used this to name himself. But the first time Yahweh (יהוה) appears is in *Genesis* 2, in which book

---

Yahweh Elohim is the first name used, followed by Elohim three times, and the remaining eight times are Yahweh Elohim. So it is clear in chapters 2 and 3 that the names can be used interchangeably, and the semi-alternating usage of Yahweh determines that even Elohim is referring to Yahweh Elohim in chapter 1.

[164] Bolding mine.

it occurs a total of 185 times, and in Exodus 340.[165] From there the sacred name becomes increasingly more prevalent as the Hebrew canon of the Tanakh progresses.

Thus again, in all ten of Job's divinely enscripturated discourses, there is no evidence of polytheistic beliefs on his part or his companions'. Also, in all 36 chapters of arduous dialogue between Job and them (3-37), never once did Job assert the oneness of God to them. He didn't need to. Although none of them were Jews per se, they were clearly not polytheists like most of the peoples of the Near East and the rest of the world were. Indeed, nearly all of the peoples of the world everywhere at that time were polytheists, pantheists or

---

[165] In light of these *Genesis* references, *Exodus* 6:3 presents an apparent problem over which my Muslim friend Ibrahim and I have wrestled. In it the LORD states to Moses, "I appeared to Abraham, to Isaac, and to Jacob, as God Almighty [El Shaddai], but by my name the LORD [YHWH יהוה] I did not make myself known to them. At face value this seems to be a contradiction. In his commentary, Norbert Link proffers as the best explanation that this statement should actually be translated as a rhetorical question— "…but by my name did I not make myself known to them?" (Yes.) Scofield and Clarke both offer this as a reasonable possibility, and Jamieson, Fausset and Brown agree with Ed Nelson with confidence:

"In reading the Hebrew Bible, often we do not know if a question is being asked or not until we read the whole context of the passage. Does the sentence make sense without it inferring a question is being asked? Then it is likely a statement. Does the sentence make sense only by understanding it to be a question? Then it is probably a question. Often an interrogative statement, that is, a question, will include a negative word like 'not' to offset it from the rest of the declarative statements. If we find a negative in a sentence that translates as 'not,' we should consider if the negative is to be understood as a flag to alert us that a question is being asked. …This is the case with Exodus 6:2-3. It has a negative 'not' in it, whereas the other sentences around it do not.

"This explanation appears to be the only logical and convincing one, which is consistent with and takes into account all pertinent Scriptures—and it is also compelling in light of the fact that there is no punctuation in the original Hebrew text. Further, the original does not use the words "but by" (in "BUT BY My name [YHWH] was I not known…") rather, it says: "as to", in "AS TO My name [YHWH] (compare Young's Literal Translation) was I not known…" The misuse of the word "but" could signify a difference in God's statement ("I revealed Myself to the fathers as El Shaddai, BUT not as YHWH"), but the original wording "as to…" does not contain the thought of such a difference ("I revealed Myself to the fathers as El Shaddai, and as to My name YHWH, was I not (also) known by that?").

"Whether a sentence is meant to be an affirmative statement or an interrogatory, can only be determined by the context. Here, it appears that Genesis 6:3 contains indeed a self-explanatory rhetorical question ("Did I not make Myself known to them as YHWH?"), which does not need or deserve an answer: God had revealed His name YHWH to the fathers, as well as others, and now He is revealing it again to Moses." www.eternalgod.org/q-a-13026/

panentheists, spiritists, or animists.[166, 167] Then, four of the five final chapters (38-41) are consumed almost entirely with the words of the LORD, Yahweh himself who had an awful lot to say to a self-righteous yet humbled and repentant Job. This one-of-a-kind divine monologue starts with these words: ***"Then the LORD answered Job out of the whirlwind and said…"***[168] In it His singular point seemed to be that He alone possesses the power, knowledge, and wisdom to determine the best series of events for a man, and for the world. But, in concert with Job and his cohorts, his oneness was not at all a part of his disquisition. It didn't need to be.

Now, with the general context as a backdrop, we can also reject polytheism because of the next several things Job says in the passage at hand. Let's look at the second and third stanza:

> *And after my skin has been thus destroyed,*
> *yet in my flesh I shall see God,*
> *whom I shall see for myself,*
> *and my eyes shall behold, and not another.*

Here Job obviously speaks of his own death. No doubt Job expected to die from the combined stress of his calamity, including the grievously painful boils all over his body.

Seeing God?

Nevertheless, Job had another expectation, a hopeful one. Not only did he seem to believe he would live on in some sense, he expected to *see* God ('ĕlvôha, el-o'-ah). This might seem strange, for not all figures of the Tanakh apparently anticipated life after death. And who expects to *see* God? Indeed, the LORD told Moses, *"…you*

---

[166] There were probably no Jews yet. Jews, or Hebrews, did not exist before Jacob moved his family to Canaan, and arguably not until Jacob's whole clan moved to Egypt.

[167] Nor were they any Muslims since Islam would not emerge for another 3000 years.

[168] Bolding mine.

cannot see my face, for man shall not see me and live." (Torah, *Exodus* 33:20) In the New Testament both Jesus and the Apostle John echoed this when they said, *"No one has ever seen God."*[169] On the other hand, the next three verses tell us that Moses *did* see something of the form and glory of God, just not His face.

> *And the LORD said* [to Moses], *"Behold, there is a place by me where you shall stand on the rock, and while my glory passes by I will put you in a cleft of the rock, and I will cover you with my hand until I have passed by. Then I will take away my hand, and you shall see my back, but my face shall not be seen."* (vv. 21-23)

Now, to see any 'part' of God, as it were, in the temporal dimension is still to see God, if only in a limited sense. So at least on one occasion a great prophet, a man, *was* allowed to see God. Some Muslims and others might be quick to point out this apparent contradiction with *1 John* 4:12, and I admit that it seems like one. But it doesn't bother me. Why? I assume that it is not an actual contradiction, along with the many other Christians who affirm the inerrancy of the scriptures of both testaments. In the same gospel Jesus also said that *"the scriptures cannot be broken,"* as I said in an earlier footnote. (*John* 10:35) On Jesus's account, certainly he knew the Tanakh inside and out, so he undoubtedly knew this passage about Moses and every other passage that I am going to present. John too. Besides that, he actually heard Jesus say it, and recorded it in his gospel, and then wrote it into the first of his own inspired epistles. Neither of them could have been wrong. That's why the solution must have to do with the possible meanings of "seeing God." Without going neck-deep into the proverbial weeds, I take Jesus's and John's words to mean that no man with his naked eye has seen the *essence* of God, only limited manifestations of

---

[169] *Gospel of John* 1:18 and *1 John* 4:12

Him, and only then by His self-disclosure.[170]

In Moses's case, this was a very special privilege from the LORD, to be sure. But it had restrictions. Moses was allowed to experience some kind of visual perception of God in the temporal dimension, but even then he was restricted from seeing the *face of God*. Also, this restriction would not necessarily apply to the dimension of the afterlife. Neither was it a restriction on seeing God in visions as we discover from the book of the great Prophet Isaiah.[171] In chapter 6:1-2 of this book we read…

> *In the year that King Uzziah died **I saw the Lord** sitting upon a throne, high and lifted up; and the train of his robe filled the temple. Above him stood the seraphim.*

Isaiah was not dead at this point, nor was he speaking about what he would see in the afterlife. Rather, Isaiah was seeing a vision of the LORD in His heavenly realm. Other prophets of the LORD had similar visions that they recorded in their respective books that are wholly contained in the Tanakh but not in the Qur'an, such as Zechariah, Joel, Daniel,[172] and Ezekiel[173]

---

[170] See Barnes notes on the Bible at biblehub.com/commentaries/john/1-18.htm

[171] Isaiah (أشعياء *Ishaʿyāʾ*) is not mentioned in the Qur'an or Hadith, but appears frequently as a prophet in Islamic sources, such as Qisas Al-Anbiya and Tafsir. Tabari (310/ 923) provides the typical accounts for Islamic traditions of Isaiah. He is further mentioned and accepted as a prophet by other Islamic scholars according to which Isaiah predicted the coming of both Jesus and Muhammad, although the reference to Muhammad is disputed by other religious scholars. wikipedia.org/wiki/Isaiah

[172] Daniel was also a Jewish exile to Babylon slightly before Ezekiel whose book of revelation contains twelve chapters. He ascended to great prominence in a manner similar to Joseph in Egypt, in the late 7th century BC. The Qur'an contains no mention of the Prophet Daniel (Daniyal, دانيال) though he is contained in Muslim tradition and legend (Isra'iliyyat). He is absent from sunni ahadith who regard him as a 'saintly man, but present in shia collections who regard him as prophet. wikipedia.org/wiki/Daniel_in_Islam

[173] Ezekiel was a Jewish exile to Babylon which later became Persia, early 6th century BC. His book of revelations contains 48 chapters which are not contained in the Qur'an, neither is there any mention of Ezekiel by name. However, there are two mentions of a figure named *Zu al-Kifl* or *Dhū al-Kifl* (ذو الكفل) whom some Muslims equate with Prophet Ezekiel (Surah 21:85-86 and 38:48). Whether they are one and the same, still Ezekiel is listed as a prophet in Islam. wikipedia.org/wiki/Dhu_al-Kifl and wikipedia.org/wiki/Ezekiel#Islamic_tradition

Three books after the *Book of Isaiah* we have the book of the Prophet Ezekiel. Ezekiel was a Jewish priest in Babylon/Persia during their 70-year captivity. In the first verse of chapter 1 of his book he revealed…

> *In the thirtieth year, in the fourth month, on the fifth day of the month, as I was among the exiles by the Chebar canal, the heavens were opened, and I saw visions of God.*[174]

But Ezekiel's vision was either more explicit than Isaiah's or he simply reported more of the visual details. First he described the appearance of four "living creatures" with wings and multiple other impressive features befitting celestial beings that stir the imagination, but which I will leave out for the sake of brevity. (vv. 4-25) These were probably cherubim or the seraphim that Isaiah saw too. Then Ezekiel describes an "expanse" over their heads, above which was the likeness of a throne the color of sapphire (probably blue). And above that was

> *…a likeness with a human appearance. And upward from what had the appearance of his waist I saw as it were gleaming metal, like the appearance of fire enclosed all around. And downward from what had the appearance of his waist I saw as it were the appearance of fire, and there was brightness around him. Like the appearance of the bow that is in the cloud on the day of rain, so was the appearance of the brightness all around.* **Such was the appearance of the likeness of the glory of the LORD.** *And when I saw it, I fell on my face…* (vv. 26-28)

This was Ezekiel's awesome vision of the LORD. Strangely, He had a "human appearance."

---

[174] Or *from* God

Finally we look at the vision of the Prophet Daniel who was a contemporary of Ezekiel. His equally apocalyptic book immediately follows Ezekiel's in Protestant Christian Bibles and is 22nd in the Jewish Tanakh. Daniel's vision is equally descriptive as Ezekiel's albeit in some different ways.

> *"As I looked,*
> > *thrones were placed,*
> > > **and the Ancient of Days took his seat;**
> > *his clothing was white as snow,*
> > > *and the hair of his head like pure wool;*
> > *his throne was fiery flames;*
> > > *its wheels were burning fire.*
> > *A stream of fire issued*
> > > *and came out from before him;*
> > *a thousand thousands served him,*
> > > *and ten thousand times ten thousand stood before him;*
> > *the court sat in judgment,*
> > > *and the books were opened.*
>
> *"I saw in the night visions,*
> > *and behold, with the clouds of heaven*
> > > *there came one like a son of man,*
> > *and he came to the Ancient of Days*
> > > *and was presented before him.*
> > *And to him was given dominion*
> > > *and glory and a kingdom,*
> > *that all peoples, nations, and languages*
> > > *should serve him;*
> > *his dominion is an everlasting dominion,*
> > > *which shall not pass away,*
> > *and his kingdom one*
> > > *that shall not be destroyed.*

In Daniel's vision God is called the "Ancient of Days." Personally, I especially like that title. As with Ezekiel, Daniel saw particular features of God unique to his vision—His clothing and His hair. Yes, I know that this rubs some people the wrong way who champion His invisibility, but I am not making this up. All these great prophets saw visions, and all of them saw manifestations of God in them. Also, in Daniel's it probably did not escape your notice that there was another figure besides God, "one like a son of man." That resembles what Ezekiel saw in his vision. We shall return to this mysterious figure and perhaps other aspects of these intriguing passages.

One final prophet that had extensive visions was the Prophet Zechariah, whose visions take up five-and-half of his fourteen chapters. Although he did not see the LORD as the other prophets did, he saw the angel of the LORD, plus Satan, four horses, a rider, a man with a measuring line, a golden lampstand, and a second angel. He also saw someone called Joshua the high priest who seems to have had no counterpart in the temporal dimension. He, and the horse rider, was either a man in the celestial dimension or he was a celestial being in that dimension. For now, our basic observation is this: In the LORD's desire to be known He granted some of his prophets the privilege of seeing Him and other things that are usually invisible features of his celestial realm, both in temporal manifestations and in visions.[175]

All this suggests that Job was in good company. He was the first, or one of the first, men of God to have experienced such an extended discourse with the Almighty, and also to have received such a speccially revealed notion of God as Redeemer, and thus of redemption itself. Or, perhaps it would be another member of the Elohim designated for this purpose like the Angel of the LORD who appeared to Prophets Abraham and Moses. Both prophets received a visitation

---

[175] In the New Testament era the LORD also granted this great privilege to the Apostle John whose revelations he recorded in the *Book of Revelation*, the very last book of the Bible, the combination of the Old Testament (Tanakh) and New Testament. It was also granted to the deacon Stephen whom we have already encountered, in *Acts* 7:56.

from a special angel called the "Angel of the LORD" (Torah, *Genesis* 22:11 and *Exodus* 3:2) as did numerous other prophets and even ordinary people. This Angel was apparently not Gabriel, and he didn't just convey messages. He performed functions with the authority and recognition of the LORD himself.[176]

Job's Afterlife

Evidently, Job believed in an afterlife, and a conscious one at that. It was one where at least some of his senses would be operational, i.e. where he could *see,* or at least see *God*. Furthermore, Job apparently did not expect to end up in some place so dismal that God was absent, such as hell or even sheol.[177] Rather, he seemed to expect to find himself in a place where God Almighty was personally present and where He could be "seen."

In the next two stanzas of this passage Job reinforces this when he says, "…whom I shall see for myself, and my eyes shall behold." This is called parallelism and is very prevalent in the Hebrew writing of the Tanakh. So, three times Job said he expected to *see God*. This makes his statement of belief quite emphatic.

Ah, but we skipped over something in the second stanza:

> *And after my skin has been thus destroyed,*
> *yet **in my flesh** I shall see God...* (v. 26)

---

[176] Throughout the whole Tanakh there are some 77 references to this angel as distinct from other, 'generic' angels or messengers.

[177] Sheol was the Hebrew concept of the afterlife that was prevalent in the Tanakh, perhaps similar to the Greek hades. The entire Hebrew canon contains 63 occurrences of the word throughout it, 7 of which are from the lips of Job himself. It is always used in a very nebulous way indicating that the Jews did not have a clear understanding of it due to minimal revelation. It certainly was not a place of reward where someone expected to find God, despite one reference to the contrary by Prophet David in Psalm 139:8. But neither was it a place of punishment to which only the wicked were sent, condemned in torment. Rather, probably everyone expected to go there, even if they were to have a subsequent destination following divine judgment.

Here Job says, "...in my <u>flesh</u> I shall see God." What does *that* mean? But wait, he just said that his flesh will have been destroyed. Shouldn't he make up his mind? This seems like a classic contradiction too. Job apparently believes that first his flesh will be destroyed and later, in sheol or wherever he expects to land in the afterlife, his flesh will be *restored*. But that's impossible. Nobody gets to keep their flesh in the afterlife, much less to see God! It must be a translation problem. No, it's not. In another review of the same 30 English translations plus 23 more, there is a virtual unanimity, even more than there was on the previous verse, and several of them are Jewish. Indeed, the most disparate translation we saw was a Jewish one that translates God as "Judgment." But this is a very small minority of them, and even it translates the previous phrase as "from my flesh." That's quite a consensus.

One other Jewish translation we have already seen that is otherwise in complete harmony with the majority renders that phrase as "without my flesh"—the exact opposite.[178] But that's it, the only one like it that I could find. Therefore, the most common rendering among Jewish translations agrees with the vast majority of today's English translations:

וְאַחַר עוֹרִי נִקְּפוּ־זֹאת וּמִבְּשָׂרִי אֶחֱזֶה אֱלוֹהַּ:[179]

This, after my skin will have been peeled off. But I would behold God while still in my flesh...

The phrase in question utilizes the Hebrew preposition that most commonly translates as "in" or "from." It is therefore evident that Job, in the throes of his misery, is making an unprecedented declaration that although his flesh/skin will be destroyed (i.e. peeled or stripped off, decayed) in death or leading to it, yet somehow in his flesh he would behold God nevertheless. He clearly had a hopeful confidence for the afterlife, which is exactly a part of what true faith

---

[178] Tanakh: The Holy Scriptures, published by JPS, Sefaria.org.
[179] Ibid.

is in the Tanakh. Job seems to have believed he would get his body back, or perhaps a new one. Either way, he believed it would be a material body of flesh in which he would *see* God. To my knowledge, there is no place in all the rest of the Tanakh that is equally explicit about this belief, so I think this should really resonate with those who share in the faith of Job, or at least one similar.

Also, it was obviously important to Job to make this declaration and to specify the key terms of his belief. He could have just said something like, "I hope in God to save me" or "I trust in God to redeem me." Or maybe even, "I am confident that God will accept me into the good side of sheol." But no. Although we might wish he had been *more* explicit and had given us more information, the amount he did give was unprecedented, especially for a book that is possibly the oldest in the Tanakh. On the chronological timeline from oldest to younger there is absolutely no declaration like it from any other figure of the patriarchal period to which Job belonged, nor from before—not Adam or Eve, not Cain or Abel, not Enoch or Seth, not Noah, not Abraham or any of his progeny. Neither are there any comparable expressions from any figure of the next era, beginning with Joseph in Egypt over the next 900 years. It wasn't until the time of Prophet-King David (1010–970 BC) and his divinely-inspired *Book of Psalms*, (*Zaboor*) that we begin to see glimpses of such 'heavenly' language, and even there it is scant.

> *If I ascend to heaven, you are there!*
> *If I make my bed in Sheol, you are there!*
>
> *Psalm* 139:8

Take a moment to look closely at the following timeline again to locate the *Psalms*.

Of course, Job didn't use either the word heaven *or* sheol, so in one sense the revelation given to David is more explicit than Job's.

OLD TESTAMENT TIMELINE

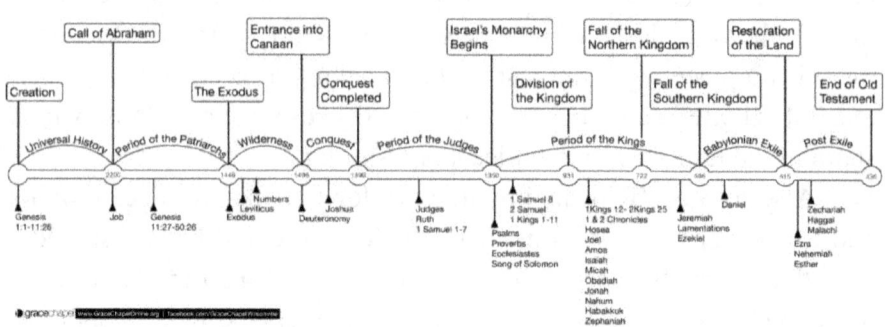

On the other hand, David's is hypothetical, it says "If I ascend" or "make my bed." David's oracle expresses that God is present both in sheol and in heaven (of course), just not that David was certain of landing there[180] or of ever seeing God as Job was. In Job's oracle, he is *certain,* or at least he is using the language of certainty: After he dies he will see God in his flesh, in his new or restored body. No comparable language appears again in the Bible until the teachings of Jesus and his Apostles in the New Testament.[181]

But is the God in verse 26 the same as the "redeemer" in verse 25? Now that is a good question, and a hard one. Some readers will see it that way immediately, and others not. I confess that upon close inspection it is not obvious. For that reason there is no definitive consensus on this question to the present. Yes, many interpreters in history have held that the redeemer is God. Others have concluded that he was some other human who was alive at Job's time and was within proximity to him. A third group have seen him as Jesus. Indeed, many Christians who have any opinion seem to believe this today. Finally, a small minority understands Job to be his own redeemer. Again I refer you to Silvy Nasrat's extremely thorough Master's degree thesis—"Job As His Own Go'-el: Interpreting Job 19:25." From his

---

[180] But we do get a general sense of that from 2 Samuel 12:23.

[181] See *Gospel of Luke* 16:19-26 and *Revelation* 21.

impressively detailed analysis of all the elements of our passage in focus, Nasrat determines that Job's redeemer was, most reasonably, neither God, nor Jesus, nor any other human. Therefore, Nasrat concludes that it was Job himself. Job, he argues, became his own redeemer by restoring his own good name after God restored his health and fortune.

The other researcher whom I included in the footnotes was Emke Jelmer Kuelen in his scholarly study, "God-talk in the *Book of Job:* A biblical theological and systematic theological study into the *Book of Job* and its relevance for the Issue of Theodicy." Kuelen agrees with Nasrat that the redeemer was neither God nor Jesus. But he doesn't entertain the notion that it might have been Job himself. Rather, he concludes that it was another man, possibly a contemporary of Job, or possibly someone who emerged much later. Both analyses of our passage are meticulous and complex, to say nothing of the studies of many others who have attempted it. The extensive details of these studies and how they arrived at their conclusions are too detailed for this book, but I commend them to you and encourage you to delve into them yourself.

As for this study, my own view is one that I think has been overlooked by these two researchers and most others that I've read. In some respects it is a both-and solution: Job's redeemer was at once God *and* the Messiah. Well, perhaps not the actual Messiah since there was hardly any other signs of a messiah yet. Rather, I'm talking about a faintly emerging 'prefiguration' of that which I've been pointing to all along—the messiah-in-relief, or *motif.* Just as a plant starts as a small sprout that can easily go unnoticed unless you are looking for it, so it was with the Messiah Motif.

Whether you are a Christian or a Muslim who agree that the Messiah was Jesus, or a Jew who utterly rejects that idea, either way it is a premature conclusion. In Job's day it was impossible to form that specific notion. My argument is far more modest.

Chapter 9

Job's Reverse Messiah Complex

Redeemer ⟷ Messiah

Does my conclusion in the last chapter mean that I reject every other interpretation? No, not necessarily. In a sense I am proposing a different kind of option that does not have to exclude the others: The *messiah motif* is on a different plane of meaning, a whole other category akin to a mold, if you recall. In the simplest terms a motif is a design or pattern. Adding more dimension, it is a distinctive feature or dominant idea in an artistic or literary composition. So does that suggest that it cannot be real as in the common understanding of myth,[182] or fantasy, or other kinds of fiction?

No, not at all.

A historical motif can certainly point to something real in the future, and even in the present. But in Job's case I am asserting that it is prophecy, and so it is a 'prophetic motif.' Like *true myth* it is "a controlling grand narrative," not only in the *Book of Job* but also in the whole of the Tanakh.[183] Let's call it a 'master narrative' with its 'master idea' of redemption as we have begun to see from the stories of Noah, Jonah, and Moses. And remember, redemption entails multiple other ideas including deliverance, liberation, rescue, ransom, salvation, and often substitution, most of which things the Messiah would later come to represent as well. Although, "messiah" (lit.

---

[182] As we shall see in chapter 11, myths can be real in some senses. C.S. Lewis coined the phrase "true myth."

[183] McGrath, *The Intellectual World of C.S. Lewis*, p. 62.

anointed one) is a word not found in *Job*, the idea is found richly embedded in the notion of redeemer that we have been studying. This is why I say that Job had a 'reverse' messiah or redeemer complex. It's not that he thought *he* was that figure in any sense, it's that he had an otherworldly expectation and confidence in one.

There were only two reasons for Job to have had either of these expectations. One was on account of his personal confidence in the trustworthy character of God, which was being shaken but not destroyed. The other reason was prophetic revelation, which was possibly even more significant than the first. In the midst of his unthinkable suffering, Job's God had given him divine foresight into the happy conclusion of the whole ordeal. There was indeed a ga'al or go'el, a redeemer who had favor toward Job. Although God was allowing his terrible affliction in the moment, the redeemer would not ultimately abandon him, for he would see God. Rather, Job's redeemer would rescue him, perhaps not in life but in the afterlife. Therefore, it seems obvious to me that the redeemer and God, if not one and the same, were in league with each other for Job's good, and Job was banking on that. **But most of all, Job was introducing all future generations of his readers to his redeemer, his messiah**. By doing this he was the first to introduce the redeemer motif which would eventually merge with the messiah motif.

I am arguing, therefore, that Job's redeemer was both a symbol and a real being at the same time. Was it God himself? I certainly do not reject this in principle. Actually, I think He is the best candidate given the parameters of the question. And, as I have said, I do not accept that Job had begun to think that God was his enemy. But if God was the Redeemer, that doesn't preclude the other options also. We saw from our studies of Noah, Jonah, and Moses that God is always the ultimate Redeemer, even when he uses human instruments as well, such as prophets. Again, take the Moses for example—was God a Redeemer? Yes. Was Moses a redeemer? Also yes. Did that make Moses the Messiah too? No, not *the* Messiah, but *a* messiah figure, or type. He contributed to the Redeemer Motif that also became the Messiah Motif.

A Noahide Prophet

Due to chronology, if Job was drawing upon any of the three prophets it was probably not Moses because Job likely predated him. And it was certainly not Jonah who came a millennia later. It would have been Noah, the only one who probably lived before Job. Indeed, this chronology could explain a lot about Job's theology. We know that Noah was a worshiper of Yahweh.

Then Noah built an altar to the LORD (Yahweh) ...

Torah, *Genesis* 8:20

So was Job. After the great flood, paganism was wiped out but not for long. It soon proliferated in the Ancient Near East so fast that the worship of Yahweh and any possible other forms of monotheism were dwarfed, but not extinguished. Therefore, it's reasonable to believe that Job's religion was a near descendent of Noah's in the third millennia BC. Some call it the "godly line" that extended from Seth, the third son of Adam and Eve. Indeed, in their respective texts of the Tanakh, very similar accolades are said of Noah and Job both:

These are the generations of Noah. Noah was a righteous man, blameless in his generation. Noah walked with God.

Torah, *Genesis* 6:9

And the LORD said [of Job]... *"there is none like him on the earth, a blameless and upright man, who fears God and turns away from evil.*

Tanakh, *Book of Job* 1:8

This also makes it reasonably certain that Job had an ample knowledge of Noah and of the way that Yahweh used him to cleanse the earth and redeem the human race from extinction:

> *The LORD saw that the wickedness of man was great in the earth, and that every intention of the thoughts of his heart was only evil continually. And the LORD regretted that he had made man on the earth, and it grieved him to his heart. So the LORD said, "I will blot out man whom I have created from the face of the land, man and animals and creeping things and birds of the heavens, for I am sorry that I have made them." But Noah found favor in the eyes of the LORD. [11] Now the earth was corrupt in God's sight, and the earth was filled with violence. [13] And God said to Noah, "I have determined to make an end of all flesh, for the earth is filled with violence through them. Behold, I will destroy them with the earth.*

Torah, *Genesis* 6:5-8, 11, 13

And in the very next verse the LORD initiates his twofold plan of destruction/redemption and tells Noah...

> *Make yourself an ark of gopher wood. Make rooms in the ark, and cover it inside and out with pitch.* (v. 14)

Think about it: When the ark became the vessel of redemption for Noah and his family, and therefore of all of humanity and all animal life with it, can we reasonably imagine that the theological significance of that event was lost on Job? I think not. Its theological import was supplemented by the animal sacrifices that Noah offered after the ark finally rested on land and its passengers came out.

> *Then Noah built an altar to the LORD and took some of every clean animal and some of every clean bird and offered burnt offerings on the altar. And when the LORD smelled the pleasing aroma, the LORD said in his heart, "I will never again curse the ground because of man, for the intention of man's heart is evil from his youth. Neither will I ever again strike down every living creature as I have done.*

Torah, *Genesis* 8:20–21

According to what we can read in the text, God never told Noah to make animal sacrifices. So how did he know to do it? Logically we either have to surmise that he learned the practice from previous members of the godly line or, as a prophet, it was revealed to him directly from God, even though we can't determine it from the text. Those are the only two options. Either way it is reasonable to conclude that Noah understood the theological value of animal sacrifice, else why would he do it? The ritual seems to have captured the whole flood/redemption event he had just endured.

As for Job, if he was really as righteous as the text says he was—and especially if he was a prophet—then he was most certainly conscious of that redemption act and the enormous motif that it created. Indeed, if Job was a prophet, then he didn't even *need* to have personal knowledge of the flood and the ark, passed down to him by oral tradition or preserved in writing. He only needed God to reveal it to him. Either way, his knowledge of this *redemption motif* was evident. It can be seen by his own acts of sacrifice on behalf of his ten children before they all died by catastrophe:

And when the days of the feast had run their course, Job would send and consecrate them, and he would rise early in the morning and offer burnt offerings according to the number of them all. For Job said, "It may be that my children have sinned, and cursed God in their hearts." Thus Job did continually.

Tanakh, *Book of Job* 1:5

Somehow, Job believed in the value of vicarious substitutionary sacrifices. How did *he* come to know and believe this? Again, logically in one of the two ways that Noah did, or both. Whichever, it was a *redemption motif* that had at some point been revealed by the LORD, then re-revealed and/or transmitted to later members of the godly line leading to Job. And, as I am arguing, the redemption motif became equivalent to the *messiah motif*. The former was revealed and demonstrated very early on in human history by God himself. The latter was simultaneously introduced although it required the passage of time to become distinctly recognizable on its own terms. From Job's words, "...I know that my redeemer lives..." it is evident that he had a grasp of redemption. Clearly, he also associated the act of redemption with a personal redeemer. This was Job's *messiah figure,* even though he didn't use the word "messiah". I do not claim that Job had a clear conception of *messiah.* Again, this would not become a clear theological concept for centuries to come. For Job there was only a *redeemer* who carried the theological DNA, or seed, of messiah. This seed would slowly develop over millennia into the full-blown messiah figure that would eventually become a dominant prophetic figure and motif in Jewish thinking.

Who Was Job's Redeemer?

So again we ask, who was Job's redeemer? Was it God himself? Yes. That is my firm conviction. As I've said, I do not believe that Job saw God as his enemy insofar that he no longer trusted Him to deliver him. But even if Job had lost some of his faith, he knew that only God *could* deliver him, in this life and the next. And in the final analysis, Job was dead right about that. It was the LORD who *did* deliver him and restore his health, wealth, and reputation. But given the circumstances, Job could not possibly have foreseen that outcome. There weren't any indicators. Still, I am convinced that he clung to the belief that Yahweh was a benevolent God whose very nature it was to rescue and redeem the desperate.

But as clear as this is to me, and possibly to you, it is not clear to others. More importantly, I don't think it was obvious to Job. For one, there was understandably a serious strain in the relationship of Job and God, from Job *toward* God. It's safe to say that Job was severely questioning God's favor toward him at the very least. In his account, much of his language of his account gives evidence of this.

> *"Oh that my vexation were weighed, and all my calamity laid in the balances! ...For the arrows of the Almighty are in me; my spirit drinks their poison; the terrors of God are arrayed against me."* Chapter 6:2, 4
>
> *"But I would speak to the Almighty, and I desire to argue my case with God."* Chapter 13:3
>
> *"Oh, that I were as in the months of old, as in the days when God watched over me...when the friendship of God was upon my tent..."* Chapter 29:2–4
>
> *"God has cast me into the mire, and I have become like dust and ashes. I cry to you for help and you do not answer me; I stand, and you only look at me. You have turned cruel to me; with the might of your hand you persecute me."* Chapter 30:19–21

Yes, Job was sorely perplexed, as any of us would be. That's why we can have respect for those such as Nasrat and Kuelen for taking painstaking efforts to come to the most logical conclusions they could, even though I disagree. So if, in my view, Job's redeemer was God himself, I doubt that Job expected Him to redeem him in this life. Rather, it seems that Job pretty much expected God to let him die in his suffering and shame. So, in my opinion, the fact that God *did* redeem Job in this life was a happy surprise to him! But until the last eight verses of the last chapter the reader cannot know this; there is no indication at all. Even in the preceding six verses which comprise Job's final words to the LORD, we can discern nothing of his material restoration. As to that he was clueless, but the LORD's words to him had hit their mark.

> *Then Job answered the LORD and said:*
> (2) *"I know that you can do all things,*
>   *and that no purpose of yours can be thwarted.*
> (3)...*Therefore I have uttered what I did not understand,*

> *things too wonderful for me, which I did not know.*
> **(5) ...I had heard of you by the hearing of the ear, but now my eye sees you;** (6) *therefore I despise myself, and repent in dust and ashes."*
> –chapter 42:1–6

From this passage we can observe that something Job had lost through his ordeal was here restored after four chapters of almost total monologue from the LORD. Job's words reveal that if he had lost any confidence in God's ability to prevent his calamity or rescue him from it, it was restored. His subsequent words show that he also received an attitude adjustment with a renewed sense of humility about his limited knowledge and understanding, accompanied by heartfelt repentance. So, even though we are told in chapter 2:10 that Job "did not sin with his lips" up to that early point (2:10), it is clear by the end of the book that either he had, or he had sinned in his heart, and he was now fully aware of it. But verse 5 which I bolded is a little odd. At first pass it may seem a little out of context, until one considers that its main idea is a poetic expression of better 'knowing' God, not just knowing *about* him.

Because of his ordeal and God's final 'in your face' confrontation with him, Job had a better understanding of God himself. If you are also a student of the Bible you know that Yahweh seems to care a lot about *being known.* It is a pattern that plays out with His prophets and other people of God over and again. As I see it, this is something that differentiates genuine biblical Christianity and its experience from much of Islam and Judaism. Except for Sufism, Islam prizes the idea that God is unknowable and does not reveal *himself,* only his laws. But consistent with the whole Tanakh, this very well may have been the LORD's highest goal for Job, or one of them. For that matter, almost the entire discourse between God and Job is absent from Islamic literature. Moreover, Muslims commonly believe that with the exception of Moses, Allah does not speak directly to anyone, not even to prophets; not even to its own final prophet, Muhammad. Rather,

Allah has dictated revelation through an intermediary only, the angel Gabriel. What Job experienced was unheard of.

The second line of verse 5 is especially peculiar. If I take it at face value it says that by this time Job was *seeing* God. Although I said it seems out of context for this section, it hardly seems so with the whole book in view. For our passage of special interest in chapter 19 does record Job as saying, "in my flesh I shall see God" (v. 26b). Then in the next verse he adds emphasis by stating, "whom I shall see for myself, and my eyes shall behold…" So this was no small detail for Job. If we are to take this literally, then verse 42:5 would appear to be a direct fulfillment of 19:27, a rather short-term prophecy. And thus, even if Job intended to predict that he would see God in the afterlife only—which would be impressive enough—he apparently did not have to wait until then. It is possible that both statements are figurative, but in light of other passages we have looked at, I don't see why they must be.

As we discussed in the last chapter, I do not presuppose philosophically that God is never seeable *absolutely.* He did allow visual manifestations of himself. The main point is that it was *God* who brought Job to his senses. That is another reason why I think Job's redeemer was God in the most real and literal sense. But I also think there was something else going on. Job's redeemer was a prophetic glimpse into the messianic future, for Israel and for the world.

Through his affliction and his excruciating crisis of faith, Job was given a priceless gift—a prophecy, a vision, and a motif all rolled into one. It was for him, but not just for him. It was a gift for Job's progeny too, possibly the Edomite and/or Midianite Arabs as we observed in chapter 2. But it wasn't restricted to his progeny alone, it was also for Abraham and his progeny, especially the descendants of Jacob such as Joseph and the twelve tribes of Israel that were taken into Egypt and saved from almost certain starvation under his reign.[184]

---

[184] Joseph himself was a 'redeemer'. Because of his divine gift of dream interpretation he was taken from prison and exalted to second-of-state who wisely stockpiled grain for a severe regional famine. The Torah's *Book of Genesis* devotes 12 chapters to Joseph beginning

After four centuries, these circumstances gave rise to Moses the great prophet-redeemer who sojourned in Midian and then led the children of Israel out of Egypt. Then, by direct divine revelation to Moses, the LORD codified redemption theology and practices for all Israelites and Israelite prophets for generations to come, thus giving shape and substance to an ever-more developed *Redeemer-Redemption Motif.* Through this codification process, and by virtue of other forms of divine revelation over millennia, this motif merged organically with Jewish messianic expectations and its great Motif forming an intermingled theological stream. Within this Jewish context it was later reinforced by Jesus and his Apostles to be passed on to Christians and Christendom. Still later, according to Surah 37:107 and other verses of the Qur'an, Muslims inherited some of it too, or should have, albeit in a limited and more obscure sense.

Therefore, we should see that the Redeemer Motif was the seed of the Messiah Motif, which two became synonymous. From the time of Noah it was revealed demonstrably to the prophets in the pre-Jewish era, and no less demonstrably to Job in the midst of his grievous suffering. Through him it was 'made real' by speech in the hearing of his companions, then captured in scripture, and then divinely transmitted and 're-revealed' to us. But it was Job who first articulated it and injected it into the stream of scripture for the posterity of a great multitude of multitudes from then until now.

---

starting with chapter 37. The Qur'an devotes a whole surah (chapter) to Joseph, surah 12, one of the few surah's with a complete and continuous narrative. (Another is surah 19.)

Chapter 10

Job's Redemption and His Friends'

The Burnt Offering

At the University of Michigan–Dearborn, between 2015-17, I audited several political science courses with a particular professor, Dr. Michael Rosano, whose teaching style I found engaging. I both agreed and disagreed with him on many things. He often made reference to the Old Testament of the Bible, or Tanakh, including Job. Once he made the claim that the *Book of Job* originally ended with verse 42:9 and excluded the last eight verses in which Job's fortune is restored. I had not heard that before. I often visited him in his office to discuss such things as, say, the Bible's view of nature, but I never got the chance to talk with him about this particular view, so I'm not sure why he believed it. In any case, all of today's versions of the Bible, and all historical ones that I'm aware of, contain the concluding segment with the final eight verses, vv. 10-17. It is outside the scope of my investigation to prove this segment is original to the book, but I would like to make several observations about it.

I have already mentioned that this section comprises a happy ending. In chapter 42:6 Job's very last words to the LORD are

> "...*therefore I despise myself,*
> *and repent in dust and ashes.*"

And then Job is vindicated. In verses 7-9 the LORD confronts Eliphaz and his two friends with "burning anger" toward them.[185] But why? What did they do wrong?

> "...for you have not spoken of me what is right, as my servant Job has," He said. (v. 7)

For this reason He required of them a burnt offering, an animal sacrifice.[186] In the Torah we see that a burnt offering might require only a single animal,[187] but in this case it was substantially more—seven bulls and seven rams! With this sacrifice the LORD also required a prayer of forgiveness; but not from *them*, rather from Job on their behalf, which He promised to accept.

> *And the LORD excepted Job's prayer."* (v. 9)

But wait, why did they need a sacrifice, and why couldn't they just pray to God directly and ask His forgiveness? As to the former, it's another example of a pre-Jewish act of animal sacrifice and redemption *by blood* in relation to Yahweh, except this was the first time in the Tanakh we are told that He required it. Although they believed firmly in one God and defended his honor, it was apparently not good enough. Despite their piety, the men had sinned against a holy God who told them, "...you have not spoken of me what is right, as my servant Job has." (v. 8b) Even if unwittingly, they had incurred His strong disfavor (i.e. "burning anger"). So their sins were apparently not minor. Indeed, they were serious enough that the LORD was unwilling to just forgive them without some extra measure of satisfaction, or atonement. What about their repentance? The text doesn't mention it. Perhaps we can assume their repentance once the LORD reproved them, but it seems as though even that would not have been

---

[185] As for the fourth interlocuter, Elihu, just as he is not numbered among Job's three friends in the beginning, so he is not in the end. He does not seem to have earned the LORD's disfavor with them, and so apparently does not need redemption by sacrifice.

[186] From the *Book of Exodus* 29:15-18 we learn that a burnt offering was a special kind of animal sacrifice in which the animal/s were first killed and then burnt on the alter.

[187] *Books of Genesis 22:13* and *Leviticus 1:3,4*

enough to obtain His forgiveness. As I see it, then, this looks like a core principle, that the LORD does not forgive as easily as many people want to believe, Muslims and non-Muslims. Sure, He is merciful and gracious, but this text seems to show that He demands a basis or grounding for His forgiveness. It isn't free.

According to the narratives of the whole book, these men seemed to be theologians, but they spoke wrong things. This has to mean that they had bad theology, or wrong beliefs about Yahweh. They obviously believed in *tawhid,* one God who was the absolute master of the universe, like Job did. But there must have been some major problems with the details. Could it be that they did not believe in redemption, and God's penchant for redemption? And could it be that they did not believe in His special role as Redeemer? Moreover, might they have dismissed out-of-hand Job's prophetic anticipation of a Redeemer? Might they have shrugged off his oracle of *the future redeemer?*

...Personally, I think this was the problem.
....

The next eight verses tell us that Job lived 140 more years and regained everything he had lost and more.

> *¹⁰And the LORD restored the fortunes of Job [and gave him] twice as much as he had before. ¹¹Then came to him all his brothers and sisters and all who had known him before, and ate bread with him in his house. And they showed him sympathy and comforted him for all the evil that the LORD had brought upon him. And each of them gave him a piece of money and a ring of gold. ¹²And the LORD blessed the latter days of Job more than his beginning.*
>
> Job 42:10–12

Following verse 9, the abruptness of verse 10 gives the reader a "happily-ever-after" kind of ending. You know, it's an abbreviated, fast-forwarded impression of the next 140 years, and especially the next 20. Here is what I see in my mind's eye using the precious gift of reasoned imagination. First, though it's possible that he was instantly healed, I can imagine that it took Job some period of time to heal and regain his strength. Let's say a week or two. But his permanent losses were catastrophic. Remember, perhaps aside from his personal dwelling and its furnishing, Job seems to have lost all of his wealth and livelihood. He also lost all ten of his children and the benefit of their assistance. As for Job's wife, after the first time she appears in chapter 2 there's no further mention of her. It's reasonable to imagine that she stayed with him, but also that she didn't. Either way, the text tells us that LORD blessed Job with ten more children, so he apparently still had a wife, or maybe he took a new wife (or wives). Assuming only one wife, think about the years it took him to repopulate his household and for all ten children to reach adulthood—at least 22½ for the youngest of them to reach the age of 14. Hypothetically, if he had multiple wives the number of years could have been as low as 14, but no less.[188]

What about Job's financial recovery? Well, unless one believes the hadith that I introduced in chapter 2 (which I don't), that would have taken some time too. On the other hand, it must have helped a lot that all his siblings and everyone who knew him "gave him a piece of money and a ring of gold" (v. 11b), and much more believable. Not only that, the previous sentence says that "they showed him sympathy and comforted him…" So for a while they scorned him, but they later corrected their error. To me this speaks to the larger-than-life kind of respect Job had within his family and community before his catastrophe, that although it was damaged during his affliction, it was evidently restored.[189] That alone is astonishing, that a person

---

[188] If he had ten wives who each got pregnant and had a child at the same time then they would all reach the age of 14 in fourteen years. If he had only one wife who got pregnant every nine months she could have borne Job ten children in 8.5 years. 14 + 8.5 = 22.5.

[189] Four verses tell us this: 12:4, 16:20, 19:19 and 19:14, which for example says, "My relatives have failed me, my close friends have forgotten me."

could first become a pariah due to the prevailing (false) interpretation of misfortune but could recover in what may have been a rather short period of time. Indeed, we can surmise that within only several months his health had returned, his wife was pregnant with his first new child, and he had received of the generosity of his community. Then, if Job was as good a businessman as his previous wealth allows us to suppose, with his newly acquired bounty he might easily have regained much of it within the year. This is a superlative example of what's called a 'rebound.' But what explains this? My take is the burnt offering that Job made on behalf of his three friends.[190] As I see it, this one act was monumental!

Again, just imagine it. First, these three older and 'wiser' men of the community come to him in his grief, and instead of consoling him they condemned him for having 'obviously' brought all his calamity upon himself. But then, after they had emptied their scorn on him, (and a fourth man, Elihu, does too), the LORD himself comes onto the scene in the theophany of a whirlwind to deliver His speech to Job, presumably in full sight of the four other men. After His speech, as we have noted, he turns to Eliphaz as the apparent spokesman for the three, to rebuke them. He also commands them to provide the aforementioned fourteen animals for the lavish burnt offering that Job was to make for them, probably in full view of the whole community. Is this not staggering to your imagination? Talk about a vindication! Let's single out the key elements:

1. God commanded it.
2. He required it at their expense.
3. He required it of Job on their behalf.
4. He required Job to offer prayer with it.
5. Its purpose was for their forgiveness.
6. Thus it was an act of *their* redemption.

---

[190] Apparently not including Elihu who seems to have been approved of by God.

7. The burnt offering happened in full view.
8. It was an act of severe humiliation for the men.
9. It was an act of extraordinary vindication for Job.
10. Job's vindication was also his redemption.

Thus we may observe that this was an act of double redemption. Do you see what the LORD did and what he spectacularly achieved for all four men here? First, can we suppose that there was any possible way Job could have convinced his three friends to do what God told them to do? No way. Had the LORD not shown up in so dramatic a way and had He not himself demanded of them what he did, what actually unfolded is the least expected thing. Job's friends must have been utterly humiliated. In my view they were probably not really his friends at all, but friendly enemies or rivals. If he really did count them among his friends, then they were fair-weather friends at best, which Job had now learned painfully. In my view they came mainly to gloat over Job's misfortune, which was evil enough.[191] But they also had bad theology, which I'm sure contributed to their gloating. As if Job's suffering and losses were not intolerable enough, these false friends only poured salt in his wounds and magnified his public shame. But in the end God achieved the impossible for Job—He completely turned the tables. Not only did He restore Job's health and wealth, He also restored his honor; and yes, partly at the expense of theirs. By means of His rebuke of Eliphaz and company, the burnt offering, and Job's prayer for them, God transferred Job's shame to them. Then, to demonstrate that He is "oft-forgiving" as the Qur'an often puts it, He provided a means of their forgiveness. Yes, by all indications throughout the Tanakh, Yahweh was a God of means.

"He redeemed them with a great sacrifice."

---

[191] a) Jesus, Sermon on the Mount, *Gospel of Matthew* 5:7, New Testament; Apostle Paul, *Letter to the Romans* 12:15, New Testament. b) Recall from a previous footnote that Dr. Kyle Dunham believes that Eliphaz was a true friend to Job, albeit misguided.

This was no small sacrifice, and it was the decisive game-changer. By it the LORD demonstrated himself as the Grand Redeemer by redeeming all parties in a big way.

He redeemed Job first by vindicating him. But in doing so He also made him into a redeemer himself, a kind of priest. Notice that the men were not commanded to pray *directly* to God, as though they were not worthy. They *weren't* worthy, so they weren't even allowed to. Instead, they needed a go-between, a mediator, an intercessor. They needed *Job* to offer up prayer for them, and God had predetermined to accept Job's prayer. Even though Job had sinned against God too, he had repented and humbled himself publicly "in dust and ashes."[192] And from a great many other verses in the Tanakh we know that Yahweh delights in repentance and humility.

So through the facets of this ending God was true to his character throughout the Hebrew scriptures, and He brought much glory to himself. Indeed, through Job's redemption the LORD did even more to redeem His own name from perhaps temporary 'tarnish' and magnify it for all ages to come as the Grand Redeemer. He also further established the *redeemer principle*. In the epic of *Job*, not only did God exalt redemption and reinforce his own Redeemer identity, He also elevated the redeemer motif. And for the first time in the Tanakh, this one included an explicit and dual act of redemption involving a commanded blood sacrifice.[193] Finally, in chapter 19:25, in Job's own words, it included the first prophetic statement about a coming Redeemer who lives and will stand on the earth. I have been arguing that it pointed to God, but not God only. It also pointed to a future redeemer figure akin to the figure of *Genesis* 3:15. He was revealed to Job in a way similar to how he was revealed centuries later to his

---

[192] Everybody has sinned, even prophets. "All have sinned and fall short of the glory of God." (Apostle Paul, *Letter to the Romans* 3:23)

[193] Later in the chronology of the biblical timeline we can see the first explicit *repetition* of Yahweh's command to sacrifice animals, given to Abraham after he first arrived in Canaan, recorded in the *Book of Genesis* chapter 15:9-17. Still later, through Prophet Moses, many forms of animal sacrifice would be institutionalized for the Israelite people by divine revelation and the explicit command of the LORD.

Midianite descendant, the pagan prophet Balaam.[194]

> *I see him, but not now;*
> *I behold him, but not near:*
> *a star shall come out of Jacob,*
>   *and a scepter shall rise out of Israel;*
> *it shall crush the forehead of Moab*
>   *and break down all the sons of Sheth.*[195]

This verse is part of a fascinating account spanning three whole chapters in Moses's *Book of Numbers*. I strongly encourage you to read it. Balaam was a pagan prophet-for-hire who was hired to curse the children of Israel in the land of Moab. But instead he blessed them with these words. Who exactly did Balaam "see"? Clearly, someone in the future who had not come onto the scene yet. Many Christians and some Jews understand this as another messianic vision, and prophecy. The Jewish commentator HaChaim wrote…

> [This] entire prophecy concerns the Messiah and is best understood in light of *Sanhedrin* 98 where the Talmud discusses the meaning of the apparently contradictory prophecy בעתה אחישנה, "at its appointed time I will hasten it" (Isaiah 60,22). The Talmud explains that the timing of the arrival of the Messiah depends on the conduct of the Jewish people.[196]

Thus the story of Balaam contributes to the great Messiah Motif in the focus of our attention. Not unlike Job's companions, HaChaim connected the return of the Messiah to human conduct as though it

---

[194] When I call Balaam a "Midianite prophet" I do so loosely. The text says he was hired by a coalition of Moabites and Midianites who were probably related peoples. If neither of these then he was a Canaanite.

[195] Torah, *Book of Numbers* 24:17, bolding mine.

[196] Sefaria.org. www.sefaria.org/Numbers.24.17?lang=bi&with=Commentary&lang2=en

could be hastened by their good behavior. From my perspective, which I believe is the Bible's, it is just the opposite. It is the people's debauchery that would hasten his coming, for that is when a messiah is most desperately needed to bring deliverance and/or judgment to those in bondage to their own sin. This is precisely what Job's 'advisors' got wrong too, but in reverse. Job's suffering was not brought on by his own sin, so it could not be alleviated by his own goodness. Rather, it was brought on by Satan, by the primaeval sin-induced curse on the world, and by the effects of collective human sinfulness on humanity.

In conclusion, even if Job did not know that God would redeem him from his earthly afflictions, he knew by revelation that he would have a redeemer at some time and in some circumstance, even if not until the somehow physical afterlife. And he knew that the LORD would be the one to provide his redemption.

Addendum

I came upon this interesting, related post in Reddit:

Ending of Job

Does anyone else feel a little disappointed by the ending of Job?

I think the greatness of the story is that it powerfully portrays that life isn't fair, that suffering is real and that we can't dance around these realities by using religion to make sense for ourselves why some people get it bad. And when God finally speaks to Job and asks: "where were you when I laid the earth's foundation?" and He goes on to detail how powerful and creative and in control He is of everything through the wide-ranging description of nature. Incredible!...and then the Lord restored Job's fortune and gave him twice as much as he had before. Perhaps the reason I am disappointed with the ending is that it is similar to a parent teaching a lesson to a child, and in order for the lesson to be learned (God is powerful and in control) the child can't have everything his way. Then we get the powerful lesson and Job is humble and he learns! ...and then he gets everything back. Perhaps I am interpreting the story teller's choice of ending as a way of saying that the restoration of Job's fortunes is a greater act than when Job speaks with God and gains a new perspective on his own life and better understands God's sovereignty

In a way I can appreciate this person's sentiments. Sure, there is something noble about Job's endurance in the face of God's apparent unfairness, not having any reason to believe there would be a happy ending to his story, at least not until his death. And since then, in our common human experience, we know that very bad things happen to people with no happily-ever-after. There are countless people, rich and poor, who have lost everything and never gotten it back. And then they die. Sure, we can admire those who uphold their dignity, their ethics, and their hope against all odds. Like this person, some might admire Job *not* because he was righteous in God's eyes, but because of his virtue in suffering, the virtue we often ascribe to those who 'suffer well' having become victims of injustice. Some theists might understand the whole story of Job in terms of God's sovereignty and inscrutability. In terms of theodicy,[197] I don't think it explains much, at least not to anyone's satisfaction. It only shows that it is God's prerogative to allow human suffering without having to explain or justify it to us.

However, in real life when someone is suffering, is it commendable to be glad about it, or worse yet to wish it because of the good example they might set for the rest of us? I think not. What could possibly be more charitable on our part than to wish for their 'redemption'? That is what I think the *Book of Job* is mostly about. Before his calamity, if Job was as faithful to God as the divine narrative

---

[197] The question of why a good, all-powerful God allows evil and suffering.

tells us, then he *knew* the LORD was a Redeemer by nature. He does not inflict suffering capriciously, and He does not take pleasure in it, even though He allows it. Rather, it is usually Satan and humans moved by Satan and sin who cause most suffering. For him it is entirely capricious and he always revels in it. Job had reason to trust in the redeemer-character of Yahweh and to believe that He would either *be* his Redeemer or would provide one.

There are many greater and some lesser strands of meaning in this story, but the greatest one is the *Redeemer-Redemption* motif. The most poignant emblem of this motif was the burnt offering which happened well *before* Job could have known that his life would be redeemed and restored. In that bloody act demanded by God, Job became the redeemer-type for his three errant friends, and they were spared the divine judgment that God assigned to them. But best of all, through this priestly act and his earlier prophetic declaration, the Redeemer-Redemption motif was further poured into the theological streams that fed the Jewish consciousness. This then fueled the sublime Messiah Motif that emerged predominant in Judaism and seeped into Islam as well, albeit more obscurely.

Part 2

Descent-to-Ascent

The Grand Motif of Four Biblical J's:

—Job, Jacob, Joseph, and Jesus

Chapter 11

Job As True Myth and Motif

> *"Oh that my words were written!*
> *Oh that they were inscribed in a book!*
> *Oh that with an iron pen and lead*
> *they were engraved in the rock forever!*
>
> Job, *Book of Job* 19:23-24

Thankfully, Job's prayer was answered. His words *were* written and preserved forever. Now, thousands of years later the world still possesses the complete *Book of Job* and his gut-wrenching account of his ordeal. To this day it is one of the most captivating and treasured literary works of all time, religious and otherwise, whose story is etched into the collective consciousness of the West and much of the world. Thousands have written about him from ancient times to the present. For example, between 578 and 595 Gregory the Great wrote his six-volume commentary, *Moralia, sive Expositio in Job,* or *An Extensive Consideration of Moral Questions*.[198] That's a lot to write about just man and one book of the Tanakh! Much more recently, Rabbi Harold Kushner wrote two books about Job that became bestsellers: *When Bad Things Happen to Good People*, and *The Book of Job: When Bad Things Happened to a Good Person,* both in 1981. He was rather focused on this question, which I am not. Still, people are still writing books about him, as you can see. The Encyclopedia Britannica's brief article on Job captures it well:

---

[198] Found at litpress.org/Products/GetSample/CS249H/9780879071493

> The *Book of Job* is not only the finest expression of the Hebrew poetic genius; it must also be accorded a place among the greatest masterpieces of world literature… Among ancient texts, it is the supreme example of speculative wisdom in which a man attempts to understand and respond to the human situation in which he exists, and protests vehemently against the rationalistic ethics of the sages.[199]

Through the westward spread of Judaism and Christianity especially, the story of Job has gained a wide audience in the West and has become a permanent cultural icon to this day. Indeed, it has come to saturate Western culture. Its cultural prevalence is real even for those who *don't* see it as scripture or divine revelation, which I do. Regardless of its historicity, its story endures and remains relevant because it captures some of the most pervasive and perplexing problems of the human condition: pain, suffering, evil, the devil, and the nature of God. Job represents perhaps the first character in human history who articulated the hard questions as to why bad things happen to good people, and related questions. By the wonder of textual preservation, Job's words have been preserved and memorialized for hundreds of generations up to the present. Elie Wiesel wrote that Job "has fascinated innumerable storytellers and commentators through the centuries…and he who perhaps was never born, seems to have achieved immortality."[200]

But like many books of the Tanakh, the *Book of Job* is a product of the Ancient Near East, even before any Jews existed. And so it is an Eastern book. There it gained prominence, first with non-Jews such as the Edomites, then with Jews, then with Christians, and still later with Muslims. The man, the prophet Job and his story became part of their collective religious memories as it has ours today in the West. This shows up in myriad examples of cultural expression, high, low, and everywhere in between. In keeping with our consistent

---

[199] Britannica.com/topic/biblical-literature/Job
[200] Wiesel, *Messengers of God,* 212-213

attention to culture, the anonymous author of this impressive Wikipedia segment has expressed it eloquently and thoroughly.

A Wikipedian Tribute to Job

The *Book of Job* has been deeply influential in Western culture, to such an extent that no list [of examples] could be more than representative.

Musical settings from Job include Orlande de Lassus's 1565 cycle of motets, the *Sacrae Lectiones Novem ex Propheta Job*, and George Frideric Handel's use of Job 19:25 ("I know that my redeemer liveth") as an aria in his 1741 oratorio *Messiah*. Modern works based on the book include Ralph Vaughan Williams's *Job: A Masque for Dancing*; French composer Darius Milhaud's *Cantata From Job*; and Joseph Stein's Broadway interpretation *Fiddler on the Roof*, based on the Tevye the Dairyman stories by Sholem Aleichem. Neil Simon wrote *God's Favorite*, which is a modern retelling of the Book of Job. Breughel and Georges de La Tour depicted Job visited by his wife, and William Blake produced an entire cycle of illustrations for the book.

Writers Job has inspired or influenced include John Milton (*Samson Agonistes*); Dostoevsky (*The Brothers Karamazov*); Alfred Döblin (*Berlin Alexanderplatz*); Franz Kafka (*The Trial*); Carl Jung (*Answer to Job*); Joseph Roth (*Job*); Bernard Malamud; and Elizabeth Brewster, whose book *Footnotes to the Book of Job* was a finalist for the 1996 Governor General's Award for poetry in Canada. Archibald MacLeish's drama *JB*, one of the most prominent uses of the Book of Job in modern literature, was awarded the Pulitzer Prize in 1959.

Verses from the book of Job figured prominently in the plot of the film *Mission: Impossble* (1996). Job's influence can also be seen in the Coen brothers' 2009 film, *A Serious*

Man, which was nominated for two Academy Awards. Terrence Malick's 2011 film *The Tree of Life*, which won the Palme d'Or, is heavily influenced by the themes of the Book of Job, as the film starts with a quote from the beginning of God's speech to Job. A 2014 Malayalam film called "Iyobinte Pusthakam" tells the story of a man who is losing everything in his life and also has parallels with Dostoevsky's (*The Brothers Karamazov*). Joni Mitchell composed The Sire of Sorrow (Job's Sad Song.) The Russian film *Leviathan* also draws themes from the Book of Job. In 2015 two Ukrainian composers Roman Grygoriv and Illia Razumeiko created the opera-requiem IYOV. The premiere of the opera was held on 21 September 2015 on the main stage of the international multidisciplinary festival Gogolfest.[201]

To this list, two that I wish to add include a magnificent song called "Job Suite" by singer/songwriter Michael Card on his 1990 album entitled "The Way of Wisdom",[202] and a beautifully illustrated book-length poem by John Piper entitled *The Misery of Job and the Mercy of God* (78 pages).[203] Also, Dr. C.J. Williams in his own recent book quotes Samuel Terrien who said,

> As a historical testimony to this understanding of Job's role, there are over forty statues of "Saint Job the Priest" preserved in Western Europe..."[204]

When I found this particular tribute and related anecdote I was taken aback. Why? Well, sure I'd had a sense that Job was familiar to many people, but I honestly had no idea his story had become so

---

[201] wikipedia.org/wiki/Book_of_Job

[202] Produced by Phil Naish

[203] Crossway, 2005

[204] *The Iconography of Job Through the Centuries* (149) as quoted by C.J. Williams, *The Shadow of Christ In the Book of Job*.

embedded in Western culture. The next author continues to elucidate Job's legacy in Islam and in Arab folk tradition.

> Job (Arabic *Ayyub* [or Ayoub] ايوب) is one of the 25 prophets mentioned by name in the Quran, where he is lauded as a steadfast and upright worshipper (surah 38:44). His story has the same basic outline as in the Bible, although the three friends are replaced by his brothers, and his wife stays by his side. In Palestinian folklore Job's place of trial is Al-Joura, a village outside the town of Al Majdal (Ashkelon). It was there that God rewarded him with a Fountain of Youth that removed whatever illnesses he had and restored his youth. Al-Joura was a place of annual festivities (four days in all) when people of many faiths gathered and bathed in a natural spring. In Lebanon the Muwahideen (or Druze) community have a shrine built in the Shouf area that allegedly contains Job's tomb. In Turkey, Job is known as *Eyüp*, and he is supposed to have lived in Şanlıurfa. There is also a tomb of Job outside the city of Salalah in Oman.[205]

As with the golden grasshopper of chapter 2, I can't help feeling incredulous about the fountain of youth part and asking the same question about its source, since this is nowhere to be found in the canonical *Book of Job*. But this is beside the point. What we are marveling at here is the enormous span of Job 'consciousness' across time and cultures, facts, legends, and myths all included.

Job as True Myth

Speaking of myth, in an earlier chapter I noted that along with its dating and historical provenance, the story of Job has been understood by various scholars either as *a*historical myth or as true

---
[205] wikipedia.org/wiki/Book_of_Job

historical narrative rooted in space and time. But in later chapters I have hinted that it is not necessary to choose one of these views to the exclusion of the other. Now I'll come right out with it: Even if one accepts it as historical fact, as I do, that does not divorce it from the power of its 'myth-like' truth value. On the other hand, if one understands it as pure myth, or mostly myth, with limited-to-no historical veracity, that does not make it 'untrue.' ...Myths can be true.

Whether fact or fiction, the story of Job *is* myth. But it is 'true myth' as I C.S. Lewis would have called it. Simply put, myth is story. Like legends, myths are old, traditional stories that have special power to capture the collective memory of a culture and to explain both religious and human experience. It is common these days to think of myths as false by definition, but that is outside of their core meaning. Myth is not necessarily false; that is a non-essential accretion of the Enlightenment era. A particular myth may very well be historically true. But the question of its historical truthfulness is not what makes a myth powerful and memorable. In addition, or instead, it is its power to teach and explain transcendent things in ways that resonate with the universal elements of human experience, such as suffering and the joy of redemption.

C.S. Lewis (1898–1963) was an expert on myth. He came to believe that the purpose of myths was to arouse the longing for transcendence. As an Oxford and later Cambridge scholar of renaissance literature, he was widely respected as an author, philosopher, lay theologian, and for many other reasons. Thus he was adept at analyzing the literatures that comprise the Bible. For example, he wrote about the mythical power of the Christian story as contained in the four gospels of the New Testament, and I think his ideas are every bit as applicable to the story of Job.

Many scholars and popular writers have written about Lewis, including Bruce Young in his piece, **"Lewis on the Gospels as True Myth."** Here, allow me to quote extensively from him with particular application to *Job*. In it, Young (and Lewis) are exploring the gospels, not Job. But for our focus I will take the liberty to apply his examination of True Myth in the gospels to the story of Job by way of inserting my own phrases in brackets. First, we want to know what are the **essential characteristics of myth** according to Lewis. Then we want to dig deeper. Young writes…

> In the chapter "On Myth" in *An Experiment in Criticism* Lewis uses "numinous" as essentially synonymous with "awe-inspiring" and lists it as one of the six characteristics of myth (44)…For most myths, historical validity is not even a question. Myths are essentially fictional, even if they have some historical basis. According to Lewis, the essential characteristics of myth include **(1)** the fact that they are "extra-literary"—that is, they do not depend on a particular literary rendition but have a powerful effect as stories with a "simple narrative shape," an effect that comes through in either simple summaries or more elaborate versions; **(2)** the related fact that they depend "hardly at all on such usual narrative attractions as suspense or surprise," so that, even if we know the story, its mere shape will continue to affect us deeply; **(3)** the minimizing of human sympathy—by which, as I understand it, Lewis means that the figures in myth have a universal quality leading us, not to analyze their individual personalities or pity or identify with their individual circumstances, but rather to see their stories as being the stories of "all men"; **(4)** content made up of the "fantastic" or "preternatural," things impossible in ordinary circumstances; **(5)** the fact that they are "grave"—serious, weighty, solemn—whether the events are joyful or sad; and finally **(6)** the fact that they are "numinous" or "awe-inspiring" (42-44).

Not surprisingly for Lewis, I think these six characteristics beautifully capture the essence of myth. Young goes on to say,

> **…Lewis believed there is something about myth that empowers it to convey truth in an especially effective way, and says, "In the enjoyment of a great myth we come nearest to experiencing as a concrete what can otherwise be understood only as an abstraction."** It is as if the images and events of myth convey universal truths which we

> experience not so much intellectually as emotionally and imaginatively. Thus, "myth is the isthmus which connects the peninsular world of thought with that vast continent we really belong to"—namely the world of direct, concrete experience. Myth is "not, like truth, abstract; nor is it, like direct experience, bound to the particular." ("Myth Became Fact," 66).
> ...In *Perelandra*, Lewis suggests that the split "of truth from myth and of both from fact" is an unfortunate result of the Fall [i.e. the fall of Adam and Eve—Torah, *Book of Genesis* chapter 3] (143-44)...[but] in the [final and ultimate] New Creation that split will be overcome: "the dry bones [will be] clothed again with flesh, the fact and the myth remarried" [cf. Tanakh, *Book of Ezekiel* 37:1-14] (*Miracles*, 263). The transcendent reality hinted at in myth will actually be present in the "New Creation"; the longing that Lewis calls "Joy" will finally find its fulfillment.

Here is where Young brings in the New Testament's four Gospels according to Lewis. It's not that Lewis believed they were fiction in the least (though before his conversion he did). It's that, even as true history he saw the essential elements and patterns of myth embedded in them. It is not my intent to examine the story of the Gospels per se, but to extrapolate these elements and patterns from them to the *Book of Job*.

> ...The Gospels [and the *Book of Job*] give us not only a preview of the glory God has in store for those who love him, but a key to the meaning of the world we now inhabit. For, though it is fallen, this world retains, according to Lewis, the main features of the divine meaning with which God endowed it as its creator. The Gospels [and *Job*] help us see this divine meaning, especially if they are read mythically...
> In Lewis's book, *Miracles*...the most concentrated exposition of this idea is the chapter on "The Grand Miracle." ...According to Lewis, the incarnation [i.e. the entrance of Jesus into the world] encompasses **four patterns**—what might be called mythic or archetypal patterns—that illuminate the meaning of the world as a whole [which I apply to

Job also]: **(1) the uniting of apparently contrary or incommensurable elements**—[such as] the divine and the human, and, in our own experience, our spiritual and animal natures (*Miracles,* 176-78);

In the next segment, scan your eyes down to point (4) to which I have already given much attention, in the previous chapter especially. Now give special focus to point (2) because it is a central idea in this part of the book, and I will spill a lot more ink on it before we're done, as they say.

(2) the pattern of descent and reascent or death and rebirth…found in various ways through all of nature (178-81); **(3) selectivity** [found in Job's highly favored status with God and as one who was 'singled out' by God for his trial]…and found also even in apparently brutal ways in the selectivity of natural processes (187-90); and **(4) vicariousness**—[where Job in some sense experienced his suffering and redemption symbolically and vicariously for all who suffer without explanation and yearn for redemption], with a similar pattern found through all of nature, where everything is interdependent, where all lives [are lived] through or from something other than itself (190-91).

To read the Gospels [and *Job*] mythically would for Lewis be in part to read them with an eye to patterns such as these. In the "simple narrative shape" of the Gospel accounts [and *Job*] we would see something of the shape of the universe as a whole, something of the pattern that runs through all of nature…

In this final segment Young and Lewis advocate for the reading of some literatures mythically *and* historically, that the two categories are not mutually exclusive. This, Lewis argues, applies especially to the Gospels which teach us about divine Redemption. It is through this lens, this Motif, that I also include *Job*.

What we learn from the Gospels [and *Job*] if we read them mythically but also historically, is thus something about the nature of reality. Here...Lewis says, is "the comment which makes that crabbed text plain: or rather, proves itself to be the text on which Nature was only the commentary." In other words, what the Gospels [and *Job*] reveal is not only the meaning of nature —not only a sense of the patterns that govern the universe. **What they reveal is that the story of the universe is in fact the story of God's working to redeem human beings, and with them all of creation...**The patterns we see in nature, through everyday observation or scientific discovery, are, as it were, allusions to or secondary reflections of this central story about the universe. "In science we [read] only the notes to a poem; in Christianity [and yes, in the story of Job] we find the poem itself" (212).

In Lewis's view it is crucial that we understand these realities not simply or primarily as mental abstractions. We must understand them with our imaginations and emotions. Hence, Lewis suggests, **God speaks to us through events, through stories.** These stories will have a symbolic or mythic dimension, for—as Lewis puts it in a discussion of the poet Edmund Spenser—"symbols are the natural speech of the soul. (137) But it is also crucial that this symbolic dimension not be separated off into the never-never land of imagination. God speaks to us through actual people and events, things that actually happen.[206]

That is what happens when we read the gospels, according to C.S. Lewis. And, I assert, it is also what happens when we read *Job*. To Lewis, although the gospels meet all the criteria for great myth, they also meet the criteria for historical documentary. Therefore they are "true myth." The *Book of Job* is similar to the gospels in some chapters (1-2, 42), but vastly different in the rest, which is poetry (3-41). In my analysis, there is a strong case to be made for the historical veracity of *Job*, and I stand by it. But I don't think that is the story's main intent, so I don't think it matters for the sake of my thesis. It is non-essential. The main intent of *Job* is to teach us certain theological truths and to give us the **'Job Motif.'** This is both a redeemer motif

---

[206] Young, "Lewis on the Gospels as True Myth." All bolding mine.

and a messiah motif. In the Tanakh it is a 'meta-motif', and it is one of the main purposes of all Hebrew scripture and the revelation it contains—to progressively develop this motif.

In the early chapters of this book we have talked extensively about specific 'micro-motifs' in the *Book of Job*. Now I want to talk about the Prophet Job *himself* and his story as Motif, with a capital 'M'—a *'macro-motif.'* I call it that because it encompasses the lesser ones and creates a cast, or a mold, for them, and all their respective elements. In the previous paragraph, I called it a 'meta-motif' because it is one that provides the theoretical framework for messiah-ness in the Tanakh.[207] For these reasons we can also call it a 'master-motif' because it serves to control the way the various micro-motifs found throughout the Tanakh come together and form the composite of the messiah, or messianic composition. I think it's true that you cannot see it except in retrospect, but that's true of many things. As soon as the present became the past and contributing events became history, people could begin looking back on them, and the potential to see the messianic motifs was activated. It's possible, if not probable, that years later Job's friends and other contemporaries could look back on his crisis and see the archetype.

The Job Motif in Myth and Pop Culture

So, what *is* this archetype, or Motif? As we saw in point (2) from Lewis's *Miracles*, it is that of descent and reascent, of falling then rising, of losing then winning, of suffering then coming through it, and even of death and rebirth, or rising again. All of the above.

As a needed reprieve from the density of last four pages, I now offer five representative examples of myth, fairytale, and other popular fiction that exhibit the Motifs that we have been discussing.

---

[207] "Any subject can be said to have a *metatheory*, a theoretical consideration of its properties, such as its foundations, methods, form and utility, on a higher level of abstraction." wikipedia.org/wiki/Meta

The Phoenix

The well-known myth of the phoenix comes to mind. Here again, "myth" does not have to mean something untrue but a "symbolic narrative."[208] It seems to emerge especially in the Greek and Egyptian collections, but **one source attributes it to Arabia**.[209] The phoenix was a singular, exotic, bird with magic powers. There has only ever been one at a time, and it cannot be killed. Well, like Fawkes in the Harry Potter films, it actually could be, but it would not stay dead. It will always come back alive. Depending on the provenance of the particular legend, the lifespan of a phoenix was 500 years or more, at the end of which, in many versions, it would burst into flames and burn to ash. But soon after, a new one would rise out of the ashes to take its place. Many other cultures have had the phoenix in their folklore as well. It has commonly symbolized multiple things including renewal, the sun, time, life in Paradise, Christ, certain aspects of Christian life, and resurrection in general. "Some scholars have claimed that the poem *De ave phoenice* may present the…phoenix motif as a symbol of Christ's resurrection."[210] This is very interesting to me.

The **suffering hero or heroine motif** has always been prevalent in our collective imagination to the present day. Stories that contain it span across cultures and have easily found their way into children's literature and movies. Disney has excelled in this.

Cinderella

Possibly the most famous example is *Cinderella* which has had multiple versions over the centuries, and eventually reached its height of popularity through Charles Perrault in 1697 and the Brothers Grimm in 1812. You know the story: Due to her father's remarriage to a nasty new wife with equally nasty daughters, a previously happy

---

[208] britannica.com/topic/myth. See also dictionary.com/browse/myth

[209] quora.com/What-are-all-the-myths-and-stories-related-to-Phoenix

[210] wikipedia.org/wiki/Phoenix_(mythology)

young girl—Cinderella—is plunged into a life of humiliating servitude and affliction. With the help of her fairy godmother, she is discovered by the prince who marries her. Thus she emerges from her period of suffering in victory and splendor. In a word, she is *redeemed*. Among others, there are several versions of the Cinderella story contained in the medieval ***Arabian Knights*** collection but with a different name, or none at all. Sometimes the central figure is a male. It doesn't matter.[211] Thus we can speak of the probably universal **'Cinderella Motif'** even when there are minor variations, as long as the same essential contour of descent-to-ascent, or suffering-to-redemption is present. I encourage you to read more about the history and especially the variations of this fascinating folktale.

Iron John

These examples remind me of the lesser-known story of Iron John, originally Eisenhans, which was introduced to me by my good friend Elias in 2000. It's a German fairy tale found in the collections of the Brothers Grimm, tale number 136, about a wild, iron-skinned man and a boy prince.[212] The story also became the basis for the book *Iron John: A Book About Men* by Robert Bly (1992). Briefly put, having encountered Iron John who represents a guide to discovery, a young prince follows him away from his home to which, he is told, he can never return. He gives up everything. His was a quest to find himself and meaning, at least that's my summation of it. His journey takes him through difficult trials and hardships that mature and transform him, giving him humility and gratitude. Like the hobbit Frodo in the next example, the young prince had first to *descend* into doubt and despair before he could later *ascend* into resolution. Eventually he does return home as the man he was meant to be.

---

[211] wikipedia.org/wiki/Cinderella. Also known as *One Thousand and One Knights,* a collection of medieval folktales of Arabic, Egyptian, Indian, Persian, and Mesopotamian origins. wikipedia.org/wiki/One_Thousand_and_One_Nights

[212] wikipedia.org/wiki/Iron_John

Lord of the Rings

Another, more modern example of this Motif is from just the last century—*The Lord of the Rings* trilogy by English author J.R.R. Tolkien (1954/1954). Between 2001 and 2003 Tolkien's trilogy was released as three Academy award-winning films directed by Peter Jackson. An epic novel of high fantasy, in 2003 the BBC named it Britain's best novel of all time. The plot is very complex but has a very simple plotline, or contour. A happy young named fellow, Frodo, lived in a happy place. But his shire was in danger, and he was urged to leave it. He was thrust into a mounting crisis in which the whole world needed saving, and apparently only he could save it. In the end he succeeded, with much help, but first he had to 'descend'. Frodo had to give up everything and be willing to die for a higher cause. He could not know if he would ever return to his good life, or even if he would live. Hardly could he have foreseen what he must endure: to go *down* into the depths of darkness, danger, and privation before any hope of success could become possible.

But with a noble heart, and curiously brave, Frodo embraced the mission and let go of everything dear. It was an adventure, but also a kind of foreboding self-denial. His mission was to carry an enchanted but cursed ring that had intruded into his life, back to the mountain where it was forged, to destroy it. Along the arduous journey he was tested to the extreme and suffered severely. And he faced death multiple times. But with the help of his friends and what some would see as divine assistance, he finally *ascended*—he prevailed. With enormous internal struggle, he cast the ring into the fire whence it came. Thus the world was saved, and he was rewarded.

Another major character who experienced his own descent-and-ascent was "Strider", or more properly Aragorn. He was the son of the last king of Gondor, a kingdom in decline. Thus he was the heir and rightful king should he every choose to claim it. But he was in a self-imposed exile. At the beginning of the saga we meet him in this state of descent, of self-pity and depression. But by virtue of his noble character and by the hand of 'providence', he would slowly ascend.

By the end of the third book (and film), *The Return of the King*, Aragorn, having overcome untold dangers with remarkable courage and selflessness, is restored to wholeness. At long last, he embraces the crown and returns his kingdom to prosperity.

Resurrection

In the first book of the Lord of the trilogy, *The Fellowship of the Ring*, not long after we meet Frodo we are introduced to one of the other essential main characters that would help Aragorn ascend, the wizard Gandalf the Grey, played by Ian McKellen. His role is prominent from beginning to end. In a fierce battle with a demon monster, the Balrog, the wizard Gandalf kills it but at a great cost, the cost of his own life. Later, having risen from death, he re-enters the saga in *The Two Towers* as Gandalf the *White* (book/film 2).

And then there's Superman, whom I already mentioned in chapter 1. In DC's "Batman v Superman: Dawn of Justice" (2016) he (Henry Cavill) dies at the hands of a huge super-monster created by Lex Luthor. The next year in "Justice League" (2017) he is reanimated with 'super-electricity' by five other superheroes who need his help to defeat yet another, but more ancient mortal enemy. In other words, he was resurrected. Such are our modern-day myths.

In pre-Christian mythologies there are multiple examples of so-called dying-and-rising gods: Osiris (Egyptian), Tammuz (Sumerian),[213] Adonis (Greek/Mesopotamian), Attis (Greek), Dionysus, or Bacchus (Greco-Roman), Quetzalcoatl (Mesoamerican),[214] Izanami

---

[213] "Tammuz, or Dumuzid, was a Mesopotamian deity widely seen as a prime example of the archetypal dying-and-rising god. But the discovery of the full Sumerian text of *Inanna's Descent* in the mid-twentieth century appeared to disprove the previous scholarly assumption that the narrative ended with Dumuzid's resurrection, and instead revealed that it ended with Dumuzid's death. However, the rescue of Dumuzid from the underworld was later found in the text *Return of Dumuzid*, translated in 1963." wikipedia.org/wiki/Dumuzid

[214] Pre-Spanish Central America, e.g. Aztec and Mayan Mexico and Guatemala

(Japanese), and Baldr (Norse).[215] It was the last one that especially captured Lewis's imagination and eventually led to his conversion to Christianity. In it, and many others, he became enamored with the dying-and-rising archetype, or motif. The many elements of these myths and their notion of gods who died only to rise again gave him a sense of the transcendent that often filled him with a powerful but fleeting sense of joy that he longed to sustain. But for a long time he never took these myths for anything more than mere fiction. That's all they were and ever could be.

> But, despite the value he placed on them, Lewis considered the mythic stories and figures he loved to be wholly imaginary. "Nearly all that [he] loved [he] believed to be imaginary; nearly all that [he] believed to be real [he] thought grim and meaningless"; he "care[d] for nothing but the gods and heroes, the garden of the Hesperides, Launcelot and the Grail" but "believe[d] in nothing but atoms and evolution and military service." (*Surprised by Joy,* 170, 174)[216]

Naturally, Lewis also considered the well-known accounts of the dying-and-rising Jesus on which Christianity is founded, contained in the four gospels of the Bible's New Testament—*Matthew, Mark, Luke,* and *John*. He initially classified the rising-Christ event as fiction with all the others because he presupposed that resurrection was impossible. But as the renowned Oxford literary scholar that he was, he compared the details of the gospel accounts meticulously with the aforementioned stories that he so savored, and he came to recognize that there was something qualitatively different about the gospel narratives. They just didn't read like fiction, he thought. ...But I'm getting ahead of myself.

---

[215] "The existence of the 'dying-and-rising god' archetype has been largely rejected by modern scholars." wikipedia.org/wiki/Adonis

[216] Young, "Lewis on the Gospels as True Myth". Ibid

The main point is that dying-and-rising is a type of descent-to-ascent, the most superlative type. Taken together, this type of Motif has been enormously pervasive throughout the world's cultures and religions over the ages. It is distinguished from tragedy because in tragedy, as with the fate of Socrates, Icarus, and Hussein, the hero dies but does not rise again; he descends but does not ascend. By contrast, the story of Job is a classic tale of descent-to-ascent, possibly the world's first, but certainly one of them. And, as we have seen, it is arguably the most well-known and beloved example of this Motif whose renown has stood the test of time.

The Quintessential Icon

To Elie Wiesel and many others, Job is the quintessential icon of patience-in-descent, and for no reason known to Job. He wished for death, or never to have been born, but it was not granted him.

After this [his disasters] Job opened his mouth and cursed the day of his birth. And Job said:

> *"Let the day perish on which I was born,*
> *...Why did I not die at birth,*
>> *come out from the womb and expire?*
> *...Or why was I not as a hidden stillborn child,*
>> *as infants who never see the light?*
>> *...who long for death, but it comes not,*
>> *...and are glad when they find the grave?"*
>
> –Job 3:1–22 (excerpts)

He was pious and resolute, but utterly helpless. He was neither a wizard, a traveler, or a superhuman, as could be said of Samson, a later figure in the Tanakh who had his own descent that ended in a kind of tragedy.[217] Neither was Job given any great mission with an epic quest to save humanity from evil forces of darkness.

Job's book tells us next to nothing about the rest of the world. From it we are given a narrow view of Job's world only. He was in one sense a normal man, but in other senses he was extraordinary, as we have already seen. He was not a god, but he was godly, and perhaps even god-like in the eyes of his people. He was "the greatest of all the people of the east" (1:3), and there was "none like him on the earth." (1:8) He was exceedingly rich, the Elon Musk of his day, so like him we can surmise that he was a very shrewd businessman, as one person pointed out to me on Facebook. Above all he was superlatively good: "blameless and upright, one who feared God and turned away from evil." (1:1) It's the very first thing that is said of him, so it is clearly the most important thing about him.

Whether Job was a prophet in the strict, biblical sense can be debated in Judeo-Christian circles, though I have already referred to him as one. Muslims seem to have no such debate. It is possible that Job was a king, or at least it has been speculated.[218] But even if he

---

[217] See the book of Judges chapters 13-16.

[218] Williams, *The Shadow of Christ in the Book of Job* "Some have speculated that Job actually was a king. The Septuagint version of Job adds an appendix of supplemental information drawn from Genesis 36 and an unnamed Syrian book*, essentially identifying Job with King Jobab of Edom (Gen 36:33).** However, this lengthier Septuagint ending to the book is clearly a later addition. It was likely added in order to supply historical and genealogical information that is not present in the canonical Hebrew text of Job, and perhaps to offer an explanation for the royal imagery in the book. The Septuagint addition, and the identification of Job with Jobab, can safely be dismissed as the creative gloss of a later Greek editor. The motif of kingship imbued in Job's character is too overdrawn to reflect historical reality."

*I do not know what book Williams refers to here, but I suspect it may be The Testament of Job to which I have made reference in the footnotes of earlier chapters. This apocryphal work does indeed identify Job as King Jobab of the sons of Esau.

**The LXX (Septuagint) version of Job 42:17 reads, "And Job died, an old man and full of days. And it is written that he will rise again with those the Lord raises up. This man is interpreted from the Syriac book as living in the land of Ausitis, on the borders of Idumea and Arabia, and previously his name was Jobab; now he took an Arabian wife and fathered a son, whose name was Ennon, and he in turn had father Zare, a son of the sons of Esau, and as mother Bosorra, so that he was the fifth from Abraam. And these are the kings who reigned in Edom, which country he too ruled: first Balak the son of Beor, and the name of his city was Dennaba, and after Balak, Iobab, who is called Iob, and after him Hasom, who

was not, he was certainly 'kingly', and highly revered as some of his own language reveals in chapters 19 and 29.[219] The point is that before his descent he was at the highest height, the pinnacle of earthly glory and success. And according to God it had not gone to his head. Then came his descent. But it was not a 'fall' like Adam's when he and Eve defied the LORD's one command and ate from the forbidden tree, resulting in their banishment. As I said in the previous chapter, Job's descent had nothing to do with his own sin. At first he is depicted as though he were 'sinless' if such a thing was possible; but not at the end, as we have seen. Job's descent was of an entirely otherworldly nature, as the text of chapter 1 tells us.

In his exceptional book, *The Shadow of Christ in the Book of Job,* C.J. Williams captures it both succinctly and poetically:

> The story begins with Job living an ideal existence, pious and prosperous beyond any other man on earth, and enjoying the unique favor of God. Job is then, all at once, cast down to

---

was a leader from Thaimanite country, and after him Hadad son of Barad, who cut down Madiam in the plain of Moab, and the name of his city was Geththaim. Albert Pietersma and Benjamin G. Wright, eds., *A New English Translation of the Septuagint,* 696.

[219] Job: "My justice was like a robe and a turban. ...I chose the way for them, and sat as chief...So I dwelt as a king in the army..." (Job 29:14b, 25a) "He has stripped me of my glory, and taken the crown from my head." (19:9). Verses 7-11 and 21-23 say...

> [7] When I went out to the gate of the city,
>   when I prepared my seat in the square,
> [8] the young men saw me and withdrew,
>   and the aged rose and stood;
> [9] the princes refrained from talking
>   and laid their hand on their mouth;
> [10] the voice of the nobles was hushed,
>   and their tongue stuck to the roof of their mouth.
> [11] When the ear heard, it called me blessed,
>   and when the eye saw, it approved,
> [21] Men listened to me and waited
>   and kept silence for my counsel.
> [22] After I spoke they did not speak again,
>   and my word dropped upon them.
> [23] They waited for me as for the rain,
>   and they opened their mouths as for the spring rain.

such depths of suffering and humiliation that no other man had theretofore experienced. This was no gradual run of providential difficulties; Job's entire world came crashing down in a moment. He lost his family, his health, and his possessions. His wife and his friends turned on him. He was brought to a point where he literally had nothing left to lose but his life, and there he sat in an ash heap, scraping his diseased skin with a potsherd, wondering why he was still alive. [But] At the conclusion of the book, we find that "the Lord gave Job twice as much as he had before", [220] and "the Lord blessed the latter days of Job more than his beginning".* ...If, in the beginning, Job was the greatest man in the east, and there was none else like him on earth, his later years of life must have been nothing short of idyllic—even glorious.

There is nothing ordinary about this story. It is extreme in every way. ...The story of Job truly has no earthly equal. Here we see the sequence of humiliation and exaltation in its extreme. **It is not a [gradual] providential process, as with other Old Testament examples.** Job's experience moved from extreme [descent] to extreme [ascent], in such a way that there is no doubt that God's hand moved these events directly and purposefully. Job was divinely moved from the outermost limits of the human experience of suffering on earth, to the outermost limits of the human experience of blessing on earth—**all as if to illustrate something *beyond* the limits of human experience.**[221]

Some may take issue with the author's wording here. According to the text of *Job* 1 and 2, Satan himself was directly responsible for Job's afflictions, on two occasions (1:12 and 2:6,7). But clearly what Williams is expressing is the other side of the coin: The LORD *allowed* Satan to afflict Job. And He allowed it for a purpose, albeit one that is never spelled out to Job or to us. Without said permission it

---

[220] Book of Job 42:10. *42:12

[221] Ibid, bolding mine.

appears obvious that Satan would not have been able to do it. Moreover, it appears to have been at the LORD's inducement when He first said to Satan, "Have you considered my servant Job…? (1:8) Either way, this is deeply troubling to many people, and it is the very crux of the so-called problem of evil—Why would God *ever* allow this kind of thing to happen and the innumerable variations of it? It is a difficult question worthy of much consideration.

While I don't think this is the core question of the Book of Job, I offer two brief thoughts. One, there *are* good answers on multiple levels, just probably no 'pat answers' that some people crave. Two, it is a compound problem with a compound explanation that does not satisfy everybody. But they satisfy me. On one level, that of the verbiage of the text itself, the answer that Yahweh gives Job (and us) is essentially, "I am God, and that should be good enough for you." These days not very many people are satisfied with that. Another answer, on another level of consideration, is that the LORD esteems the descent-to-ascent Motif, and through Job's ordeal He was memorializing it forever. Logically, without descent there can be no ascent, so if ascent is the goal then descent must take place. A hero cannot become a hero without a crisis, and without crises there can never be heroes. Likewise, a champion cannot become a champion without defeating his enemies, whether they are other persons or circumstances. We do not get this from the verbiage of the text, we get it from the contours of the story that produce the Motif. We readers of the 21st century, with all of *Job's* readers over the millennia, can readily see these contours and their Motif. In retrospect, I think Job would have been able to see it too, over time. In the big picture, this is the main thing the story of Job contributes to the problem of evil.

Chapter 12

The Descent-to-Ascent Motif in the Tanakh

—Jacob and Joseph

> *Where then is my hope?*
> *Who will see my hope?*
> *Will it go down to the bars of Sheol?*
> *Shall we descend together into the dust?"*
>
> Job, *Book of Job* 17:15–16

Why do I say that the LORD esteems the descent-to-descent Motif? Well, it's because of the sentence I bolded in Williams' quote two pages earlier where he makes reference to "other Old Testament examples." The fact is that there are multiple examples of the descent-to-ascent Motif in the Tanakh. Let's look at some of them and compare them to the pattern we see in Job.

I already mentioned Adam and Eve a few pages back, but in my opinion, they're not a good example of this Motif. Why? Because as far as the text of *Genesis* 1-4 tells us, they only *descended*. I would like to think they ascended later, after the murder of Able by his brother Cain, but we cannot know that. All we can assume of Adam and Eve is that they lived out the rest of their lives in exile, subject to God's curse on the ground that would forever make life hard. Moving forward there was Noah, to whom I have already devoted an entire chapter (+). He is a far better example of the full Motif cycle. As we have seen, he and his family experienced deep descent into the darkness of a year-long flood before they were brought up and out of it.

Noah received Yahweh's blessing with a covenant for all humanity, and he lived another 350 years (a total of 950).[222] Beyond that we are told almost nothing about his progress or development, so he is still not the best example. We have also extensively covered the prophets Moses and Jonah, who both exemplify our Motif exceptionally well. Moses was exiled to later return as redeemer, lawgiver, and prophetic ruler of the people of Israel during their desert sojourn. As for Jonah, I think you remember his experiences vividly enough from chapter 6, and we will come back to him again in chapter 14. Now I want to offer some other examples from the Tanakh that we have not considered yet at all—Jacob and Joseph.

Jacob in the Tanakh

In chapter 25 of the *Book of Genesis* we meet Jacob for the first time, the son of Isaac and grandson of Abraham. Verses 22-26 tell of his birth to Rebekah moments after his fraternal twin brother Esau who, as we have seen, became the progenitor of the Edomites and the possible ancestor of Job himself. But Jacob, or *Israel* as he was later called by God, became the father of the Israelites.[223] To Muslims he was a prophet, but to Jews and Christians, a patriarch. When Jacob had about 70 descendants, they all moved to Egypt during a famine,[224] and when they came out 430 years later they numbered in the possible millions.[225] In the next two chapters we are told that Jacob was favored over Esau by his mother, and he cheated Esau twice, first out of his birthright and later his other firstborn blessings. The first time was Jacob's own idea,[226] and the second time was his mother's which hinged on her deceit. Not only did they conspire together to

---

[222] *Book of Genesis* chapter 9

[223] *Book of Genesis* 35:10

[224] *Book of Genesis* 46:26, 27

[225] *Book of Exodus* 12:37, and verse 40

[226] *Book of Genesis* 25:29-34

cheat Esau, they had to deceive Isaac to do it. It was so serious an offense that Esau determined to kill Jacob. As a consequence of their conspiracy we find Jacob fleeing for his life at the urging of Rebekah, all of which is recorded in chapter 27 as the following passage shows.

> *Now Esau hated Jacob because of the blessing with which his father had blessed him, and Esau said to himself, "The days of mourning for my father are approaching; then I will kill my brother Jacob." But the words of Esau her older son were told to Rebekah. So she sent and called Jacob her younger son and said to him, "Behold, your brother Esau comforts himself about you by planning to kill you. Now therefore, my son, obey my voice. Arise, flee to Laban my brother in Haran and stay with him a while, until your brother's fury turns away—until your brother's anger turns away from you, and he forgets what you have done to him. Then I will send and bring you from there. (vv. 41-45)*

וַיִּשְׂטֹ֤ם עֵשָׂו֙ אֶֽת־יַעֲקֹ֔ב עַל־הַ֨בְּרָכָ֔ה אֲשֶׁ֥ר בֵּרֲכ֖וֹ אָבִ֑יו וַיֹּ֨אמֶר עֵשָׂ֜ו בְּלִבּ֗וֹ יִקְרְבוּ֙ יְמֵי֙ אֵ֣בֶל אָבִ֔י וְאַֽהַרְגָ֖ה אֶת־יַעֲקֹ֥ב אָחִֽי׃

וַיֻּגַּ֣ד לְרִבְקָ֔ה אֶת־דִּבְרֵ֥י עֵשָׂ֖ו בְּנָ֣הּ הַגָּדֹ֑ל וַתִּשְׁלַ֞ח וַתִּקְרָ֤א לְיַעֲקֹב֙ בְּנָ֣הּ הַקָּטָ֔ן וַתֹּ֣אמֶר אֵלָ֔יו הִנֵּה֙ עֵשָׂ֣ו אָחִ֔יךָ מִתְנַחֵ֥ם לְךָ֖ לְהׇרְגֶֽךָ׃

וְעַתָּ֥ה בְנִ֖י שְׁמַ֣ע בְּקֹלִ֑י וְק֧וּם בְּרַח־לְךָ֛ אֶל־לָבָ֥ן אָחִ֖י חָרָֽנָה׃

וְיָשַׁבְתָּ֥ עִמּ֖וֹ יָמִ֣ים אֲחָדִ֑ים עַ֥ד אֲשֶׁר־תָּשׁ֖וּב חֲמַ֥ת אָחִֽיךָ׃

עַד־שׁ֨וּב אַף־אָחִ֜יךָ מִמְּךָ֗ וְשָׁכַח֙ אֵ֣ת אֲשֶׁר־עָשִׂ֣יתָ לּ֔וֹ וְשָׁלַחְתִּ֖י וּלְקַחְתִּ֣יךָ מִשָּׁ֑ם לָמָ֥ה אֶשְׁכַּ֛ל גַּם־שְׁנֵיכֶ֖ם י֥וֹם אֶחָֽד׃[227]

---

[227] Sefaria.org/Genesis.27.41-45? The Contemporary Torah, JPS. For this passage and the next, I include the Hebrew for the sake of flourish, not because I expect any Hebrew-only readers to depend on the translation.

In the next chapter (28), verses 1-5 tell us that Isaac agreed with Rebekah, Jacob's mother in this urging, but not for the same reason only. Yes, he had been deceived by Jacob, but oddly that seems not to have been driving his thinking. He and Rebekah both wanted Jacob to find a wife from among his cousins as Isaac had done 20 years earlier, not from the local women as Esau had done, to his parents' disapproval. So they had mixed motives.

Then Isaac called Jacob and blessed him and directed him, "You must not take a wife from the Canaanite women. Arise, go to Paddan-aram to the house of Bethuel your mother's father, and take as your wife from there one of the daughters of Laban your mother's brother. God Almighty bless you and make you fruitful and multiply you, that you may become a company of peoples. May he give the blessing of Abraham to you and to your offspring with you, that you may take possession of the land of your sojournings that God gave to Abraham!" Thus Isaac sent Jacob away. And he went to Paddan-aram, to Laban, the son of Bethuel the Aramean, the brother of Rebekah, Jacob's and Esau's mother.

וַיְהִי כִּי־זָקֵן יִצְחָק וַתִּכְהֶיןָ עֵינָיו מֵרְאֹת וַיִּקְרָא אֶת־עֵשָׂו ׀ בְּנוֹ הַגָּדֹל וַיֹּאמֶר אֵלָיו בְּנִי וַיֹּאמֶר אֵלָיו הִנֵּנִי:

וַיֹּאמֶר הִנֵּה־נָא זָקַנְתִּי לֹא יָדַעְתִּי יוֹם מוֹתִי:

וְעַתָּה שָׂא־נָא כֵלֶיךָ תֶּלְיְךָ וְקַשְׁתֶּךָ וְצֵא הַשָּׂדֶה וְצוּדָה לִּי (צידה) [צָיִד]:

וַעֲשֵׂה־לִי מַטְעַמִּים כַּאֲשֶׁר אָהַבְתִּי וְהָבִיאָה לִּי וְאֹכֵלָה בַּעֲבוּר תְּבָרֶכְךָ נַפְשִׁי בְּטֶרֶם אָמוּת:

וְרִבְקָה שֹׁמַעַת בְּדַבֵּר יִצְחָק אֶל־עֵשָׂו בְּנוֹ וַיֵּלֶךְ עֵשָׂו הַשָּׂדֶה לָצוּד צַיִד לְהָבִיא:

So Jacob made the 550-mile trek to his uncle's estate in Haran, which is today a village in southeastern Turkey. This was the city where, as a young man, Abraham (Abram) and his family settled after having emigrated from Ur in southern Mesopotamia, until he left there for Canaan at age 75.[228] The text does not say how old Jacob was, but I will assume he was about 40. (Some 60 years earlier, Abraham too was determined not to allow Isaac to marry a Canaanite woman, but he did not send him there. Rather, he sent his servant on a mission to find a willing bride from among his relatives and bring her back for Isaac, to which story is devoted an entire chapter.)[229] There Jacob spent his next 20 years, partly in exile and partly building his family from within his bloodline. **It was his descent.** Apparently, his parents never did call him back home, as if they could just email him or something. The next five-and-a-half chapters (28-33) chronicle Jacob's experiences starting with his journey to Haran, his entire sojourn there, and his return to Canaan twenty years later. It's a lot of material with a substantial amount of detail, so allow me to condense and summarize it for you.

Again, the main idea is that Jacob was in-descent the entire time. A number of very striking things happened, most of which I will not cover in detail. On his way to Haran Jacob had a spectacular vision of angels, ironically, ascending and descending between heaven and earth. Upon his return he wrestled all night with perhaps an angel whom Jacob determined to be God himself.[230] Following this he had to face Esau and his army of 400 men who had almost certainly come to destroy him. Thankfully, God had blessed Jacob and assuaged Esau's wrath by means of Jacob's generous gifts and heartfelt humility toward him. There was also God's invisible work on Esau's heart, of course. That was part of Jacob's **path to ascent.** For in the 20 years between the two celestial encounters he was in a low place, trapped by his circumstances resulting from his uncle's trickery. True, he

---

[228] Torah, *Book of Genesis* 12:1-7

[229] Ibid. chapter 24

[229] Ibid. chapter 32:22-32 The text is ambiguous about what kind of being it was, but at the end Jacob said, "For I have seen God face to face, and yet my life has been delivered." This was the first time Jacob was given the name Israel, assigned by the celestial being.

amassed a large family and great wealth during this time, but it was at the cost of his freedom. He was essentially an indentured servant to his uncle Laban, a kind of slave. Jacob had bound himself to 14 years of labor for Laban's two daughters Rachel and Leah in marriage (though he was cheated on the first one),[231] and another period of six years for his share of the livestock that fortunately he was able to keep.[232] During this last period Jacob and his wives decided they'd had enough, and Jacob said to them:

> *"I see that your father does not regard me with favor as he did before. But the God of my father has been with me. You know that I have served your father with all my strength, yet your father has cheated me and changed my wages ten times. But God did not permit him to harm me." Then Rachel and Leah answered and said, "Is there any portion or inheritance left to us in our father's house? Are we not regarded by him as foreigners? For he has sold us, and he has indeed devoured our money.* (31:5-7, 14-15)

At this time the LORD actually told Jacob to return to Canaan.[233] For all these reasons, and seeing that Laban had no intention of letting them go easily, they decided to escape.[234] When Laban found out, of course, he was not ok with this. In fact he was furious! For over two decades he had exploited Jacob and enjoyed the benefits of his cheap labor. With his kinsmen he pursued them, and on the seventh day apprehended them. From a position of power,[235] Laban charged Jacob essentially with stealing his daughters and grandchildren, as well as

---

[231] Ibid 29:16-30

[232] Ibid 30:25-43

[233] Ibid 31:3

[234] Ibid 31:17-21

[235] He said, "It is in my power to do you harm." (31:29) Had not God warned Laban not to harm Jacob he may have killed or enslaved him and repossessed his daughters, grandchildren, and all his flocks.

his family idols.[236] As is common with slaveowners, Laban clearly believed that all Jacob had accumulated belonged to him (Laban).

But Jacob's rebuttal was equally impassioned:

> *"These twenty years I have been with you. Your ewes and your female goats have not miscarried, and I have not eaten the rams of your flocks. What was torn by wild beasts I did not bring to you. I bore the loss of it myself. From my hand you required it, whether stolen by day or stolen by night. There I was: by day the heat consumed me, and the cold by night, and my sleep fled from my eyes. These twenty years I have been in your house. I served you fourteen years for your two daughters, and six years for your flock, and you have changed my wages ten times. If the God of my father, the God of Abraham and the Fear of Isaac, had not been on my side, surely now you would have sent me away empty-handed. God saw my affliction and the labor of my hands and rebuked you last night."* (31:38–42)

With that, Laban let Jacob and his company go. It has all the marks of a miracle. This appears to have been the first time Jacob had the nerve to stand up to his uncle, and from his words we can see clearly that Jacob believed he had been in affliction all those years. But now, with the LORD's command and His promise to be with him, Jacob finally received the nerve to leave Laban, to *ascend*. And ascend he did. Similar to Aragorn's in the *Lord of the Rings* trilogy, it was a gradual ascent, but ultimately Jacob became father to a king! Well, not the head king, but not far from one at all. As we will soon see, perhaps the least likely of all Jacob's sons became the "lord of all Egypt" and its savior-redeemer.[237]

---

[236] Rachel did in fact steal them (31:32b)

[237] *Genesis* 45:9 plus 8 and 13

Following this harrowing but favorable encounter with Laban—and the even scarier one with his estranged brother Esau and his army (chapter 33)—Jacob was finally free from his partly self-inflicted period of bondage in a foreign land. He and his four wives,[238] his 12 children, and his numerous livestock returned to Canaan. They initially settled in Shechem, the first place his grandfather Abram had built an altar to offer burnt offerings to Yahweh.

> *"And Jacob came safely to the city of Shechem, which is in the land of Canaan...and he camped before the city...There he erected an altar and called it El-Elohe-Israel."*

There Jacob also built an altar for burnt offerings.[239] But soon a scandal took place and God told Jacob to move his family to Bethel where he built another altar, and called the place El-bethel meaning "House of El, or House of God."[240] These two chapters (34-35) give account of Jacob's life in these temporary locations where his grandfather and father had both lived where they were feared by the neighboring peoples. They ultimately reached Mamre, or Hebron, where his father Isaac was still living at the full age of 180. When Jacob arrived, Isaac died.[241] (Then, chapter 36 gives us the lineage of Esau.) In the remaining 14 chapters of *Genesis* Jacob's name occurs 33 times for a grand total of 160. In Canaan, he and his sons continue to dominate the plotline of God's providence until Jacob's death is recorded in chapter 50. Like his forbearers, they were strangers everywhere they settled, but with God's favor and protection, Jacob became great like

---

[238] Only one of which he had actually wanted to marry, the others foisted upon him.

[239] Ibid 33:18, 20 אֵל אֱלֹהֵי יִשְׂרָאֵל: El-Elohi-Jisrael ʼĒl ʼĕlôhêy Yisrâʼêl, ale el-o-hay' yis-rawale'. It means "the Mighty God of Israel," a generic title, not a proper name.

[240] Again, like "Elohim," not a proper name, but a generic one similar to the Arabic "Allah" meaning "the God," akin to the way "God" is used generically in English and "Got" in German. My Muslim friend Ibrahim argues that "El" was the proper name for the main god of the ANE pantheon. I assert that just as "Allah" is used interchangeably as a proper name in Islam, it is possible that "El" was also used this way by Jacob and others.

[241] Ibid. 35:27-29

his father and grandfather before him.[242] And he became the third-generation progenitor of a great people with a long line of Hebrew prophets over the span of two millennia.

At the age of 130 Jacob was personally invited by Egypt's king, or pharaoh, to move his whole family to the land of Goshen in Upper Egypt, "the best of the land."[243] (Abraham had also sojourned there two centuries before during a sever famine in Canaan. After having emigrated from his native Ur of Chaldea some decades earlier, Upper Egypt was as far south as he ever went. [244]) In the throes of another severe regional famine, Jacob's family was sustained by the Egyptian government and allowed to pasture their flocks in peace. So Jacob ascended still higher. Through no effort of his own he reached a station much higher than either Abraham or Isaac had before him. Apparently his early bondage and sufferings were prerequisite to making him the man God wanted him to be. Like Job, Jacob had been sorely humbled, and like Job he had been elevated to the highest echelon of society.

"How did this happen?" one would rightly be curious to know. There must be a backstory. Indeed there is a rich one, found in abundant detail in chapters 45-47:12 of the *Book of Genesis*. And there is a backstory to that too, which we will explore shortly.

It should be interesting to note that on his way south to Egypt, Jacob and his clan stopped in Beersheba and offered sacrifices to God, presumably on the altar that his father Isaac had built. Beersheba was a special place where more than a century earlier God spoke to Hagar and showed her a well of water.[245] Later, after a resolved dispute with the local Philistines, Abraham had "called on the

---

[242] Ibid 35:5

[243] Ibid 45:10,11, 17-20; 47:6,11 Qur'an surah 112:93 and 99

[244] Ibid 12:10-20. Probably Zoan, but On (Heliopolis) and Memphis were also in that region.

[245] Ibid 21:14-21 Muslims call this well "Zam Zam" but locate it 868 miles south of Beersheba in today's Mecca, Saudi Arabia. Today a mosque, the Masjid Al-Haram is built over top of it. The non-Muslim cannot help wondering how and why this event could have happened so far south of Abraham's land of sojourn in Canaan, especially when the original text states its location so clearly. The conclusion should be commonsensical.

name of Yahweh" and planted a tamarisk tree there.[246] He settled there for some time.[247] Decades later Isaac also dug a well there and built an altar where he also "called on the name of Yahweh."[248] It also appears that he and his family lived there at the time of Jacob's departure to Haran.[249] Now, having been summoned to Egypt, it made perfect sense for Jacob to "make hajj" as Muslims say, or pilgrimage, there to worship Yahweh by blood sacrifice as he had learned from his father (and it was on the way this time.) In Beersheba we are told that God spoke to Jacob a fourth time.[250]

> *So Israel took his journey with all that he had and came to Beersheba, and offered sacrifices to the God of his father Isaac. And God spoke to Israel in visions of the night and said, "Jacob, Jacob." And he said, "Here I am." Then he said, "I am God, the God of your father. Do not be afraid to go down to Egypt, for there I will make you into a great nation. I myself will go down with you to Egypt, and I will also bring you up again... (Book of Genesis 46:2-4)*

Then he continued on to Egypt in the wagons that Pharaoh and Joseph had sent to carry him (45:27 and 46:5).

> *The sons of Israel carried Jacob their father, their little ones,*

---

[246] Ibid 21:31-34

[247] Ibid 22:19

[248] Ibid 26:23-25; 26-33

[249] Ibid 28:10

[250] Ibid 46:2-4 Note: Although the Qur'an contains this detail of Jacob's journey to Egypt (surah 112:94), it omits his stop at Beersheba and any of the related details that *Genesis* mentions such as God's words to Jacob. *Also, whenever God spoke to Jacob he didn't speak to him through an angel (with the possible exception of *Genesis* 32:22-32). Also, although it is without dispute that Jacob worshiped the one God Yahweh, his oneness was never a part of His words to Jacob. Apparently it was unnecessary to say, and He seemed to have more specific things to tell him. This is also true with respect to the words of God to Abraham and Isaac as contained in the rich texts of Genesis. In them, could/would the parts speaking about 'Tawhid' possibly have been edited out so universally? If so, why?

and their wives, in the wagons that Pharaoh had sent to carry him. They also took their livestock and their goods, which they had gained in the land of Canaan, and came into Egypt, Jacob and all his offspring with him, his sons, and his sons' sons with him, his daughters, and his sons' daughters. All his offspring he brought with him into Egypt. (46:5–7)

Jacob in Islam   Ya'qub   يعقوب

The narrative I have presented in this chapter so far is a condensed version of the scriptural text found in the *Book of Genesis* in the Tawrat, or Torah. Much of it will be agreeable to Muslims as compared with **The Story of Ya'qub** (Jacob), one of 29 *Stories of the Prophets* by one Ibn Kathir (c. 1300–1373) whom we already met in chapter 2.[251] His full name was much longer—Abu al-Fiḍā 'Imād Ad-Din Ismā'īl ibn 'Umar ibn Kathīr al-Qurashī Al-Damishqī إسماعيل بن (عمر) بن كثير القرشي الدمشقي أبو الفداء عماد الدين. Ibn Kathir was a highly influential Muslim historian, exegete and scholar during the Mamluk era in Syria (1250–1382). He was an expert on Tafsir (Quranic exegesis) and Fiqh (jurisprudence), and wrote several books, including a 14-volume universal history entitled *Al-Bidaya wa'l-Nihaya (The Beginning And The End)*.[252] Although his piece on Jacob ends before that contained in the *Book of Genesis* (at the death of Isaac), and therefore also mine, it resembles the original Torah's account from some 2000 years earlier. And why shouldn't it, one might ask? Exactly. There was only one Jacob. For me, the question that arises next is, from whence was it obtained? Ibn Kathir doesn't say specifically. With respect to non-Qur'anic and otherwise non-Islamic material, it was apparently not his standard practice. Granted, this was far more common in those days, but that leaves us to discover or

---

[251] sunnahonline.com/library/stories-of-the-prophets/296-story-of-prophet-yaqub. See also islamguiden.com/arkiv/stories_of_the_prophets.pdf

[252] wikipedia.org/wiki/Ibn_Kathir

deduce his possible sources. Unless he was claiming divine revelation, which he was not, he must have had a source.

The first logical candidate is the Qur'an itself. According to my best search of Muhammad Pickthall's English translation there are 16 explicit references to Ya'qub in ten surahs (not including verses with the word "Israel" which in the Torah can refer to Jacob after he was renamed, including *Genesis* 2:132, 133, 136, and 140; 3:84; 4:163; 6:84; 11:71, 12:6, 38, 68, 83; 19:6 and 49/50; 21:72/73; 29:27, and 38:45/46.[253] This is corroborated by Yusuf Ali's translation which contains all of these verses plus two more in surah 12 that are implied (in parentheses) and another one that I cannot account for. Here, for example, is verse 27 of surah 29 called "The Spider":

وَوَهَبْنَا لَهُ إِسْحَاقَ وَيَعْقُوبَ وَجَعَلْنَا فِي ذُرِّيَّتِهِ النُّبُوَّةَ وَالْكِتَابَ وَآتَيْنَاهُ أَجْرَهُ فِي الدُّنْيَا ۖ وَإِنَّهُ فِي الْآخِرَةِ لَمِنَ الصَّالِحِينَ

> And We gave (Abraham) Isaac and **Jacob**, and ordained among his progeny Prophethood and Revelation, and We granted him his reward in this life; and he was in the Hereafter (of the company) of the Righteous.

This single verse speaks of Jacob in relation to Abraham and Isaac and affirms him among the righteous who produced prophets and was rewarded in this life. In my judgment, this verse is emblematic of all the other verses: It offers very little of the rich and complex details of the Torah's narratives of Jacob's life. If all we had was the Qur'an we would know next to nothing of his story, every bit as much a saga as that of his grandfather Abraham.[254]

---

[253] As found in www.perseus.tufts.edu and stated in wikipedia.org/wiki/Jacob_in_Islam. According to Yusuf Ali's translation, Surah 12 also has two or three that are implied, e.g. vv. 13 and 66. Specific verse numbers (ayas) found in search-the-quran.com/search/Jacob.

[254] 159 occurrences of Abram (49) and Abraham (110) to which the LORD changed it. (*Genesis* 17:5) Taken together, the *Book of Genesis* contains 14 chapters devoted to the life of Abraham, and 20 of the last 26 to the life of Jacob; or 23 if we count the three chapters (39-41) where Jacob is not named but still follow his overarching metanarrative through the story of Joseph that becomes prominent beginning in chapter 37. More on that.

The Islamic website IslamReligion.com contains a much shorter article on the story of Jacob by Aisha Stacey whom we met in chapter 2 in a similar vein. In her piece Stacey includes five of the verses that I listed, another in which Jacob is implied because he speaks (12:86), plus two that speak of the children or descendants of "Israel". As before she also references Ibn Kathir's account:

> Notable scholar of Islam, Ibn Kathir mentions that Prophet Jacob left his family and travelled to his maternal uncle where he married two of his cousins, Leah and Rachel, and worked as a shepherd for his father-in-law. He was the father of twelve sons and their dynasties later became known as the 12 tribes of Israel.[255]

Even if we add in the verses that contain the word "Israel" we know little more about Jacob, because they usually refer to the children or people of Israel, not Jacob himself.[256] In a third Muslim website called IslamforChristians.com we get basically the same 'skeletal' coverage of Jacob. The unnamed writer of this piece cites four Qur'anic passages in my list plus another that is not in my list—37:112/113. Upon examining the immediate context, however, verse 109 makes it clear that this passage is not about Jacob at all, but rather about Abraham, so only four are actually about Jacob. To me, what's really interesting about this piece is that the first 3/5ths of it are about Jacob in the Bible, or the Torah more specifically. The author lists five passages from the *Book of Genesis* highlighting five instances from Jacob's life that s/he finds, at best, unflattering of him, or even sacrilegious toward such a great prophet in Islam. Indeed, s/he is actually *offended* by the Torah's presentation of Jacob, for in the fourth paragraph s/he writes:

---

[255] Stacey, islamreligion.com/articles/10811/story-of-prophet-jacob/

[256] My search for "Jacob" resulted in about 35 occurrences of "Israel" in 33 verses, as well as the word "charity." search-the-quran.com/search/jacob

Therefore, Jacob's character in the Bible can never be that of a prophet sent by God but rather that of a usurious, deceitful, conceited Jew who begot comparably usurious, deceitful, conceited offspring.[257]

S/he is largely on the mark, at least with respect to his *pre-ascent*. Very few Christians or Jews would defend the character of Jacob in his younger years, his life before his *descent*. And the writer of the *Book of Genesis* himself (Moses) apparently made no attempt to whitewash the details to make Jacob look good (a characteristic that accurately describes the whole of the Tanakh.) Surely he could have. And if he had presupposed Jacob's prophet-hood, or that prophets cannot sin or have a questionable youth, he may have had motive to do so. But the text of the Tanakh teaches no such things. That's one reason why Christians and Jews are far more interested in the unvarnished details about Jacob and other biblical figures, and why neither insists that Jacob was a prophet. The Hebrew scriptures of the Torah never tell us that he was, *or* that he wasn't for that matter. (For my fellow Christians who insist that Jacob wasn't a prophet, he prophesied on one occasion at least: Chapter 49:1-27 of *Genesis* captures his last words foretelling the futures of his twelve sons and their respective tribes.) It's quite possibly true that Jacob was as bad as this anonymous writer described him from the narratives of *Genesis—before* his ascent that is. But through his descent into bondage he eventually ascended to become a man who had encountered Yahweh personally and worshipped Him the way all the greatest prophets did.

Based on their narratives, certainly Jacob believed in the one God of his father and grandfather, even in his questionable youth. But monotheism alone does not guarantee one's moral integrity. It takes much more than that. We can learn from his story that it takes a personal encounter with the Almighty, even multiple encounters. And sometimes it takes divine discipline through hardship. Through his confrontation by Yahweh—when He spoke to Jacob directly—and

---

[257] Anonymous, islamforchristians.com/greatest-prophets-christianity-islam-prophet-jacob/

through his descent into suffering, Jacob's faith in the one true God was clearly strengthened. And the LORD brough him up out of that valley with a true relationship with Him such as Abraham and Isaac had. In all their detail, the scriptures of the Torah never tell us that Jacob preached or proclaimed the one God, nor that he received verbatim revelations that he recited to his family or to the surrounding peoples. For that matter, neither did Abraham or Isaac if we take the scriptures at their word. But what we can see is the hand of God providentially shaping and leading Jacob to fulfill His divine mission for him. He was to become great as the father of Joseph and of the children of Israel. And thanks to the Torah's detailed account, the life of Jacob has become a witness to the world for all posterity, just as Job's story has: A testimony to the faithfulness of God Almighty.

Most Jews and Christians couldn't care less whether Jacob was a prophet or not—or Abraham,[258] or Isaac, or Noah, or even Job for that matter. If Jacob was a prophet, well and good. In our view, the sins of one's youth do not permanently disqualify one for God's favor and use, so Jacob's would not disqualify him for prophethood. (Also, who knows what kind of life Abraham led in his younger years before his calling in *Genesis* 12:1; we know almost nothing of him before he was 75. For all we know he was an intemperate pagan along with all the rest of his people of Ur, and later had a conversion to righteous Yahwism.) But prophets were not the only 'cream of the crop.' Either way, these men were unquestionably among God's 'saints.'[259] The Christians I know are far more interested in seeing how God accomplished His goals through them, and how He changed them in the process, often painfully. In the case of Jacob, the Torah shows us how the LORD led him down a path of descent, into a place of suffering,

---

[258] In Genesis 20:7 the Philistine king Abimelech called Abraham a "prophet," which is the only time he was ever called one in the Tanakh.

[259] A word study of 'saints' throughout the Tanakh is very interesting. Two examples: **Psalm 16:3** – "As for the **saints** in the land, they are the excellent ones, in whom is all my delight." **Daniel 7:18** – "But the **saints** of the Most High shall receive the kingdom and possess the kingdom forever, forever and ever."

so He could bring him up on the other side, a better man who knew and trusted Him. And He never abandoned him.

Jacob's story, of course, is not identical to Job's. Before his ascent, it cannot be said of Jacob that he was "blameless and upright, one who feared God and turned away from evil." (Job 1:1 and 8) Also, I don't think Jacob suffered as acutely as Job did, but he languished longer.[260] The main point of the comparison is that we can see in the story of Jacob our Motif. The next example will be even more pronounced.

But first, let's return briefly to the question about Ibn Kathir's sources. The Qur'an gives us some general facts about Jacob, and some very high praises, but it certainly cannot be the source of what Ibn Kathir wrote about him. Also, whatever ahadith exist about Jacob, they too would be based on preexisting sources, not divine revelation, which Muslims do not claim for this material anyway. And they could not possibly compare to the Torah in their breadth and depth of detail. Therefore, the most logical source for Ibn Kathir's history of Jacob, and the preponderance of what Muslims know about Jacob's life, would have to be the Torah itself. After all, it is the original source. On the other hand, if the Torah were the *only* source of his account, it should be identical. But it is not.[261] As similar as it is, it is divergent enough for us to wonder why. Throughout the narrative, "from the People of the Book" appears six times in the subheadings. Most likely the *Stories of the Prophets* are in-part a product of oral tradition, as well as a collection of Qur'anic and other Islamic source materials. If this book were a Volume 2, I would be compelled to explore Talmudic and various apocryphal sources.

---

[260] If my estimated timeline of Job's suffering in the Book of Job is correct which calculates to weeks or perhaps months, and certainly less than a year.

[261] The narrative is significantly Islamicized as compared to the Genesis account, replacing "Yahweh" with "Allah." It also changes or leaves out other details as in the time that Jacob wrestled with "a man" but believed he had "seen God" (*Genesis* 32), which text does not say Jacob "wrestled with an angel." Also, in Ibn Kathir's account some of the geographical facts are blatantly wrong. In one place it says that Shechem was actually Jerusalem, which it was not. Another place says that Bethel would become Jerusalem, which it did not ever become. Both those places were north of Jerusalem.

Joseph Yusuf يوسف

If the Qur'an is short on details about the life of Jacob, it has much more to say about Jacob's 11th son, Joseph, the last one born in Haran.[262] In fact, the Qur'an contains an entire surah devoted to his story—surah 12 called "Ya'qub" (which continuous narratives are very *un*characteristic of the Qur'an).[263] Both it and the *Book of Genesis* show that the anonymous writer was wrong on one essential count when s/he said that Jacob "begot comparably usurious, deceitful, conceited offspring." S/he was right on the broad strokes, but s/he overgeneralized. I am confident s/he would admit that s/he neglected to make exception for Joseph. We turn now to his story, first in the Qur'an and then in the Torah's *Book of Genesis*.

Surah 12 contains 111 verses exclusively about Joseph, son of Jacob. It parallels the last 14 chapters of Genesis (37-50, minus chapter 38 which is about his older brother, Judah). In the Islamic *Stories of the Prophets*, Ibn Kathir includes some 22 pages on Surah Yusuf (112) with detailed commentary on all its verses.[264] In the Qur'an the story of Joseph appears abruptly. The preceding surah (11) says nothing about Joseph *or* Jacob, nor do the first ten surahs. But in the Torah's narrative there is a mounting metanarrative, or 'super-narrative' all throughout. Starting with Abraham in *Genesis* 12, it has been gradually building up to the story of Joseph, which seems to be the 'grand finale' of the whole book. So, beginning in *Genesis* 37 the main focus of the narrative shifts from Jacob to Joseph, though Jacob is still part of Joseph's story. Jacob's name still occurs another 33 times until his death at the conclusion of *Genesis* (chapter 50), but Joseph clearly takes center stage. In these final chapters his name occurs 211 times.

---

[262] *Book of Genesis* 30:24-25. Until Benjamin was born in Canaan, Joseph was the youngest son who birth precipitated Jacob's demand of Laban to let him leave.

[263] The only other comparable surah devoted to one continuous narrative is surah 19, or "Maryam", containing the Qur'anic version of the nativity.

[264] https://www.islamguiden.com/arkiv/stories_of_the_prophets.pdf

As with Job, and now Joseph, the pattern I want us to see in both sources is that of ***descent-to-ascent***. Differences between the Qur'an and the Torah aside, they largely agree on the macro-details of the essential storyline. It is beyond debate that Joseph descended into a period of acute suffering before ascending out on the other side. In my evaluation, Joseph's descent was more gut-wrenching even than Job's, and certainly more than his father's. On the other side, his ascent was steeper and markedly more spectacular. Not only did he become a great ruler of Egypt, he also became its *redeemer*—the primary Motif of this book.

The basic outline and many of the general details of Joseph's life in Surah 12 fairly closely match the Torah's. Still, with 26% of the latter's content, it is a highly condensed version of the Torah's fuller and much older, original narrative.[265] Below is my general outline of the macro-details of Joseph's *descent-to-ascent* plotline in chiastic form followed by a more detailed version with references and some of the micro-details in the footnotes.[266]

Life of Joseph, v. 1

a) Young Joseph had a good life with his family in Canaan.
   b) His jealous brothers sold him as property to traders who in-turn took him to Egypt and sold him (age 17).
      c) At first he was in a good place and he prospered, but then ill fortune found him and he was falsely accused of a crime.
         d) He spent the next 10-13 years in prison.
      e) While in prison he gained a reputation for interpreting dreams, and Pharaoh summoned him to interpret his.
   f) Joseph did interpret Pharaoh's dreams, after which he swiftly

---

[265] 111 verses in surah 12 ÷ 416 verses in *Genesis* 37, 39-50 = 26.6%. By number of chapters it is lower—1 ÷ 13 = 7.6%

[266] See wikipedia.org/wiki/Chiastic structure and chiasmusxchange.com/explanatory-notes/

g) brought him out of prison and elevated him to the second highest position in his government (age 30).
h) In this post Joseph had enormous power. He implemented a plan that saved all of Egypt from certain starvation during a famine, as well as his entire family. He reigned for 80 years.[267]

Obviously, the lowest point of Joseph's descent was his heartbreaking imprisonment on false charges **(d)**. Equally obvious, his highest, most radical, and most unexpected path of ascent was from e to f. With this level of generality the Torah and the Qur'an are in near-perfect agreement. Now let's look at the slightly longer and more detailed version including references.

Life of Joseph, v. 2

1) While in Canaan, young Joseph dreams a dream in which his parents and brothers bow down to him. (Qur'an, surah 12:4-7 and *Book of Genesis* 37:5-10)[268]
    2) Due to his dreams and for other reasons, Joseph's brothers become jealous of him and plot to kill him. (Q 12:9-10 and *Gen.* 37:2-4, 8, 10 -11, 18-20)
        3) Instead of killing Joseph, his brothers decide to sell him. (Q 12:9-19 and *Gen.* 37:21-28)
            4) He is purchased by a band of travelers. (Q 12:19-20 and *Gen.* 37:25-28)[269]
                5) They take Joseph to Egypt and he is purchased by an Egyptian. (Q 12:21; *Gen.* 37:28, 36, 39:1)

---

[267] According to *Genesis* 50:26 Joseph died at age 110, so 110 minus 30 = 80. The Qur'an does not tell us Joseph's age at any points of his life.

[268] *Genesis* 37:1 tells us that Jacob and his family lived in Canaan; verse 2 tells us that Joseph had two consecutive dreams at the age of 17.

[269] *Genesis* 37:25, 27-28 tell us that they were Ishmaelites, specifically Midianite traders on their way to Egypt.

6) "The LORD is with Joseph" in this situation. (*Gen.* 39:2a and 3). He is rewarded with "wisdom and knowledge" (Q 12:22)[270]

7) Potiphar recognizes that the LORD is with Joseph who finds favor with him and becomes successful. (*Gen.* 39:2-6)

8) **Potiphar's wife accuses him of attempting to seduce** *her* (Q 12:23-36; *Gen.* 39:6b-20); **Potiphar sends him to prison where he remained for 10-13 years. At this low point we can imagine Joseph's sense of despair.** (Q 12:35 and *Gen.* 39:19-20)[271]

9) But the LORD was with Joseph there and gave him steadfast love and much favor. (*Gen.* 39:21-23; not in Qur'an)[272]

10) While in prison he gained a reputation for interpreting dreams by interpreting the dreams of two of Pharaoh's servants. (Q 12:36-43[273] and *Gen.* chapter 40)

---

[270] *Genesis* 37:36 tells us the buyer's name was Potiphar, while the Qur'anic text does not name him. However, the footnotes in two English versions call him Al-Aziz, or al-Azeez, which one translates as Potiphar, the "chief minister in Egypt". (The Clear Qur'an) The other footnote calls him the "minister in charge of supplies". (Sahih Int'l)

[271] On this point the micro-details between the Qur'an and Torah are noticeably different, although the outcome is the same. In the latter Joseph is imprisoned on Potiphar's belief of his wife's accusation, while in the former he is exonerated but imprisoned anyway for unclear reasons, perhaps on the weight of the gossip and/or the lust of the other women.

[272] Genesis 39:21–23: "But the LORD was with Joseph and showed him steadfast love and gave him favor in the sight of the keeper of the prison. And the keeper of the prison put Joseph in charge of all the prisoners who were in the prison. Whatever was done there, he was the one who did it. The keeper of the prison paid no attention to anything that was in Joseph's charge, because the LORD was with him. And whatever he did, the LORD made it succeed." The Qur'an does not include this passage or anything like it.

[273] Verse 43 in the Clear Qur'an translation has a footnote stating that the term "pharaoh" should have been "king" because the time of Joseph was the Hyksos period that had kings instead of pharaohs. However, in this section of the *Book of Genesis* the two titles are used interchangeably as in chapter 41 and verse 46.

11) In keeping with Joseph's interpretation, one of them (the baker) was killed[274] but the other (the cup-bearer) was restored to his office and later revealed Joseph's gift to the Pharaoh. (Q 12:45 and *Gen.* 41:1-13)

12) When Pharaoh had two dreams of his own he summoned Joseph to interpret them, which he did and was promptly pardoned and elevated to the second highest position in his government. (Q 12:46-56 and *Gen.* 41:37-46)

13) In this exalted position Joseph became God's special instrument of salvation, a type of savior. He implemented a plan that saved all of Egypt from certain starvation during a famine, as well as his entire family. He reigned for 80 years. (Q 12:54-56 and *Gen.* 41:33-56)

14) Thus Joseph, like Job, having descended to his very lowest point, and even lower, had been exalted by the LORD to greatness and to a position of *redeemer*. He had ascended higher than he ever could have imagined. Arguably, he had descended deeper and ascended higher. And, like Job, it was none of his own doing. It was God's. God had redeemed Joseph so that he in turn could become an instrument of redemption.

For some months, while his brothers were coming back and forth to him from Canaan, they did not recognize Joseph who maintained his anonymity. But when he could bare it no longer, he revealed himself to them with deep emotion:

Then Joseph could not control himself before all those who stood by him…And he wept aloud, so that the Egyptians heard it, and the household of Pharaoh heard it. And Joseph said to his brothers, "I am Joseph! Is my father still

---

[274] Strangely, verse 41 states that Joseph told him that he would be "crucified", a form of execution that would not exist for another 1500 years.

alive?" But his brothers could not answer him, for they were dismayed at his presence. (Gen. 45:1-3)

The Qur'an's version is thus:

قَالَ هَلْ عَلِمْتُم مَّا فَعَلْتُم بِيُوسُفَ وَأَخِيهِ إِذْ أَنتُمْ جَـٰهِلُونَ ۝

قَالُوٓا۟ أَءِنَّكَ لَأَنتَ يُوسُفُ ۖ قَالَ أَنَا۠ يُوسُفُ وَهَـٰذَآ أَخِى ۖ قَدْ مَنَّ ٱللَّهُ عَلَيْنَآ ۖ إِنَّهُۥ مَن يَتَّقِ وَيَصْبِرْ فَإِنَّ ٱللَّهَ لَا يُضِيعُ أَجْرَ ٱلْمُحْسِنِينَ ۝

He said, "Do you know what you did with Joseph and his brother when you were ignorant?" They said, "Are you indeed Joseph?" He said "I am Joseph, and this is my brother. Allah has certainly favored us. Indeed, he who fears Allah and is patient, then indeed, Allah does not allow to be lost the reward of those who do good."[275]

How dramatic that must have been! Here is how Joseph understood and described his experience to them, with my bolding.

*So Joseph said to his brothers, "Come near to me, please." And they came near. And he said, "I am your brother, Joseph, whom you sold into Egypt. And now do not be distressed or angry with yourselves because you sold me here, **for God sent me before you <u>to preserve life</u>**. For the famine has been in the land these two years, and there are yet five years in which there will be neither plowing nor harvest. **And God sent me before you to preserve for you a remnant***

---

[275] Surah 12:89-90, Sahih International. legacy.quran.com/12/89-101

on earth, and to keep alive for you many survivors. So it was not you who sent me here, <u>*but God*</u>*.* **He has made me a father to Pharaoh, and lord of all his house and ruler over all the land of Egypt.** *Hurry and go up to my father and say to him, 'Thus says your son Joseph,* **God has made me lord of all Egypt.** (*Genesis* 45:4–9)

Note the sentences that I bolded and underlined. Together they comprise five statements in which Joseph attributes his whole experience to the will and plan of God—to preserve life, especially the progeny of his eleven brothers and presumably his own. Many of the more Reformed sorts of Christians, and others, see the Joseph story as a special example of 'divine providence,' or just providence, although the exact word is nowhere in the scriptures. It's when the invisible 'hand of God' seems to become almost visible, and it becomes apparent that His will is behind the chain of events, usually from a long-range perspective looking back. I don't know if Muslims talk about providence amongst themselves, but I wouldn't be surprised to learn that some do.

Here is the comparable passage from the Qur'an, in my judgment. It's quite different from the Genesis passage, but it does capture Joseph's acknowledgements of God's working as I have bolded.

وَرَفَعَ أَبَوَيْهِ عَلَى ٱلْعَرْشِ وَخَرُّوا۟ لَهُۥ سُجَّدًا ۖ وَقَالَ يَـٰٓأَبَتِ هَـٰذَا تَأْوِيلُ رُءْيَـٰىَ مِن قَبْلُ قَدْ جَعَلَهَا رَبِّى حَقًّا ۖ وَقَدْ أَحْسَنَ بِىٓ إِذْ أَخْرَجَنِى مِنَ ٱلسِّجْنِ وَجَآءَ بِكُم مِّنَ ٱلْبَدْوِ مِنۢ بَعْدِ أَن نَّزَغَ ٱلشَّيْطَـٰنُ بَيْنِى وَبَيْنَ إِخْوَتِىٓ ۚ إِنَّ رَبِّى لَطِيفٌ لِّمَا يَشَآءُ ۚ إِنَّهُۥ هُوَ ٱلْعَلِيمُ ٱلْحَكِيمُ ﴿١٠٠﴾

$$\text{رَبِّ قَدْ ءَاتَيْتَنِى مِنَ ٱلْمُلْكِ وَعَلَّمْتَنِى مِن تَأْوِيلِ ٱلْأَحَادِيثِ ۚ فَاطِرَ ٱلسَّمَـٰوَٰتِ وَٱلْأَرْضِ أَنتَ وَلِىِّۦ فِى ٱلدُّنْيَا وَٱلْـَٔاخِرَةِ ۖ تَوَفَّنِى مُسْلِمًا وَأَلْحِقْنِى بِٱلصَّـٰلِحِينَ ۝}$$

"And he raised his parents upon the throne, and they bowed to him in prostration. And he said, "O my father, this is the explanation of my vision of before. **My Lord has made it reality. And He was certainly good to me when He took me out of prison and brought you [here]** from bedouin life after Satan had induced [estrangement] between me and my brothers. Indeed, **my Lord is Subtle in what He wills. Indeed, it is He who is the Knowing, the Wise. My Lord, You have given me [something] of sovereignty and taught me of the interpretation of dreams.** Creator of the heavens and earth, You are my protector in this world and in the Hereafter. Cause me to die a Muslim and join me with the righteous." [276]

Notice the very last sentence. If you are a Muslim I'm sure you didn't even blink when you came to that. "Of course Joseph was a Muslim," you say, "All the prophets were Muslims." But if you're a Christian or Jew you probably winced. There is no such indication in all of the Torah, nor in the Psalms (Zaboor), nor in any of the Hebrew prophets and writings contained in the Tanakh. Yes, they worshiped one God, Yahweh, but does that make them Muslims? No. There were no Muslims per se and no Islam before the 7th century A.D. From Adam to Jacob we do not have a name for them besides followers of the one true God and general monotheists. Surely being a "Muslim" entails more than that by today's standards. Beginning with Jacob they became known as children of Israel, and then

---

[276] Surah 12:100-101, Sahih International, legacy.quran.com/12/89-101

Hebrews during their Egyptian era. So Jews and Christians see the Qur'an's claim that Joseph was a Muslim as an anachronism and an unjustifiable backwards projection.[277] As for the entire narrative itself, why would God give new revelation for a story that already existed in the Torah at that time? If He did, and if it came from an eternal tablet in heaven, wouldn't it be equal in length instead of only 1/4th as long; and wouldn't it match that of the Torah in every detail? My answer is yes. Therefore, the most plausible source for it was Jewish tradition, i.e. that Muhammad learned it aurally from the Jews themselves in a greatly condensed form. But let's return to the main theological thrust of the narrative.

In the Qur'an, but far better in *Genesis* I believe, Joseph shows his confidence that Almighty God had wisely engineered all of his circumstances in order to bring about His desired results—for the good of Joseph, of the Egyptians, and of *all* the people of Israel. He probably could not foresee any of this while he was in prison, not until he had ascended to an unimaginable level of rulership. We recall that, at the young age of 17, he had had those mysterious, prophetic dreams before his initial descent, but we have no reason to suppose that the LORD had revealed the whole plan to him. So Joseph did not know that He would rescue/redeem him, and he did not know that He would make him a great redeemer himself. But that is exactly what Joseph became in a temporal sense.

As with Job, Joseph's story gives us insights into the character and faith of a godly man in the throes of suffering. It also raises similar questions about the problem of evil, and I think with similar answers. But most of all I think it teaches us about God. Clearly from this example and most of the others we've considered in this book, God is not *un*willing to allow his prophets and saints to suffer in order to accomplish something higher and better *through* them, *for* them,

---

[277] Another noteworthy difference between the two narratives is that Surah 12 portrays Jacob as having been blind and having his sight restored when someone casts Joseph's shirt over his face (vv. 93-96). In *Genesis* this is not in the text. There are many others, including a wolf in the Qur'an (13, 14, 17) vs. the "fierce animal" in *Genesis,* and Joseph's lack of the many-colored coat in the Qur'an (*Genesis* 37:3, 23, 32).

and for the whole world to come. The Tanakh's *Book of Psalms* testifies to this when the prophet-king David[278] wrote…

> *I will remember the deeds of the LORD;*
> > *yes, I will remember your wonders of old.*
>
> *I will ponder all your work,*
> > *and meditate on your mighty deeds.*
>
> *Your way, O God, is holy.*
> > *What god is great like our God?*
>
> *You are the God who works wonders;*
> > *you have made known your might among the peoples.*
>
> **You with your arm redeemed your people,**
> > **the children of Jacob and Joseph.**
>
> Psalm 77:11–15

And in the very next *Psalm*...

> *We will not hide them from their children,*
> > *but tell to the coming generation*
>
> *the glorious deeds of the LORD, and his might,*
> > *and the wonders that he has done.*
>
> *He established a testimony in Jacob*
> > *and appointed a law in Israel,*
>
> *which he commanded our fathers*
> > *to teach to their children,*
>
> *that the next generation might know them,*
> > *the children yet unborn,*
>
> *and arise and tell them to their children,*
> > *so that they should set their hope in God*
>
> *and not forget the works of God.*
>
> Psalm 78:4-7

---

[278] The Apostle Peter calls David a prophet in the Book of Acts 2:30. Bolding mine.

And in *Psalm 105*...

> *When he summoned a famine on the land*
> > *and broke all supply of bread,*
> *he had sent a man ahead of them,*
> > *Joseph, who was sold as a slave.*
> *His feet were hurt with fetters;*
> > *his neck was put in a collar of iron;*
> *until what he had said came to pass,*
> > *the word of the LORD tested him.*
> *The king sent and released him;*
> > *the ruler of the peoples set him free;*
> *he made him lord of his house*
> > *and ruler of all his possessions,*
> *to bind his princes at his pleasure-*
> > *and to teach his elders wisdom.*
> *Then Israel came to Egypt;*
> > *Jacob sojourned in the land of Ham.*
> *And the LORD made his people very fruitful*
> > *and made them stronger than their foes.*

Psalm 105:16-24

Although David was a prophet, he did not need God to reveal all this to him by 'divine download'. It was all facts of Jewish history. It was knowledge preserved in the collective memory of what became the Jewish people. But it was also preserved in scripture for them and everyone since then to this present day.

Speaking of King David, the scriptural narratives of his life tell us that he endured his own descent before his ascent. This part of his story is found in the Tanakh's books of *1 Samuel* chapter 16 through *2 Samuel* chapter 1. There we learn that God had chosen him as the new king to replace King Saul, only Saul was not dead yet and he felt insanely threatened by David. So before the young David could actually take the throne, he was hunted by Saul for seven years and chased into exile. Before becoming the most beloved and revered prophet-king in Israel's history he had to suffer, to descend. Indeed, he narrowly escaped death multiple times. He's yet another example of the unmistakable pattern in biblical history.

By now my point is abundantly clear. The *Descent-to-Ascent Motif* is a fixed feature in the Hebrew scriptures that resounds and reverberates through the long halls of the Tanakh. And it is the framework of the *Redemption Motif.* These Motifs were not intended to go unnoticed in ancient biblical history, nor were they intended for their immediate readers only. They were also intended for the people of the New Testament era thousands of years later, the time of Jesus and his Apostles. This is partly why the Jews understood redemption, and why we can understand it today, thousands of years later still. As with *Job-as-redeemer*, certainly Almighty God had us in mind when he orchestrated the dramatic events of Joseph—and Jacob, and Moses, and Abraham, and Noah, and Jonah, and all the Old Testament saints who experienced this kind of suffering, which was pretty much all of them. It's a recognizable pattern that had its immediate purpose in each saint's life and time, and it had collective *long-range* import for the people of first-century Palestine. There are two passages in the New Testament of the Bible that say exactly that:

> **For whatever was written in former days was written for our instruction,** *that through endurance and through the encouragement of the Scriptures we might have hope.*
>
> New Testament, *Book of Romans* 15:4

> **Now these things took place as examples for us,** *that we might not desire evil as they did.* ... [they] **happened to them as an example, but they were written down for our instruction,** *on whom the end of the ages has come. Therefore let anyone who thinks that he stands take heed lest he fall.* (Bible, New Testament, *1 Corinthians* 10:6, 11, 12)

It is on this principle I am asserting that the main reason for the story of Job is for later generations.

Chapter 13

The Prophet-Messiah Jesus
– The Ultimate Redeemer Motif

Throughout this book, so far I have made only passing references to Jesus. It is now time to shine the spotlight on him. There are thousands of years between Jesus and Job, and the other prophets or saints I have been focusing on. But Jesus had all of their best features in common. So the thesis of this chapter is exactly that. Jesus was the ultimate object to which all the previous figures pointed, whether explicitly or by virtue of their Motifs. The very purpose of the *descent-to-ascent Redeemer Motif* that so prominently characterizes the *Book of Job,* as well as the other prophet-saints we have looked at, was to give us the *Messiah Motif,* which was ultimately personified by Jesus. Therefore, the main purpose of the *Book of Job* is to prefigure Jesus the Messiah in the New Testament, including the gospels, *Acts,* and all the epistles. Yes, I am a Christian, and Christians believe Jesus was more than a prophet and Messiah, but not less. He was at once Son of God, a king, God incarnate, prophet, and Messiah.

In early first-century Israel, this idea was eventually embraced by the thousands of Jews who became Christ-followers, or Christians. This was made possible, in part, because of the existing Messiah Motif and its subordinate motifs, some of which we call *types,* with the corresponding branch of study called *typology.* Through multiple types, there was a messiah-shaped space carved into their worldview to make room in their hearts for the true Messiah when he would finally arrive. They had been collectively introduced to his profile by these types and by their accompanying prophecies, so they had been trained to wait and yearn for him for centuries. There was an Adam type, a Noah type, an Abraham type, a Joseph-type, a Moses-type, a David-type, and yes, a Job-type. We can see this in the inspired writings of the Bible's New Testament which is saturated and 'hyperlinked'[279] with references to the Tanakh with its many types and motifs. So there is enormous continuity between the Tanakh and the New Testament which, following a 'silent period,' emerged 400 years after the last prophet's book in the Tanakh, *Malachi*.

Adam   Αδάμ

In the New Testament, **Adam** is mentioned seven times in seven verses, in five different books by three inspired writers including the genealogy of Jesus in the *Gospel of Luke* chapter 3, three letters of Apostle Paul, and the *Epistle of Jude*.[280] Jesus never spoke of Adam himself. but in the *Book of Romans* Paul spoke of him as a "type" of the one who was to come:

> *Yet death reigned from **Adam** to Moses, even over those whose sinning was not like the transgression of Adam, who was a **type** of the one who was to come.* (5:14)

The next verse makes it clear who Paul was speaking of:

> *But the free gift is not like the trespass. For if many died through one man's trespass, much more have the grace of God and the free gift by the grace of that one man Jesus Christ abounded for many.* (v. 15)

In his next epistle Paul states this idea even more succinctly:

> *For as in **Adam** all die, so also in Christ shall all be made alive.* (1 Corinthians 15:22)

Noah   Νώε

Noah appears 8 times in the New Testament. These include five times in two of the four gospels, all but once from the lips of Jesus

---

[279] I got this idea from Dr. Jordan Peterson in part 1 of his lecture series on Genesis.

[280] *Luke* 3:38, *Romans* 5:14, *1 Corinthians* 15:22 and 45, *1 Timothy* 2:13-14, and *Jude* 14

himself, which are parallel passages in *Matthew* 24:37-38 and *Luke* 17:26-27. Here is the latter verse:

> *For as the lightning flashes and lights up the sky from one side to the other, so will the Son of Man be in his day. But first he must suffer many things and be rejected by this generation. Just as it was in the days of **Noah**, so will it be in the days of the Son of Man.*

The rest appear in the *Letter to the Hebrews*[281] and the two epistles of Apostle Peter.[282]

Abraham   Αβραάμ

Abraham is very prominent in the New Testament with 69 appearances of his name. 29 of them are in the four of the gospels, 15 of which come from the lips of Jesus himself.[283] Two very profound examples come from the *Gospel of John* and *Romans:*

> *Your father Abraham rejoiced that he would see my day. He saw it and was glad." So the Jews said to him, "You are not yet fifty years old, and have you seen Abraham?" Jesus said to them, "Truly, truly, I say to you, before Abraham was, I am."* (8:56-58)

> *Abraham "believed God, and it was counted to him as righteousness."* (4:3, *Galatians* 3:6, and *James* 2:23)

---

[281] The exact writer is disputed. The highest candidates are the Apostle Paul, Apollos, and Barnabas, Clement of Rome, and Luke. See britannica.com/topic/Letter-to-the-Hebrews and wikipedia.org/wiki/Authorship_of_the_Epistle_to_the_Hebrews. By comparison, none of the transcribers of the Qur'an (those who put ink to paper) are known, or certainly not all of them. In actuality they are anonymous in principle, i.e. they are not supposed to be known.

[282] *Hebrews* 11:7, *1 Peter* 3:20, and *2 Peter* 2:5

[283] Five of these are embedded in the story of Lazarus and the rich man that Jesus told in the *Gospel of Luke* chapter 16, two from the lips of the rich man appealing to Abraham to give him relief in hades, and to send someone to warn his five living brothers.

The remaining 40 occurrences are found in 7 books and letters by 5 of the inspired New Testament writers.[284]

Moses   Μωϋσῆς

Moses surpasses even Abraham appearing a whopping 77 times: 36 times in the four gospels, 18 of which come from the lips of Jesus himself (including parallel passages). The single book that contains the most references to Moses is the *Book of Acts* with 19. The remaining 22 appear in the epistles, including 4 in *Romans* and 11 in *Hebrews*.[285] The following short passage is from the *Gospel of Mark* when, 1500 years after Moses had expired (or was possibly taken up), he was seen in an 'impossible' meeting with Jesus and the prophet Elijah (dead 800 years) atop a mountain (a Judean hill).

And there appeared to them Elijah with Moses, and they were talking with Jesus. (Mark 9:4)

When I wrote this section a dear Muslim doctor friend named Ibrahim and I had been studying this gospel together by text message. We had just come to this passage and I asked him what he made of it. He said that [This] would have been an amazing sight. Jesus's supremacy was underscored among Elijah and Moses. This is certainly a text that lays claim to his unique status. Luke adds that they "appeared in glory and spoke of his departure, which he was about to accomplish at Jerusalem." (v. 31) Apparently Moses and Elijah knew the plan and they were both in on it.

David   Δαβίδ

---

[284] *The Book of Acts* (8), *The Book of Romans* (9), *The 2nd Letter to the Corinthians* (1), *The Letter to the Galatians* (8), *The Book of Hebrews* (11), *The Epistle of James* (2), and *The First Epistle of Peter* (1). For all 69 specific citations type this URL into your browser: www.esv.org/search/?q=Abraham&sort=reference&phrase=yes&forms=yes&source=bible&product=&category=&book=Matthew-Revelation&page=4

[285] *1 Corinthians* 9:9 and 10:2, *2 Corinthians* 3:13 and 15, *2 Timothy* 3:8, *Jude* 9, and *Revelation* 15:3.

David the prophet-king appears 53 times in 9 of the 27 New Testament books, including all four gospels, *Acts*, two of Paul's epistles, the *Book of Hebrews*, and *Revelation*. Including parallel passages, Jesus spoke of David 11 times. To me, one of his most interesting statements is found in the *Book of Revelation* chapter 22:16 where the ascended, heavenly Jesus says to John the Apostle:

> *"I, Jesus, have sent my angel to testify to you about these things for the churches. I am the root and the descendant of **David**, the bright morning **star**."*

This last phrase seems to me as a reference to the Torah's *Book of Numbers* 24, the fourth book of five. As we saw in an earlier chapter, the pagan prophet Balaam prophesied thus in his third and final oracle towards the people of Israel (v.17a):

> *I see him, but not now;*
>   *I behold him, but not near:*
> *a **star** shall come out of Jacob,*
>   *and a scepter shall rise out of Israel;*

Many Christians and some Jews have understood this as a messianic prophecy foretelling the coming of the Messiah.[286] In

---

[286] See biblehub.com/commentaries/numbers/24-17.htm, and evidenceunseen.com/bible-difficulties-2/ot-difficulties/genesis-deuteronomy/num-2417-does-this-passage-predict-jesus/, and chabad.org/library/bible_cdo/aid/9952/showrashi/true/jewish/Chapter-24.htm, and Ramban as follows: "[I]n this fourth prophecy Balaam continued [on the future] and saw the Messianic era; therefore he spoke of it as a very distant event, saying, *I see him, but not now; I behold him, but not nigh*, [a phrase] which he did not use [before]. He stated that this is the purpose of G-d which He had planned, to come to pass *in the end of days…*" Ramban goes on to say, "Because the Messiah will gather together the dispersed of Israel from all the corners of the earth, Balaam compares him [metaphorically] to *a star* that passes through the firmament from the ends of heaven, just as it is said about [the Messiah]: *and behold, there came with the clouds of heaven, one like unto a son of man* etc. *(Daniel 7:13)*. Balaam thus said that he saw that at a distant time *a star* would pass from the ends of heaven, and there would rise out of it the sceptre of a ruler… (sefaria.org/Numbers.24?lang=bi&with= Ramban&lang2=en) Another Jewish understanding of this passage is that it refers to King David, e.g. Ibn Ezra in sefaria.org/Numbers.24?lang=bi&with= Ibn%20Ezra&lang2=en. Still others understand it simply as "Good fortune will rise" upon Israel, e.g. Rafi in sefaria.org/ Numbers.24?lang=bi&with=Rashi&lang2=en.

this understanding, the star also seems to foreshadow the star of Bethlehem that is recorded by Apostle Matthew in chapter 2 of his gospel (vv. 2, 7, 9, 10). His narrative says that an unspecified number of "wise men" or perhaps kings from the East (literally Greek μάγοι = "magi" possibly from Persia) followed a "star" or a star-like appearance that led them to Bethlehem where they would find the young Messiah they were searching for (Greek χριστὸς = Christ); "king of the Jews" they called him (Greek = βασιλεὺς τῶν Ἰουδαίων) which is why King Herod felt so threatened by their appearance. Having discovered him, Matthew tells us, the wise men *rejoiced,* and *worshiped* him.

> *Now after Jesus was born in Bethlehem of Judea in the days of Herod the king, behold, wise men from the east came to Jerusalem, [2] saying, "Where is he who has been born king of the Jews? For we saw his star when it rose and have come to worship him."…[9] And behold, the star that they had seen when it rose went before them until it came to rest over the place where the child was. [10] When they saw the star, they rejoiced exceedingly with great joy. [11]* **And going into the house, they saw the child with Mary his mother, and they fell down and worshiped him.** *Then, opening their treasures, they offered him gifts, gold and frankincense and myrrh.*[287]

I realize it may seem that I strayed from my focus on King David. But I wanted to follow the trail that the star presented us in *Revelation* 22:16. There Jesus says **1)** He's the descendent of David the prophet-king from Bethlehem, where Jesus also was born according to prophecy (Prophet *Micah* 5:2). Obviously, a descendent of a king has royal blood, and the firstborn male descendent of a king is himself a rightful heir to the throne. **2)** He calls himself the "bright and morning star." Unlike the star of Bethlehem,

---

[287] *Gospel of Matthew* 2:11. Bolding mine.

certainly this is a metaphor, but so is the star prophesied by Balaam in *Numbers* 24:17 from which, he said, a "scepter" would emerge, a ruler, a king. It's hard not to see these as 'micro-motifs' and as puzzle pieces that fit together. We could call this *messianic complementarity*, or *messianic intertextuality*.

. . . .

Having highlighted five figures of the Tanakh so far, let's save Joseph for the next chapter, then Jonah again, and Job himself for the chapter after that.

Now I would like to look at some of the key theological terms we have discussed thus far, highlighting just five—**redemption, sacrifice, forgiveness, salvation,** and **suffering.** They overlap. These, along with some of their accompanying ideas, are enormous concepts spanning both testaments, Old and New. Even when these words are absent from a particular section of scripture, their meanings are embedded throughout the collective books of the library that comprises the Bible, tying them all together into one grand theological metanarrative. In spite of the unreasonable post-modern aversion to metanarratives, they are hard to dismiss entirely, whether from belief systems or histories. The Bible claims to contain one of the most timeless, coherent, and far-reaching metanarratives of all religions.

Redemption גְּאֻלָּה λύτρωσιν كُنْتُمْ تَعْلَمُونَ

These are words we covered in depth in chapter 5 as they appear in the Tanakh. As we noted there, as huge a motif as it is in the Tanakh, "Redeemer" appears in the New Testament only once, in the *Book of Acts* chapter 7 and verse 35, in reference to Moses.[288] But

---

[288] The writer of *Acts* is nearly universally believed to be Luke who was also the author of the *Gospel of Luke*. Luke was a companion of Paul the Apostle and a first-rate inspired historian in his own right. His writings were considered as divine revelation by the early church and by all true Christians to this day. One of the superlative virtues of the *Book of Acts* is its historical accuracy, accumulating no less than 84 confirmed geo-political facts as document-

the word **"redemption"** is more abundant in the New Testament because its purpose is to explicate pre-Christian motifs. It appears 9 times in 6 books and letters by 3 inspired writers, including once from the lips of Jesus when he was prophesying his return at the time of the final judgment of the world (*Gospel of Luke* 21:28). The rest appear in Apostle Paul's *Epistles to the Romans, 1 Corinthians, Ephesians, Colossians*, and once in the *Book of Hebrews*.[289] Paul's epistle to the Ephesians states:

> *In him [Jesus] we have redemption through his blood, the forgiveness of our trespasses, according to the riches of his grace...* (1:7)

This verse reveals that redemption = the forgiveness of our trespasses, which are sins, the outflow of sin itself, the literal infection that causes people to commit them. And the writer of the *Book of Hebrews* reveals:

> *But when Christ appeared as a high priest...he entered once for all into the holy places, not by means of the blood of goats and calves but by means of his own blood, thus securing an eternal* **redemption**. (9:11a and 12)

This verse teaches that there is an <u>eternal</u> redemption made possible by the blood of Christ. I realize that this idea is objectionable to both Jews and Muslims, but it is at the very core of Christian and New Testament theology, and indispensable. It is premised on the equally indispensable idea of sacrifice.

Sacrifice   קרבן   ὁλοκαυτεῖν   أُضْحِية

---

ed by the late near-eastern archaeologist Sir William Ramsay. Strangely, the content of *Acts* is wholly absent from the Qur'an which seems entirely indifferent to the development of the early Christian church and the activities of Jesus's Apostles.

[289] *Romans 3:24* and *8:23, 1 Corinthians 1:30, Ephesians 1:7* and *4:30, Colossians 1:14*, and *Hebrews 9:12*.

This word appears 18 times in the New Testament, 14 of them in reference to the animal sacrifices practiced since the time of Adam and later instituted by Moses in the Torah. These appear in two of the four gospels from the lips of Jesus (*Matthew* 9:13 and 12:7; *Luke* 2:24), 3 in Apostle Paul's epistles (*1 Corinthians, Ephesians,* and *Philippians*) and 7 in the *Letter to the Hebrews*.[290] "Offering" as in burnt offerings which were animal sacrifices appears 7 times in one gospel from the lips of Jesus (*Luke* 5:14), and 2 of the other inspired writers. (*Book of Acts* 21:26 and the *Letter to the Hebrews* 10:10, 11, 14, 18, and 11:17).[291]

The word **"sin"** or **"sins"** appears a striking 104 times in the New Testament in all but 7 of the 27 inspired books and letters.[292] These include 26 times from the lips of Jesus in the four gospels (including all parallel references), 38 in Paul's *Letter to the Romans*, and 11 in the *Letter to the Hebrews*. So all the NT writers talk about sin in one or more of their inspired writings, and even the books that don't contain the word still have the concept. (By comparison, it occurs 285 times in the Tanakh.) Therefore, sin and sins is an enormously important idea in both the Old and New Testaments of the Bible. Indeed, it is the central problem in humanity, not the oneness of God as it is in Islam. Human sin is the universal problem which the LORD God has expended all of his effort to resolve for the benefit of individuals and for all humanity.

Forgiveness סְלִיחוֹת ἄφεσιν مغفرة

---

[290] For all 18 citations type this URL into your browser: https://www.esv.org/search/?q=sacrifice&sort=reference&phrase=yes&*forms*=yes&source=bible&product=&category=&book=Matthew-Revelation

[291] This last verse also contains one of the abundant references to Abraham in reference to the near-sacrifice of his son Isaac, which we have previously discussed. (cf. Torah, *Book of Genesis* 22)

[292] Those that do not contain the word "sin" include the Apostle Paul's Letters to the Philippians and Colossians, 1 and 2 Thessalonians, 2 Timothy, and 2 and 3 John. For all citations type this URL into your browser: esv.org/search/?q=sin&sort=reference&phrase= yes& forms=yes&source=bible&product=&category=&book=Matthew-Revelation&page=5

What person would claim that he/she has never been in need of forgiveness, even from other people? This fundamental word appears only twice in the Tanakh, but 16 times in the New Testament, in all four gospels, 5 of which are from the lips of Jesus himself. Then it appears 5 times in the *Book of Acts*, twice in the inspired writings of Apostle Paul, and twice more in the *Book of Hebrews*. But don't be fooled by the apparent sparsity of this word. Because of the enormous 'pandemic' of sin, divine forgiveness is the essential remedy.[293] In chapter 10 of the *Book of Acts*, the sequel to Luke's gospel, Luke records these words of Apostle Peter. On this occasion he was preaching the message of forgiveness to a household of God-fearing gentiles, during which the Holy Spirit was poured out upon them, we are told.[294]

> *To him* [Jesus] *all the prophets bear witness that everyone who believes in him receives forgiveness of sins through his name.* (v. 43)

There is no 'vaccine' to prevent the 'disease' per se, only treatment, and an ultimate *cure* for those who will accept it on God's terms and conditions.[295] But the concept emerges under multiple words, one of which is our central Motif of *Redemption*. It also comes under the second word "salvation", a concept that is very similar to redemption and used by Christians almost synonymously and are both huge themes in the entire Bible.

---

[293] Gospels of *Matthew* 26:28, *Mark* 1:4, and 3:29, *Luke* 1:77, 3:3, and *24:47*, *John* 20:23, plus *Acts* 2:38, 5:31, 10:43, 13:38, and 26:18, *Ephesians* 1:7, *Colossians* 1:14, *Hebrews* 9:22 and 10:18.

[294] The Holy Spirit is enormously prominent throughout the Old and New Testaments, especially in the *Book of Acts*. In many places the scriptures state that the Holy Spirit speaks to people as He did in chapter 13:2, 20:23 (testifies), 21:11, and 28:25. In chapter 13:4 we are told that the Holy Spirit "sent out" the Apostle Paul and Barnabas, and in 15:28 that a certain decision "seemed good to the Holy Spirit." Lastly, in chapter 16:6 the Holy Spirit forbade Paul and his companions to preach in Asia. So in these seven verses the Holy Spirit speaks, testifies, sends out, approves, and forbids. These are personal verbs that require a person to perform them, one reason why the Holy Spirit is believed to be a person by Christians, i.e. the third person of the trinity.

[295] I wrote this during the second year of the Covid-19 pandemic in 2021 when there was an enormous amount of frenzy over the available vaccines, who got one and who didn't, etc.

Salvation יְשׁוּעָה σωτηρία ٱلْمُفْلِحُونَ

"Salvation" shows up 128 times in the Tanakh, and 41 times in the New Testament by every inspired writer except Matthew and Mark.[296] And like redemption and other biblical concepts, the idea appears in many places even where the word doesn't, as in the story of Joseph, and Jacob too for that matter. But Jacob was the only person in *Genesis* to speak of it, prophetically, not long before he died (49:18). Even though "salvation" occurs three times more in the Tanakh, it's also a lot bigger, so the relative proportion of the word's occurrences in the New Testament is slightly higher.[297] Here is a significant passage containing the word twice in a way that is very relevant to our study:

> *Though you have not seen him, you love him. Though you do not now see him, you believe in him and rejoice with joy that is inexpressible and filled with glory, obtaining the outcome of your faith, the **salvation of your souls**. Concerning this **salvation**, the prophets who prophesied about the grace that was to be yours searched and inquired carefully, inquiring what person or time the Spirit of Christ in them was indicating when he predicted the sufferings of Christ and the subsequent glories. It was revealed to them that they were serving not themselves but you. (Epistle of 1 Peter 1:8-12)*

This contains the same idea as the two passages at the end of the last chapter, that the divine revelation received by the prophets and saints of the Tanakh, and all the divinely orchestrated events recorded, were all pointing toward a future salvation that would be actualized in the early years of the New Testament—done so by

---

[296] *Luke* 1:69, 1:77, 2:30, 3:6, and 19:9; *John* 4:22; *Acts* 4:12, 7:25, 13:26, 13:47, 16:17, and 28:28; *Romans* 1:16, 11:11, and 13:11; *2 Corinthians* 1:6, 6:2 and 7:10; *Ephesians* 1:13 and 6:17; *Philippians* 1:28 and 2:12; *1 Thessalonians* 5:8-9; *2 Timothy* 2:10 and 3:15; *Titus* 2:11; *Hebrews* 1:14, 2:3, 2:10, 5:9 and 6:9; *1 Peter* 1:5, 9-10 and 2:2; *2 Peter* 3:15; *Jude* 3; *Revelation* 7:10 and 12:10. All bolding mine.

[297] There are 7957 verses in the New Testament compared to 31, 102 in the Tanakh, or Old Testament. The word "salvation" occurs .05% in the former compared to .04% in the latter.

the suffering of Christ around 30 AD. In fact, I confess that from one of those passages I skipped over an important part that concurs with the passage above and which I will include now:

> *For I do not want you to be unaware, brothers, that our fathers were all under the cloud, and all passed through the sea, and all were baptized into Moses in the cloud and in the sea, and all ate the same spiritual food, and all drank the same spiritual drink. For they drank from the spiritual Rock that followed them, and the Rock was Christ. ...We must not put Christ to the test, as some of them did and were destroyed by serpents...*
>
> 1 Corinthians 10:1–4, 9

It should be obvious that this passage, and the one before it, are sort of 'reverse prophesying' if there is such a thing. That is, the two inspired writers prophetically interpreted Christ into the ancient events of which they wrote, respectively. In the latter example immediately above, the Apostle Paul said essentially that Christ had been present with the Israelite people as they wandered through the desert with Moses, that he followed them, and that he was the "spiritual rock" from which they got water everywhere they camped. In the former passage the Apostle Peter said that as far back as 1500 years earlier, the various Hebrew prophets had prophesied by the *Spirit of Christ* about the grace that the post-resurrection believers would much later experience as a result of the sufferings and glories of Christ.[298] This is another profound example of intertestamental continuity.

This brings us to suffering itself.

Suffering　צָרָתָם　παθεῖν　معاناة

---

[298] The "sufferings" refers to the trial and voluntary execution of Jesus, while the "glories" refers to his resurrection from the dead three days later. So by "post-resurrection believers" I mean those disciples and others who put their faith in Jesus as Lord and Savior *after* his resurrection, and because of it.

As we have seen demonstratively, suffering is a very prominent theme and motif in the Tanakh. Even so, the word "suffering" (Hebrew: saratam) only occurs four times with reference to intense and/or prolonged pain that must be endured,[299] and the verb form 21 times. In the New Testament, besides the prior example in *1 Peter*, "sufferings" (plural) occurs 11 more times in the inspired writings of the Apostles Peter and Paul plus one in the *Book of Hebrews*.[300] "Suffering" (singular) appears 16 times in 10 of the 27 books and letters by 6 inspired authors.[301] The verb "suffer" (παθεῖν / pathein) is found 32 times. Evidently Jesus never used either the singular or plural forms of "suffering" in his teaching and discourses; or if he did it was not recorded *per se*.[302] Still, he talked about his impending suffering *a lot*. Nine of the occurrences of "suffer" are found in the four gospels, seven of which are from the lips of Jesus, the other two are narrator comments from the Apostle Matthew and from Mark the disciple of Apostle Peter, and all are in reference to Jesus himself. Five of the seven were stated before the Passion events, and two after.[303] Allow me to list them here with my own commentary on some of them:

> ***Matthew* 16:21** – *From that time Jesus began to show his disciples that he must go to Jerusalem and **suffer** many things from the elders and chief priests and scribes, and be killed, and on the third day be raised.*
>
> –Apostle Matthew

Jesus knew, and he wanted them to know.

---

[299] My attempt at a simple and concise definition.

[300] *Romans* 5:3 and 8:18, *2 Corinthians* 1:5-7, *Philippians* 3:10, *Colossians* 1:24, *2 Timothy* 3:11, *Hebrews* 10:32, *1 Peter* 1:11, *1 Peter* 4:13, *1 Peter* 5:1

[301] *Gospel of Matthew* 8:6, *Acts* 1:3, *Romans* 5:3, *Ephesians* 3:13, *2 Thessalonians* 1:5, *2 Timothy* 1:8, 2:3, 2:9, and 4:5, *Hebrews* 2:9 and 10, *James* 5:10 and 13, *1 Peter* 2:19 and 5:9, and *2 Peter* 2:13. However, it is translated from multiple Greek words and so carries multiple related meanings and connotations.

[302] According to the Apostle John, *"Now there are also many other things that Jesus did. Were every one of them to be written, I suppose that the world itself could not contain the books that would be written."* (*Gospel of John* chapter 21:25) This would presumably apply also to Jesus's words according to common sense.

[303] The events immediately surrounding and including Jesus's execution and resurrection.

***Matthew* 17:12** – *"But I tell you that Elijah has already come, and they did not recognize him, but did to him whatever they pleased. So also the Son of Man will certainly **suffer** at their hands."* –Jesus

---

***Mark* 8:31** – *And he began to teach them that the Son of Man must **suffer** many things and be rejected by the elders and the chief priests and the scribes and be killed, and after three days rise again.* –Mark

---

***Mark* 9:12** – *And he said to them, "Elijah does come first to restore all things. And how is it written of the Son of Man that he should **suffer** many things and be treated with contempt?"* –Jesus

---

***Luke* 9:22** – ..."*The Son of Man must **suffer** many things and be rejected by the elders and chief priests and scribes, and be killed, and on the third day be raised."* –Jesus

---

***Luke* 17:24-25** – *"For as the lightning flashes and lights up the sky from one side to the other, so will the Son of Man be in his day. But first he must **suffer** many things and be rejected by this generation."* –Jesus

This passage from *the Gospel of Luke* 17 is especially interesting, to which a parallel is found in *Matthew* 24. In the next five verses Jesus spoke of Noah (and Lot) and their surrounding events as prototypes of himself in his context:

> ***"Just as it was in the days of Noah, so will it be in the days of the Son of Man.*** *They were eating and drinking and marrying and being given in marriage, until the day when Noah entered the ark, and the flood came and destroyed them all. Likewise, just as it was in the days of Lot—they were eating and drinking, buying and selling, planting and building, but on the day when Lot went out from Sodom, fire and sulfur rained from heaven and*

> *destroyed them all—so will it be on the day when the Son of Man is revealed."*³⁰⁴   —Jesus (vv. 26-30)

*This is a superb example of intertextuality, or the intertestamental relationship of scripture, precisely the kind that this book has been developing, albeit with special reference to Job.

> ***Luke* 22:14-15** – *And when the hour came, he reclined at table, and the apostles with him. And he said to them, "I have earnestly desired to eat this Passover with you before I **suffer**."* —Jesus

This too is an interesting passage for somewhat different reasons. These words of Jesus were from the well-known Last Supper that all four gospel writers include. Four sentences later Jesus spoke these famous words to express the *telos* (τέλος), the purpose or end goal of his suffering:

> *And he took bread, and when he had given thanks, he broke it and gave it to them, saying, "This is my body, which is given for you. Do this in remembrance of me." And likewise the cup after they had eaten, saying, "This cup that is poured out for you is the new covenant in my blood."*³⁰⁵
> —Jesus (vv. 19-20)

The Apostle Matthew, who would have been there in person, records that Jesus added, "…for the forgiveness of sins." (v. 28b)

By every indication, then, Jesus evidently knew what was about to happen to him, and *why*. It was to initiate something called a "new covenant." This covenant even had a ritual attached to it. Forever after, Jesus's people were to commemorate the event symbolically, which all do today. (I ask, since Muslims claim to follow

---

³⁰⁴ Although Noah can be considered a prophet, no Christians consider Lot as a prophet to my knowledge. But he was "righteous" according to the Apostle Peter (*2 Peter* 2:7).

³⁰⁵ Also recorded in Matthew's Gospel chapter 26:26-29, in Mark's chapter 14:22-25.

the teachings of Jesus, why do they not practice this?) Neither Job nor Joseph knew the reason for their sufferings beforehand, but clearly Jesus did. By his own words, his suffering—his execution—was *the plan*. But how could he have known what other prophets were not given to know? Well, because he *knew* both the plan and the future. Even though there was one thing he said he did not know about the specific day and hour of the apocalypse,[306] he knew everything else. So his purpose was never to be an unwilling victim, nor was he to be rescued by divine subterfuge to deceive not only his enemies but also his followers, and even his mother. Rather, he was to be a fully-aware and fully-willing participant in the divine master plan to destroy the devil and all the powers of evil and sin in this troubled world.[307]

How did Jesus know this plan? First, he knew it because he was a collaborator in it. According to his own teaching he had been with the Father from all eternity, from "before the foundation of the world."[308] Second, he knew it because, as a man born into the world as a child (yes, miraculously), the Father "showed" Jesus his activities, which were even "seen" by him.[309] Third, he knew it because the prophets had foretold it. But this was not a private knowledge as were the previous two categories, it was a public knowledge that would have been known by all Jews who were reasonably well versed in the Hebrew scriptures. It was also knowable by some privileged non-Jews such as the Babylonian or Persian

---

[306] *Gospel of Mark* 13:32: "But concerning that day or that hour, no one knows, not even the angels in heaven, nor the Son, but only the Father. See * in note 290.

[307] *First Epistle of John* 3:8b: "The reason the Son of God appeared was to destroy the works of the devil."

[308] *Gospel of John* 17:5: "And now, Father, glorify me in your own presence with the glory that I had with you before the world existed." (See also v. 24)

[309] *Gospel of John* 5:19 and 20: "So Jesus said to them, *'Truly, truly, I say to you, the Son can do nothing of his own accord, but only what he sees the Father doing. For whatever the Father does, that the Son does likewise. For the Father loves the Son and shows him all that he himself is doing.'"* *Yes, Jesus could be "shown" things. Even as an eternal and divine being who was privy to eternal knowledge, as a simultaneous man he appeared to have had some isolated limits to his knowledge. This is owing to his full humanness in which some knowledge was 'partitioned' if you will, as in a computer.

magi who crossed the desert to worship him as a small child.[310] Messianic prophecies were accessible to all.

Finally, the words on the next page were given by Jesus *after* his death and resurrection; so logically they were not predictive as the previous seven are. He spoke them in a discourse with some of his disciples while traveling together, and it is an example of Jesus looking back "over his shoulder" if you will. It is a very interesting episode that is reported only by Luke, protégé of Apostle Paul and a 'revelatory historian' as I will call him. Basically, while these two disciples were walking together to a town called Emmaus, talking about the tragic events of the last three days, Jesus appeared to them 'incognito.' That is, he did not identify himself and they were prevented from recognizing him until they reached their destination and had a meal together. During the whole journey Jesus acted like he was unaware of the events and invited them to tell him about them, after which he said the following:

> **Luke 24:25-27, 46** – *And he said to them, "O foolish ones, and slow of heart to believe all that the prophets have spoken! Was it not necessary that the Christ should **suffer** these things and enter into his glory?" And beginning with Moses and all the Prophets, he interpreted to them in all the Scriptures the things concerning himself.* [46] ...*and* [he] *said to them, "Thus it is written, that the Christ should **suffer** and on the third day rise from the dead..."* –Jesus

Thus, in the last two passages from Luke 22 and 24, Jesus demonstrated that he *knew* the divine plan, and he embraced it. He fully expected to suffer and die, and then to rise again, *not* to be rescued. If God had had a plan to rescue Jesus from execution, then God had misled even Jesus and all the prophets before him, making them all liars, and disqualifying them as true prophets at all. But as the Luke 22 passage shows, Jesus knew and understood that this

---

[310] See *Gospel of Matthew* 2:1-12

plan had a good and glorious purpose. It was to initiate the New Covenant by which humans would be forgiven and redeemed, and their hearts would be transformed.

In the Tanakh "suffering" appears only five times—once, in the *Book of Lamentations*, the sequel to the book of the prophet Jeremiah, twice in the *Book of Nehemiah*, and not surprisingly, twice in the *Book of Job*.[311] Precious few times. But a further search for the word "suffer" gives 21 more results in eleven books of the Tanakh including the *Book of Job*.[312] As we have seen already, suffering is a profoundly deep and important subject in Judeo-Christian theology. As I have said before, it is something that we humans largely bring upon ourselves and others because of our sin, but it is also inflicted on us by Satan as we saw in *Job*, albeit it is usually impossible to tell, as it was for him. Thirdly, it is due to God's curse on the ground, or planet, following the first humans' rebellion. (*Genesis* 3:19) And, apparently it is one of God's tools, or means, to bring about both judgment and repentance. Verse 9:27 of the *Book of Nehemiah* says this of God:

> *Therefore you gave them into the hand of their enemies, who made them suffer. And in the time of their suffering they cried out to you and you heard them from heaven, and according to your great mercies you gave them saviors who saved them from the hand of their enemies.*

This was a part of Nehemiah's prayer to the LORD when he and the people of Israel (Judah), having been conquered by Babylon, were in captivity there for seventy years.[313] He was referring not only to this particular captivity but also the dozens of earlier times when the people were afflicted and oppressed by the surrounding

---

[311] *Nehemiah* 9:27, *Job* 2:13 and 9:28, *Lamentations* 1:18.

[312] *Numbers* 14:33, *Nehemiah* 2:17 and 9:27, *Job* 24:11, *Psalm* 34:10 and 88:15, *Proverbs* 11:15, 13:20, 19:15, 22:3, and 27:12, *Isaiah* 24:6, *Jeremiah* 13:22, *Ezekiel* 18:19 and 20, 34:29, 36:7 and 30, *Daniel* 6:2, *Joel* 1:18, and *Zephaniah* 3:18

[313] 597–538 BC

nations. In these cases it was Israel's enemies that brought suffering upon her, but the preceding verse tells why:

> *Nevertheless, they were disobedient and rebelled against*
> *you and cast your law behind their back and killed your*
> *prophets, who had warned them in order to turn them*
> *back to you, and they committed great blasphemies.* (v. 26)

As with the ten tribes of the northern kingdom before them, the southern Judahites' suffering was a result of their collective sin—their disobedience and rebellion against God, and yes their killing of the prophets. They had brought it upon themselves. So it was God's judgment upon them, a national punishment. But it was also a means by which He would bring the people to repentance, and thus to mercy and forgiveness.

Job's suffering, like Jesus's, was of an entirely different nature, not for their own sins. And for a different purpose. Jesus's was vicarious, and I assert that Job's was too, but in a different sense. It is obvious from Job's example, and those of the other ancient saints we have considered, that there are all different kinds and degrees of suffering, hardly contingent upon a single word for it.[314] That is to say, there are many ways to recognize and talk about suffering without the use of a particular word. In the case of Job we need not see *any* occurrences of the word "suffering" to get a gut-wrenching sense of his anguish, which is also painfully true of both Joseph and Jonah.

Like other figures of the Tanakh, each of them is woven into the texts of the New Testament as part of the Bible's 'big picture,' or metanarrative, or salvation plotline, stemming from the first Adam and leading to Jesus the Messiah himself, the "last Adam"

---

[314] Judas was the infamous disciple of Jesus who betrayed Jesus and subsequently committed suicide out of remorse. (See *Matthew* 27:3-5)

[314] This is a basic principle that applies to a great many other subjects. For example, we can observe in scripture that people worshipped even when the word "worship" does not appear. Also, when God presented himself to people, His awesome "god-ness" was clearly evident even when He did not say, "I am God". He did not need to.

as he is called in the Epistle of *1 Corinthians* 15:45-49.[315] Each of them is his own motif that contributes to the Master Motif of the Messiah, who actually descended twice, albeit in two, even three senses. He first descended from heaven to earth. (*Gospel of John* 3:13 and 17:5, *Ephesians* 4:9,10) Then, while on earth, he descended into suffering, and descended further into the "heart of the earth" before ascending into victory and glory.[316] He made his descent and ascent for the sake of the whole world.

He Came for the Whole World

Yes, despite some verses that would seem to indicate that he came only for the Jews, there are multiple verses that indicate the global breadth of his mission. Consider these 16 verses from the *Gospel of John* and other books, ten of which come from Jesus himself, and the rest from Apostles, or figures in the narrative.

> *John* **1:29** - The next day he saw Jesus coming toward him, and said, "Behold, the Lamb of God, who takes away the sin of the **world!**"   –Prophet John, the Baptizer

> *John* **3:16** - For God so loved the world, that he gave his only Son, that whoever believes in him should not perish but have eternal life.   –Jesus

> *John* **3:17** - For God did not send his Son into the world to condemn the world, but in order that the world might be saved through him.   –Jesus

---

[315] *"Thus it is written, 'The first man Adam became a living being'; the last Adam became a life-giving spirit. But it is not the spiritual that is first but the natural, and then the spiritual. The first man was from the earth, a man of dust; the second man is from heaven. As was the man of dust, so also are those who are of the dust, and as is the man of heaven, so also are those who are of heaven. Just as we have borne the image of the man of dust, we shall also bear the image of the man of heaven."*

[316] I will explain "heart of the earth" in the next chapter.

***John* 4:42** - *They said to the woman, "It is no longer because of what you said that we believe, for we have heard for ourselves, and we know that this is indeed the Savior of the world."* —Samaritans

---

***John* 6:14** - *When the people saw the sign that he had done, they said, "This is indeed the Prophet who is to come into the world!"* —People who had just been fed by Jesus

---

***John* 6:33** – *"For the bread of God is he who comes down from heaven and gives life to the world."* —Jesus

---

***John* 6:51** – *"I am the living bread that came down from heaven. If anyone eats of this bread, he will live forever. And the bread that I will give for the life of the world is my flesh."* —Jesus

---

***John* 8:12** – *Again Jesus spoke to them, saying, "I am the light of the world. Whoever follows me will not walk in darkness, but will have the light of life."* —Jesus

---

***John* 8:26** – *"I have much to say about you and much to judge, but he who sent me is true, and I declare to the world what I have heard from him."* —Jesus

---

***John* 9:5** – *"As long as I am in the world, I am the light of the world."* —Jesus

---

***John* 12:47** – *"If anyone hears my words and does not keep them, I do not judge him; for I did not come to judge the world but to save the world."* —Jesus

***John* 14:31** – *"...but I do as the Father has commanded me, so that the world may know that I love the Father. Rise, let us go from here."* –Jesus

***John* 17:13** – *"But now I am coming to you, and these things I speak in the world, that they may have my joy fulfilled in themselves."* –Jesus

***1 John* 2:2** – *"He is the propitiation for our sins, and not for ours only but also for the sins of the whole world."*
—Apostle John

***1 John* 4:14** – *"And we have seen and testify that the Father has sent his Son to be the Savior of the world."*
—Apostle John

***1 Timothy* 1:15** - *The saying is trustworthy and deserving of full acceptance, that Christ Jesus came into the world to save sinners, of whom I am the foremost.* —Apostle Paul

In light of these verses, all should acknowledge that Jesus was sent into the world *for* the whole world, not just the Jews. In the *Gospel of Matthew* chapter 15 there is an account of Jesus on a northward journey with his disciples to what even then was south Lebanon. A local Canaanite woman discovered him and somehow knew he had power to cast out demons. Apostle Matthew reports that when she implored him to deliver her daughter Jesus at first told her, *"I was sent only to the lost sheep of the house of Israel,"* the most pronounced statement that he ever made like this. But of course he was being facetious, or satirical, as he was sometimes known to be. Why? 1) Because that is the only time Jesus was reported to have ever said that,³¹⁷ and 2) the occasion for his saying it was actually outside of Israel's borders in gentile Phoenician territory—the region or Tyre and Sidon. Despite some other satirical dialogue in this encounter, the plain fact was that Jesus, a Jewish man, was there talking to a pagan woman and helping her by delivering her daughter from a demon. By all appearances, she seems to have been the only person he came for.³¹⁸ So in light of these sixteen global statements, the most reasonable conclusion is that even this is an example of Jesus's global mission too.

Sure, Jesus's primary audience at that time was the Jews, and his primary geographical area was Jewish Palestine.³¹⁹ But having a *primary* audience and geography implies that he had secondary ones too—limited numbers of proximal gentiles (and half-Jews) inside and around Israel. After his departure, of course, his mission went pan-global! Now that Jesus resides in the heavenly realms (most Muslims seem to agree), his mission field is constrained neither by geography nor ethnicity. From his vantage he can see everywhere. There are no people anywhere in the world that Jesus cannot see and does not want to reach with his message of redemption

---

³¹⁷ The parallel passage in chapter 7 of Mark's gospel does not contain this statement, which is believed by many scholars to have been written before Matthew's. In this view Matthew would have 'added in' a statement that Mark had left out. Consequently, if someone were to rigidly analyze Mark's gospel only for the sake of isolating Mark's content, they would not have this statement. It would be 'inadmissible' evidence. But if they insist on including that statement from Matthew, then of course they are allowing for gospel-harmony.

³¹⁸ The Apostle Matthew calls her a Canaanite woman, while Mark calls her Syro-Phoenician, which terms can be equivalent. The point is that she was a pagan, not a Jew. And Jesus went a long way into foreign territory to find her and grant her request.

³¹⁹ In *Matthew 15:21-28* it is obvious that Jesus was probably engaging the woman's help to teach his disciples another lesson on the 'inclusivity' of the Kingdom of God. On multiple occasions they showed evidence of being ethno-centric, as Jewish men were expected to be. But Jesus was different, and better, and he wanted to teach them that. As the master teacher that he was, first he said what he knew they wanted to hear so he could then dismantle it. The woman was clever and read his cues. When she played along and still demonstrated determined faith, he readily granted her petition. In fact, he praised her in front of his disciples stating, "Oh woman, great is your faith" (v. 28) to moderately shame them and show them that gentiles, and even gentile women matter to him. This is similar to his encounter with the Samaritan (half Jew) woman in *John* 4 1-43 who led her whole village to him, and to what Jesus said to the Roman centurion when he healed his servant and marveled at his faith in *Matthew* 8:5-13. "Truly, I tell you, with no one in Israel have I found such faith."

and eternal salvation. Yes, Jesus was, and is, the Savior-Messiah of the whole world. And a world-wide scope-of-mission is exactly what we all really expect from a prophet who is also Messiah.

As for Job, he was a very local redeemer, and not a real messiah at all. On the other hand, in his story, if we think of his companions as representatives of 'Everyman,' the whole human race, we can begin to grasp the redeemer motif that he prefigured for the world, which then feeds into the great Messiah Motif.

Chapter 14

Joseph and Jonah in the New Testament

> *"Joseph is a fruitful bough,*
>
> *a fruitful bough by a spring;*
>
> *his branches run over the wall..."*
>
> Torah, *Book of Genesis* 49:22
> Jacob's final prophetic blessing upon
> Joseph before his own death

Joseph   Ιωσήφ

In the Torah, Joseph and Moses are the two great bookend-prophets to the four-century Egyptian period. Joseph brought them in, and Moses led them out. At the end of his life, his father Jacob prophesied that Joseph's messianic "branches" of Israelite in-gathering and preservation would "run over the wall." In the New Testament, Moses looms very large, but Joseph less so. That's somewhat curious to me. Joseph was nevertheless a paragon of virtue, faith, extraordinary greatness, and the object of God's providential orchestration of events. He was a member of the great "Hall of Faith" with 19+ other prophets and saints.[320]

The name "Joseph" appears in the New Testament 34 times, including parallel references in all four gospels. However, Joseph was a popular Jewish name, so they do not all refer to our person of interest, the 11th son of Jacob.

In the *Gospel of Matthew* the first seven occurrences refer to

---

[320] Chapter 11 of the *Book of Hebrews*

Joseph the husband of Mary, the mother of Jesus,[321] and there are six such references to him in *Luke* and *John*.[322] In *Matthew*, two others refer to one of Jesus's brothers,[323] and the final two refer to a believing pharisee who was a secret disciple of Jesus, Joseph of Arimathea. This Apostle tells us that Joseph took the corpse of Jesus down from the cross and interred it in his own newly carved tomb; a remarkable and very risky thing to do considering his class and station. (27:57 and 59) In *Mark*, all three occurrences of "Joseph" refer to this pharisee for the same reason,[324] plus one in *Luke* 23:50 and one in *John* 19:38. So all four gospels name this Joseph as the 'redeemer' of Jesus's corpse, and to me that makes him a bit like the great son of Jacob who redeemed his whole extended family, his people. My young friend Emad and I argued extensively over the gospels' claim that the dead body was taken down from the cross and entombed rather than just thrown into a pit of other dead bodies, as he claimed. That debate is too extensive to go into, but I wanted to make mention of it.

The point is that the gospels clearly corroborate each other on this point. If you are a Muslim, I will say it this way, admittedly tongue-in-cheek: All four gospels name this Joseph as the claimant of the body of this crucified man who looked exactly like Jesus and whom even Joseph, Jesus's mother, and his own disciples thought was him. Not to mention that this dead man rose to life pretending to be Jesus and convincing everybody. Such extraordinary acting he must have performed! And we thought identity theft is only a problem these days.

Several additional references in the gospels refer to Josephs who are not our person of interest, the great grandson of Abraham and prophetic patriarch. That leaves only one gospel reference to

---

[321] Verses 1:16, 18, 19, 20, 24, 2:13, and 2:19

[322] *Luke* 1:27, 2:4, 2:16, 3:23, and *John* 1:45 and 6:42

[323] Verses 13:55 and 27:56

[324] Verses 15:43, 45, and 46

this Joseph, found in *John* 4:5.

So he came to a town of Samaria called Sychar, near the field that Jacob had given to his son Joseph.

I cite this verse only in-passing because it mentions both Jacob and Joseph, and corroborates the time when Jacob gave this plot of land to Joseph recorded in *Genesis* 48:21-22. But the verse above reports on something that happened there during the days of Jesus, something I already alluded to in footnote 300. I encourage you to revisit that, then read the whole account in chapter 4 of Apostle John's gospel.

Following the gospels, the *Book of Acts* contains two Josephs other than our prophetic patriarch—one that was nominated to replace Judas as one of the twelve Apostles but who was not selected (1:23),[325] and another that emerged as the apostolic partner of Paul, surnamed Barnabas. (4:36) Then in chapter 7, in his lengthy public sermon in which he recounted the history of Israel, the new deacon Stephen made four references to Joseph son of Jacob. His message was actually the history of the Messiah. This is the same passage that calls Moses a "savior" that we looked at in chapter 7. Eight verses are devoted to the story of Joseph (9-16) the first of which says…

And the patriarchs, jealous of Joseph, sold him into Egypt; but God was with him and rescued him out of all his afflictions and gave him favor and wisdom before Pharaoh, king of Egypt, who made him ruler over Egypt and over all his household.

This is the longest New Testament treatment of Joseph.

The only other two references appear gloriously in the "hall of faith" as I said, chapter 11 of the *Book of Hebrews*. Here the inspired author gives an honorary mention of some of the prophets

---

[325] Because Judas had hanged himself. (*Matthew* 27:5, *Acts* 1:18)

and noteworthy men and women of faith, including Joseph (vv. 21 and 22). He is listed in ranks with Abel, Enoch, Noah, Abraham, Sarah, Isaac, Jacob, Moses, Rahab, Gideon, Barak, Samson, Jephthah. David, Samuel, and "all the prophets." Oddly, neither Jesus nor Paul makes any recorded mention of Joseph, and the last one is in reference to his tribe found in the book of *Revelation* (7:8). All told there are 7 New Testament references to him.

....

> *"[L]et us consider whether is harder, for a man after having been buried to rise again from the earth, or for a man in the belly of a whale…to escape corruption."*
>
> St. Cyril of Jerusalem,
Catechetical Lecture 14.18 [326]

Jonah Ἰωνας

The number of occurrences of "Jonah" in the New Testament are comparable to those of Joseph, except that they all are attributed to Jesus himself. In other words, no other New Testament voice mentions Jonah besides Jesus, as recorded seven times in two of the four gospels: three times in the *Gospel of Matthew* chapter 12, once in verse 16:4, and three times in of the Gospel of Luke chapter 11. Here is Matthew's account:

> *Then some of the scribes and Pharisees answered him [Jesus], saying, "Teacher, we wish to see a sign from you." But he answered them, "An evil and adulterous generation seeks for a sign,* **but no sign will be given to it except the sign of the prophet Jonah. For just as Jonah was three days and three nights in the belly of the great fish, so will the Son of Man**

---

[326] orthodoxchurchquotes.wordpress.com/tag/prophet-jonah/

be three days and three nights in the heart of the earth. (12:38-40, bolding mine)

Here is Luke's account:

*When the crowds were increasing, he began to say, "This generation is an evil generation. It seeks for a sign, **but no sign will be given to it except the sign of Jonah. For as Jonah became a sign to the people of Nineveh, so will the Son of Man be to this generation.*** (11:29-30)

As you can see, the two respective passages in *Matthew* 12 and *Luke* 11 are similar, so we can call them 'parallel' passages meaning that they appear to be two independent accounts of the same one discourse-event of Jesus made by these two respective authors. That is, we could reasonably surmise that Jesus spoke of Jonah on only one of those two occasions reported by both writers. However, it is also possible that they are two separate but similar sermons. [327] The lone statement in *Matthew* chapter 16:4 is also almost identical to the one in 12:39 but with a different context, so we can reasonably infer that Jesus probably made that statement on a different occasion. That means that we could (possibly) subtract the Lukan verses from the total count, which would leave us with a total of four references to Prophet Jonah, three less than those of Joseph.

But it is what theses verses *say* that we should really be interested in, and what we should focus on. Because they seem to be parallel, we could largely harmonize, or blend, the substance of the meanings of the two gospels' passages. In short, in both passages Jesus uses Jonah as a *type* of himself, or as a "sign." But certainly not the part of Jonah's story where he tried to run from God. Only Jonah did that. Rather, they both are concerned with everything *other* than that embarrassing part. Just as Job and other prophets modeled redemption-

---

[327] It is not unreasonable to surmise that Jesus repeated and even repackaged much of what he taught on multiple occasions and settings, e.g. in various cities and villages. So the reader is required to conclude that this is the same discourse event. They could have been entirely different. Bolding mine.

through-descent, or through suffering, so also did Jonah. In the best sense, Jesus exploited the Jonah motif.

I. Jonah and Jesus in *Matthew* 12

In *Matthew* Jesus zeros in on Jonah's suffering, his descent, into the belly of the great fish. Refer back to the bolded part of Matthew's passage. Jesus used the three days of Jonah's descent to refer to his own. Not that Jesus was ever swallowed by a big fish; rather, he descended into death, into the "heart of the earth." Exactly where the "heart of the earth" is and what it is might seem one of the cryptic expressions of Christ, but it really isn't. The original Greek for this phrase is καρδία τῆς γῆς, literally "heart of the Earth." The majority of English translations (51 of 62) render it as exactly that, or as "belly of the earth" on one occasion, which seem obviously synonymous. Seven render it as simply "the grave" (5) or "a deep grave" (2), three as either "depths of the earth" (2) or "deep in the earth" (1), and one as "the ground." A commonsensical understanding of this phrase, then, is that at the very least, Jesus believed he would die and would be buried, exactly how the Jews understood it too.[328] According to some commentators, the phrase might mean more than that, but there is large consensus among scholars that it cannot mean less.[329] It is clearly an expression of Jesus's

---

[328] **Barnes Notes on the Bible:** In the "heart of the earth" –The Jews used the word "heart" to denote the "interior" of a thing, or to speak of being in a thing. It means, here, to be in the grave or sepulchre; **Jamieson-Fausset-Brown:** "The expression 'in the heart of the earth,' suggested by the expression of Jonah with respect to the sea (2:3, in the Septuagint), means simply the grave, but this is considered as the most emphatic expression of real and total entombment."

[329] Some commentators assert that it must mean not only that Jesus was buried in a grave or sepulcher, but also that he also descended into a much deeper place, i.e. the netherworld. Ellicot says, '"the heart of the earth," standing parallel as it does to "the heart of the seas," the "belly of hell"—*i.e.,* Sheol and Hades—in Jonah 2:2-3, means more than the rock-hewn sepulchre, and implies the descent into Hades, the world of the dead, which was popularly believed to be far below the surface of the earth.' Meyers agrees: But the question as to what Jesus meant by ἔσται … ἐν τῇ καρδίᾳ τῆς γῆς, whether His *lying in the grave* (so the greater number of expositors), or His *abode in Hades* (Tertullian, Irenaeus, Theophylact, Bellarmin, Maldonatus, Olshausen, König, *Lehre von Christi Höllenfahrt*, Frankf. 1842, p.

foreknowledge, or a prophecy—a prediction that he would die, but very temporarily—"three days and three nights" to use Jesus's exact verbiage. Not that his spirit, or soul, or real essence would die, of course, only his body. In death, nobody's real essence dies. So if Jesus was truly a divine being, God, as Christians believe, it is not requisite to infer that God would have died with Jesus's death.

A Technical Problem

But there is a technical problem to wrestle with. *If* Jesus was crucified and rose again at all, some skeptics and Muslims ask, was he really in the grave for "three days and three nights"? Short answer: no, probably not.

It is popularly believed that Jesus was executed on a Friday morning and buried on the afternoon of the same day. Then, his resurrection took place very early on the "first day of the week" which is Sunday morning.[330] The problem is, that is only two nights and one whole day. Couldn't Jesus do basic math? some mock, who also deem this reason enough to dismiss this statement as inauthentic. Even though his prediction of his own death is clearly established by these texts, as is his resurrection, some take issue with this apparent discrepancy, so much so as to dismiss the two most important event-facts entirely. Even if this were an actual discrepancy, i.e. an error, the four gospels are in perfect agreement with Jesus's prediction that he would die and rise again over the course of mere days—not years, months, or even weeks.[331] And if he foretold those two things right, who

---

54; Kahnis, *Dogmat.* I. p. 508), is determined by καρδία τῆς γῆς, to which expression the resting in the *grave* does not sufficiently correspond; for the *heart* of the earth can only indicate its lowest *depths*, just as καρδία τῆς θαλάσσης means the depths of the sea in Jonah 2:4, from which the biblical expression καρδία in our present passage seems to have been derived. Again, the parallel in the κοιλία τοῦ κήτους is, in any case, better suited to the idea of *Hades* than it is to that of a grave cut out of the rock on the surface of the earth. If, on the other hand, Jesus Himself has very distinctly intimated that His dying was to be regarded as a descending into Hades (Luke 23:43), then ἔσται … ἐν τῇ καρδ. τ. γ. must be referred to His sojourn there. (https://biblehub.com/commentares/matthew/12-40.htm)

[330] *Gospels of Matthew* 28:1, *Mark* 16:2, *Luke* 24:1, *John* 20:1 and 19, and *Book of Acts* 20:7

[331] *Gospels of Matthew* 16:21, 17:22:23, 20:17-19, *Mark* 9:31-32

would get hung up on the basic math? Still, detractors are not easily satisfied when a technical problem like this presents.

For many of us, there is a simple explanation of the math. First, although chapter 1:17 of the *Book of Jonah* reveals that Jonah was in the belly of the great fish for three days and three nights, we need not understand that as a specific duration of, say, exactly 72 hours in the precise 'scientific' or mathematical terms of our day, which would be three 24-hour days. In those terms, if he was there for three nights then he was really only there for two *whole* days: Midnight from October 1 to midnight on October 3, for example, would entail three nights but would only be 48 hours, and only one *whole* night. Or, midnight on October 1 to say 6am on October 3 would entail three nights but only two-and-a-half days. Midnight on October 1 to 10pm on October 3 would be three nights and days, but neither three *whole* days nor three *whole* nights.

The point is, if *whole* days and *whole* nights are demanded then there is no way to encompass three whole nights <u>and</u> three whole days. So in doing one's calculations, one has to decide on the definition of "day" and "night." If it is insisted that a 'day' is 24 hours, then the problems above obtain, and there is no solution. But if the definition is adjusted to mean 12 hours, or the period of daylight, then the solution is possible. And isn't that closer to the way we think of days and nights? In reality, every 24-hour day includes a day and a night, or even more precisely, one whole day from dawn to dusk, and two partial nights, one before and one after.

But in real life, even today, we aren't even *that* precise when we don't have to be. We usually use "day" and "night" loosely and imprecisely. And to the present time in history, "day" can refer to any part of the daylight hours or the 24-hour period. It was no different for the ancient Jews of Jonah's day. So the phrase "three days and three nights" could not have been a literal 72 hours even then. Rather, it was a vernacular expression indicating a round number of days and nights. The same should be understood for Jesus's expression of his time in the "heart of the earth," or grave. Therefore, Jesus's personal comparison to Jonah's time in the belly of the fish is not a discrepancy at all. Several citations from Bible commentaries should suffice to support the point, the first from Ellicott:

> The purely chronological difficulty is explained by the common mode of speech among the Jews, according to which, any part of a day, though it were but a single hour, was for legal purposes considered as a whole. An instance of this mode of speech is found in 1Samuel 30:12-13, and it is possible that in the history of Jonah itself the measurement of time is to be taken with the same laxity.[332]

Here is one from Barnes:

> This computation is…strictly in accordance with the Jewish mode of reckoning. If it had "not" been, the Jews would have understood it, and would have charged our Saviour as being a false prophet, for it was well known to them that he had spoken this prophecy, *Matthew* 27:63. Such a charge, however, was never made; and it is plain, therefore, that what was "meant" by the prediction was accomplished. It was a maxim, also, among the Jews, in computing time, that a part of a day was to be received as the whole. Many instances of this kind occur in both sacred and profane history. See 2 *Chronicles* 10:5, 2 *Chronicles* 10:12; *Genesis* 42:17-18. Compare *Book of Esther* 4:16 with 5:1.[333]

And here is a final one from Matthew Poole:

> "What we call day and night made up the Jewish nucyhmeron. It appears by Genesis 1:5, that *'the evening and the morning'* made up *a day.* Three days and three nights is with us but the same thing with three natural days, and so it must be understood here. Christ was in the grave three natural days, that

---

[332] "For he had not eaten bread or drunk water for three days and three nights." https://biblehub.com/commentaries/matthew/12-40.htm

[333] Ibid.

is, part of three natural days; every one of which days contained a day and a night, viz. twenty-four hours."[334]

This explanation alone should satisfy the reader. But there is another dimension to the problem and its possible solution: Did Jesus really die on a Friday? After all, the gospels do not specify. Therefore some are convinced that he actually died on a Thursday, or even a Wednesday, views for which there are plausible rationales, respectively. The former has to do with the plethora of events that occurred between the execution and resurrection, and the latter has to do with the reference to the "sabbath" in all four gospels.[335] The question is whether this sabbath was merely the single, weekly one (Saturday) or actually two sabbaths, for the Sabbath associated with the annual Passover may also have fallen at that time. But this is beyond the primary scope of our discussion, and I do not wish to stretch the reader's attention beyond its limits.[336] Suffice it to say, again, that Jesus *believed* he would die—*not* be delivered from death—but only for a period of days, not weeks, or months, or years, or forever. For just as Jonah would come out of the belly of the fish, Jesus believed (i.e. he knew) that he would come out of the state of death that he would enter into. Thus, in *Matthew* 12 Jesus used Jonah's descent and ascent to prefigure his own.

For those who are inclined to dismiss the story of Jonah, or at least the part where he gets swallowed by the fish and survives, it should count for something that Jesus believed it, apparently in a literal sense. Supposing he believed the story in a figurative or mythical sense, it seems hard to draw that conclusion from his words. Still, for those who insist that it was mythical, it doesn't matter. It is then ***true***

---

[334] Ibid. Gill and Bengel concur.

[335] *Matthew* 28:1, *Mark* 15:42 and 16:1, *Luke* 23:54 and 56, and *John* 19:31.

[336] For those who *are* interested see 1) nickcady.org/2017/04/17/was-jesus-in-the-grave-three-days-and-three-nights-heres-how-it-adds-up/ and 2) https://bible.org/question/were-three-days-and-three-nights-jesus-was-grave-full-72-hours. Also see Appendix 9 for a more thorough explanation of this problem and its considerations.

myth. It is quite palpable enough for Jesus to use it for his purposes, to communicate his own descent and ascent.

Immediately after this part of the passage (vv. 38-40) in the same segment comes Jesus's extension of it:

> *The men of Nineveh will rise up at the judgment with this generation and condemn it, for they repented at the preaching of Jonah, and behold,* **something greater than Jonah is here.** *The queen of the South will rise up at the judgment with this generation and condemn it, for she came from the ends of the earth to hear the wisdom of Solomon, and behold,* **something greater than Solomon is here.** (vv. 41-42, bolding mine.)

I want to say this is self-explanatory. But in the interests of clarity I shall explicate: Jesus not only compares himself to Jonah but claims to be greater. Then he mixes in the Queen of the South (i.e. Sheba, today's Yemen) and King Solomon than whom he also claims to be greater.[337] In both cases, his point is to alert them to the dire consequences of rejecting his warnings. The Ninevites repented with hardly any effort on Jonah's part, and the Queen of Sheba traveled a great distance to find true wisdom. And since Jesus is greater than them both, his audiences should feel even more convicted.

The second passage in *Matthew* referring to Jonah (16:4) consists of only one verse, and it is almost identical to the one we have already exposited. It is an example of repetition and a mark of a very good teacher, as we have noted before.

II. Jonah and Jesus in *Luke* 11

Now let's examine the second full passage in *Luke* 11. I referred to it before as a parallel passage, but on closer examination, it does not match Matthew's account exactly. Actually, this is typical of

---

[337] See *1 Kings* 10:1-13

many parallel passages in the gospels, which attests to the independence of each inspired writer. In Luke's account, Jesus does not speak of Jonah's time in the belly of the fish at all, nor does he speak of his own time in the grave. Rather, Jesus highlights a different aspect of Jonah's mission, or, well, the mission itself. In verse 30 of this passage Jesus says…

> *For as Jonah became a sign to the people of Nineveh, so will the Son of Man be to this generation.*

   Here Jesus leaves out the whole part about Jonah's being swallowed by a big fish. He refers only to Jonah's having been a "sign" to the people of Ninevah, and by analogy Jesus's own 'sign-ship' to the people of his generation and his own specific geo-historical context. As I've said before, Jesus would have reused his divine material in multiple teaching situations but would have tailored it for each particular audience, say, in each village. In this case, it wasn't Jonah's descent into death-like suffering that Jesus wished to analogize, but rather how God used Jonah as a *sign* to the Ninevites, and how God intended to use Jesus as a sign to the Israelites, Samaritans, Romans, and other gentiles within his cultural milieu.

   Then, as in Matthew's account, Luke reports Jesus's theological extension to the first two verses as follows:

> *The queen of the South will rise up at the judgment with the men of this generation and condemn them, for she came from the ends of the earth to hear the wisdom of Solomon, and behold, something greater than Solomon is here. The men of Nineveh will rise up at the judgment with this generation and condemn it, for they repented at the preaching of Jonah, and behold, something greater than Jonah is here.*

   Note that this segment is almost identical to the second part of *Matthew*'s passage including Jonah and the Queen of the South. But do you notice the one difference? Yes, they are reversed. Does that matter? No, I don't think so. As in *Matthew*, here Jesus is asserting that he is greater than both Jonah and Solomon, and that is all the more reason why his audiences should repent. So much so that if they did not, then both the Queen of Sheba and the Ninevites will rise up at the time of the final divine judgment to condemn them. Very strong words. But where did Jesus get off claiming to be greater than both prophet Jonah and King Solomon? Where indeed? Clearly Jesus believed he was the greatest of the prophets, and more than a prophet, the one-and-only Messiah, and rightful King of Israel (even though he never sought political power). If he was not then it was intolerable bravado on his part. But if he really was then God had raised him up as the cumulation of all prophets, saints, and righteous kings before him and the fulfillment of all their prophecies and prophetic motifs. And evidently, according to Jesus himself, certain elements of Jonah and his mission qualified as such. So the Job motif is a prime example of the Master Motif that we've been relishing all along.

Incidentally, there is one more comparable passage that I want us to look at, this time from the *Book of Hebrews* again.

> ...*consider Jesus, the apostle and high priest of our confession, who was faithful to him who appointed him, just as Moses also was faithful in all God's house.* **For Jesus has been counted worthy of more glory than Moses**—*as much more glory as the builder of a house has more honor than the house itself. ...Now Moses was faithful in all God's house as a servant, to testify to the things that were to be spoken later, but Christ is faithful over God's house as a son.* (3:1-3 and 5-6, bolding mine)

I say it's comparable because it's in keeping with our passages of focus in *Matthew* 12 and *Luke* 11 in which Jesus elevated himself above a prophet (Jonah) and even a great king (Solomon). The writer of *Hebrews* claims that "Jesus has been counted worthy of more glory than Moses." Even though Jesus did not say this himself, it seems entirely consistent with what he *did* say about himself in our 'twin' passages of *Matthew* and *Luke*.

And finally we come back to Job in the last chapter.

Chapter 15

Job in the New Testament

> *Like both the birth and death of Christ, the suffering of Job was a multicultural event. ...What power there is in the sacrifice of one righteous, broken, and penitent heart.*
>
> Mike Mason,
> *The Gospel According to Job*

Is Job *himself* a motif in the New Testament as he was in the Old, and as other ancient biblical figures clearly are? Well, yes and no. Again, neither Jesus nor Paul ever mentioned him, or at least it is not recorded. Someone might ask, if the main purpose of *Job* is to prefigure Christ, shouldn't we expect Jesus to have talked about him? Fair question. Frankly I don't know the answer, and I'm not sure if anyone can. Some might wonder, then, if Jesus even knew about Job. In my reasoned opinion, to imagine that seems very far-fetched, and even humorous. Job does appear in the New Testament, but only once in the *Epistle of James*. But we certainly should not understand this as a measure of his significance.

> *As an example of suffering and patience, brothers, take the **prophets** who spoke in the name of the Lord. Behold, we consider those blessed who remained steadfast. You have heard of the steadfastness of **Job**...* (5:10,11, bolding mine)

Dr. C.J. Williams offers this commentary on the passage:

> It is noteworthy that James refers us to all the prophets, then singles out only Job by name. **Not only is Job**

counted among the prophets, but he is the greatest example among them when it comes to the patient endurance of suffering. So, while Job is not mentioned in the "Hall of Faith" in Hebrews 11, he is the only one mentioned by name in the "Hall of Patience" in James 5. If Job is an example of the patient **endurance of suffering**, he is so only because he reflects the perfect patience of Christ.[338]

That is because Job was a type of Christ, not only in patience (which by itself seems trite to me), but even more in steadfastness and in the multiple other ways that I have elucidated.

Bear in mind that this James, the writer of the epistle by his name, was not the Apostle James who was martyred early on just after Stephen (*Book of Acts* 12:2). Rather, he was Jesus's younger brother who presumably grew up with Jesus for 20+ years and shared many lessons in the synagogue with him. Laying aside Jesus's prescient, and even prophetic knowledge of things, it seems reasonable to infer that if James knew about Job, then so did Jesus. There are other reasons to believe this too. Since the *Book of Job* was included in the canon of Hebrew scripture, nearly all ordinary Jews would have been familiar with his story, Jesus included. Moreover, the four gospels reveal Jesus's thorough knowledge of the Tanakh, which can also be said for Apostle Paul. Oh yes, they knew about Job.

I suppose we cannot know why Jesus never talked about Job. But I surmise it was partly because, as Hebrew literature goes, the *Book of Job* is not very Hebraic in some ways; it is not contained in the Torah (Pentateuch), and Job the man was not part of the lineage of Israel. He was not even a part of the historical timeline, which some call the 'salvation timeline' or plotline. For these reasons he bears a lot of resemblance to the mysterious figure Melchizedek in *Genesis* 14:18-20. Therefore, the *Book of Job* was kind of 'off the beaten path' as it were. I suspect that the average Jew was probably more prone to talking about any other character of the Tanakh.

---

[338] Williams, *The Shadow of Christ in the Book of Job,* p. 69. Bolding mine.

There were other figures Jesus didn't mention either. As we have observed, he never mentioned Joseph, which is even more remarkable considering his enormous place in Jewish history. Neither did he speak of the prophet Ezekiel or most of the so-called 'minor' prophets. But, as we have just seen, Jesus did speak of the prophet Jonah. There is a *Jonah Motif,* just as there is a *Joseph Motif,* and many others. By virtue of their *suffering,* the *redeemer* and the *descent-to-ascent* qualities which they share with *Job*, these capture and import much of the Job Motif from the Old Testament (Tanakh) and carry it over into the New with them. I am asserting that there is a compound Motif of these Old Testament figures that collectively blend together and reach their "crescendo" in one Meta-Motif—*the Messiah Motif.* C.J. Williams calls this the **"Messianic Trajectory."** [339]

> ...the prophetic experience of being cast down from an established position to the depths of undeserved humiliation, then to be exalted by the hand of God to a place of even higher honor than the beginning. This trajectory of experience is identified by Christ as a summary of his life and a pattern of Old Testament prophecy in *Luke* 24:25-27:
>
> > *'O foolish ones, and slow of heart to believe in all that the prophets have spoken! Ought not the Christ to have suffered these things and to enter into his glory?' And beginning at Moses and all the prophets, he expounded to them in all the Scriptures the things concerning himself.*

Among other things, this affirms our thesis way back in the first chapter: The Grand Messiah Motif, like a tapestry with its multi-stranded and interwoven component motifs, exhibits an enormous literary and revelatory coherence to Biblical scripture that collectively bears the marks of divine origin, formation, and preservation throughout the millennia to our current day.

---

[339] Ibid. p. 22.

As we have seen throughout this book, there are multiple lenses through which we can view and understand the holy books of the Tanakh. One of them is the lens of Job which I have endeavored to 'grind and polish' for us. Each of the other prophet-saints we have reviewed is also represented by his own lens as well. We can then combine them the way that a telescope and other visual devices do to zoom in and out on the subject/s of our specific interest. Through the Job lens, and especially through the alignment of them, we can clearly see the great Messiah, or Redemption Motif, of the Tanakh and of the whole Bible. Therefore, we can and should have great confidence in the Bible as divine revelation because of these self-authenticating qualities. As a veritable *library* of scripture, it is self-authenticated by the coherence and continuity of its components.

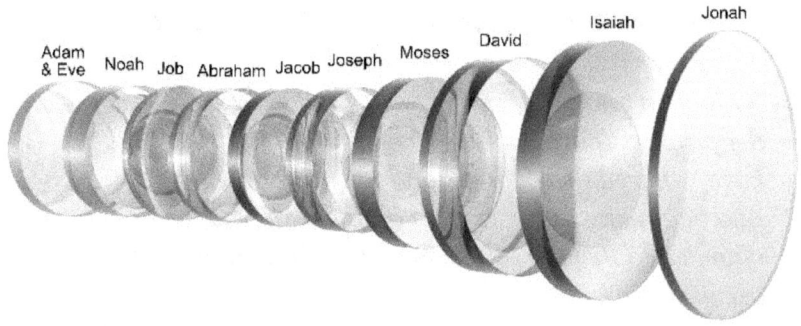

Image purchased from istock.com and altered by author.

These include its history, its prophets and prophecies, its themes and motifs, its trajectory, and its unified message—especially in view of its diversity. As a body of literature, the Tanakh and the Bible as a whole displays a remarkable historio-theological continuity between its 66 books, its segments and its two testaments, that points demonstrably to long-range divine planning and orchestration. Such continuity-within-diversity is best explained as the product of a prolonged, overarching, progressive, and divine plan consisting of complex web of 'hyperlinked' historical, geographical, and theological components which progressively develop and reach their culmination in redemption, and in the ultimate Job-like Redeemer, the Messiah. When we grasp the magnitude and intricacy of such a masterfully fine-tuned plan we should be moved with awe to appreciate its wholesale genius, and the genius of the Job Motif in its own right.

Through the lens of Job—the book and the man—together with all the prophets and saints up through Jesus the Messiah, the whole Bible is a matchless compendium of divine revelation. It is much like the varied instruments in a symphony orchestra or a complex machine with multiple, inter-working, and precision parts. It has a grand, meta-narrative replete with interconnected themes and motifs. In literature, a meta-narrative is an over-arching story line with a master plot that controls all the sub-plots, as with those in a sophisticated novel, and even moreso with a novel series, such as the *Lord of the Rings* trilogy. Despite their diversity, both the symphony and the complex machine function because they have a master purpose and plan, together with a master design and organization.

All these elements require a master designer. The elements do not occur by accident. In terms of the symphony it's the work of the composer and the conductor to bring the various instrumentalists into unity and harmony. In terms of the complex machine it's the combined work of the inventor and engineer, with the skilled craftsmen, the assemblers, and the operators. When you observe a machine such as this there can be no doubt that it is the product of a Master Inventor. The whole Bible is like this machine in many ways, including the Old and New Testaments. The Tanakh alone is an intricate collection of divine literatures with varied authors spanning 1500 years, and yet they all have continuity and coherence. Its multiple yet complementary themes and motifs are brilliantly interwoven and brought to culmination in the New Testament. Logically, this points to a Master Author and Editor-in-Chief. When seen and understood through these lenses, Yahweh himself should be the most reasonable Producer of the Messianic Job Motif in the *Book of Job* as well as in the entire Bible preserved for all ages *and us.*

In the chapters of this book we have examined multiple biblical characters as examples of and evidence for this assertion, both in the Tanakh *and* the Qur'an. We have also examined figures of the New Testament, especially those who first 'take the stage' in the Tanakh and who also appear in the New Testament. These have included the prophets/saints Adam and Eve, Noah, Abraham and Isaac, Hagar, Moses, David and Solomon, and more. In these later chapters, we have added to the roster the New Testament prophet John the Baptizer, Stephen the deacon, plus others, and the writing Apostles in whose inspired writings all the others appear. Prominently featured have been Jacob and Joseph, Jonah as spoken of by Jesus, and of course Job as spoken of by the Apostle James and personified by Jesus. Most notably is Jesus himself, the Job-like Redeemer and Messiah for the world. We have seen how all of these figures exemplify, foreshadow, and point to the Messiah in their own unique but similar ways, and how Jesus fills the mold they unknowingly created for him. In Jesus's own words He was signified by Jonah, and by extension, Job. Jesus was the realization of the Master Type and Motif to which they and the others all contributed well before his arrival. Indeed, this is so prevalent it's as if it was the primary purpose of the whole Tanakh—to create this magnificent cast of the People of the Book that leads to and finds its fulfillment in Jesus.

…We could say that Jesus was 'typecast.'

I've quoted this before, but it deserves to be quoted again.

And he said to them, "O foolish ones, and slow of heart to believe all that the prophets have spoken! Was it not necessary that the Christ should suffer these things and enter into his glory?" And beginning with Moses and all the Prophets, he interpreted to them in all the Scriptures the things concerning himself. (Gospel of Luke 24:25–27)

Now, with his personal permission, I wish to quote again from Dr. Williams at length because he has written so eloquently on this in the sixth chapter of *The Shadow of Christ in the Book of Job*.[340]

The Poetry of Suffering

Job's experience…seems to clearly distend into the realm of typology. This is a theme that exactly mirrors the **messianic suffering** described so vividly in the Psalms and the Prophets, and which came to pass in the Gospels. We see the anger and chastisement of God, the attack of wicked men, the ungodly being united against him, his own personal sorrow and isolation, yet all against the backdrop of his own innocence. In some cases, there is nearly exact phraseology linking Job's experience to that of the **Messiah**. For example, concerning the persecution of men:

They gape at me with their mouth,
They strike me reproachfully on the cheek,
They gather together against me.

***Job* 16:10**

They gape at me with their mouths,
Like a raging and roaring lion.

***Psalm* 22:13**

---

[340] All bolding throughout Williams' quotations mine.

And now I am their taunting song;
Yes, I am their byword.
They abhor me, they keep far from me;
They do not hesitate to spit in my face.

Job 30:9–10

I also made sackcloth my garment;
I became a byword to them.
Those who sit in the gate speak against me,
And I am the song of the drunkards.

Psalm 69:11–12

Key **allusions** are also prevalent, such as this thematic conjunction of bitter weeping while being persecuted, along with the claim of innocence:

My face is flushed from weeping,
And on my eyelids is the shadow of death;
Although no violence is in my hands,
And my prayer is pure.

Job 16:16, 17

I am weary with my crying; my throat is dry.
My eyes fail while I wait for my God.
Those who hate me without cause are more than the hairs of my head;
They are mighty who would destroy me, being my enemies wrongfully;
Though I have stolen nothing, I still must restore it.

Psalm 69:3, 4

Comparisons like this are numerous, and the language is vivid and familiar to anyone who is conversant with the Old Testament. This, in part, accounts for the purpose of Job's long, poetic musings on his suffering. Poetry is designed for the art of connotation, and is uniquely suited to forge the conceptual connections in typology.

Job experienced not only the general persecution of those around him, but isolation from those closest to him. This element of being shunned by family and friends was a most bitter aspect of his grief:

> *He has removed my brothers far from me,*
> *And my acquaintances are completely estranged from me.*
> *My relatives have failed,*
> *And my close friends have forgotten me.*
> *Those who dwell in my house,*
> *And my maidservants,*
> *Count me as a stranger.*
> *I am an alien in their sight.*
>
> **Job 19:13–15**

Job's experience had become, by his own description, a living picture of the **messianic suffering** so familiar in the Prophets and Psalms. There is a reason why Job speaks at length about these facets of his suffering, drawing the picture in such fine literary detail. He uses words, phrases, and images that are integral to the **messianic image** in the Old Testament [Tanakh]. Such connections are not incidental, not within the redemptive-historical unfolding of the promise of a suffering Savior, which is the very theme that binds together the written revelation of God.

What we see is a prophecy of Christ's work, joined to and illustrated by the experience of Job. When Job describes his suffering, it is in such a way that his words find their place in the unfolding promise that would finally come to rest in the sufferings of the Savior.

And so, with his lengthy complaints and poetic imagery, Job is not merely hyperbolizing his agony. He is framing it within the historically developing prophetic image of the humiliation of the Savior.

God had designed Job's experience, and the description of it, to be a part of this prophetic development.

Our Savior was to endure the wrath of God, the hatred of man, and the comfortless isolation of persecution—yet all this in perfect innocence.

Job described what he truly experienced, but he was inspired by the Holy Spirit to portray (and likely to some extent perceive) **his suffering in terms that pointed beyond himself.**

What suffering is put to such poetry? What agony and grief is so finely portrayed in chapter after chapter of evocative word pictures? It is not that poor Job just managed to keep his literary flair while losing all else. **These words carry the weight of prophecy,** with a depth and detail that gesture toward timeless significance. **Ultimately, this is an ancient reflection of what Christ would suffer for us.**

Perhaps to those around him, Job's sufferings did not immediately or distinctly bear the marks of typology, and perhaps Job himself did not fully understand this divine purpose invested in his hardships.

But now, with the blessing of the complete revelation of God before us, we can much more readily see the full purpose of Job's unique experience. We can read Job with its full redemptive-historical purpose in view **…a faint but real image of what Christ would suffer in the flesh for the sake of our redemption.**[341]

---

[341] Ibid, p. 41

My final, conclusive summary is a restatement of my own words from chapter two of this book:

> Right from the beginning the Messiah figure is introduced and progressively reappears with ever-more layers to his character until the full complement of his attributes is displayed. In the final chapters of *Job*, and especially toward the end of the whole Tanakh, we should marvel at a fully developed Messiah figure. His profile appears in the scriptural texts we have examined throughout this book, plus others such as Prophets *Isaiah* 9, 11, 42, 49, 53, and 61, *Daniel* chapter 7:9-14, and *Malachi* chapter 3:1-4 to name a few.
>
> Then, in the first century, the New Testament presents us with a man who spectacularly fits these descriptions, who claimed the messianic title, and who could support his claim with a host of enviable human qualities as well as otherworldly ones. Even if we postponed an examination of the New Testament, the Messiah of the Old Testament looms large enough. Although he was a mystery, his Motif became well-known in Hebrew culture. When one-day he would be born into the world, and 30 years later would go public, he would exhibit a full spectrum of seemingly conflicting attributes. In his voluntary death he would become the Suffering Servant and Savior to all who believed, both Jew and gentile. By his resurrection he would become the "firstfruits" of all who will have died.[342] And at his second coming he will return to execute ultimate justice and establish the kingdom of God on earth. As I first put forth in chapter 2, no disparate chain of mere human writers could have conceived of this Messiah without divine revelation and preservation of the scriptures of the Bible. And even the most gifted writers could not have inserted him so prophetically into the texts without divine oversight.

---

[342] *Book of Romans* 15:20. This is an Old Testament allusion meaning he would be the first who had died to one day rise again in the resurrection unto life.

This is the Messiah Motif, this is *the Reason of Job*.

Appendix

1. The 39 Books of the Bible's Old Testament with their traditional authors (Protestant Christian arrangement)

2. The Scriptures™ – the Jewish Arrangement of the Old Testament (Tanakh)

3. The Tanakh: Cross-reference Hebrew to English names and order with meanings

4. The 39 books of the protestant Christian canon as listed in their Jewish arrangement

5. Some of the Hebrew Prophets in the historical eras in which they prophesied

6. The Hebrew Kings and Prophets – A chronological timeline of the Hebrew kings and prophets

7. A Comparative Table of Prophets (Islamic)

8. Additional explication of the time-elapse between the reported burial and resurrection of Jesus

Appendix

Appendix 1

The main takeaway from this chart is that from left to right the conservative chronology of the books goes from oldest to youngest in terms of the historical period they cover. It also lists 20 of the 50+ prophets found in the Tanakh who wrote scripture.[343] Jews and Christians ascribe to all the same prophets.

The 39 Books of the Old Testament with their traditional authors (Protestant Christian arrangement)

A. Pentateuch / Torah	B. Historical Books	C. Wisdom Lit / Writings	D. Major Prophets	E. Minor Prophets
Genesis (Moses)*	Joshua (Joshua)	Job (Job, plus other views)	Isaiah (Isaiah)	Hosea
Exodus (Moses)	Judges (uncertain)	Psalms (David, Asaph, Moses, and others)	Jeremiah (Jeremiah)	Joel
Leviticus (Moses)	Ruth (uncertain)	Proverbs (Solomon)	Lamentations (Jeremiah)	Amos
Numbers (Moses)	1 Samuel (Samuel)	Ecclesiastes (Solomon)	Ezekiel (Ezekiel)	Obadiah
Deuteronomy (Moses)	2 Samuel (Samuel)	Song of Songs (Solomon)	Daniel (Daniel)	Jonah
*plus other views	1 Kings (Samuel)			Micah

---

[343] The exact number of prophets in the Tanakh depends on what precise criteria one uses to identify them. For example, those who are called prophets in scripture clearly qualify, such as Moses and Jonah. But some such as Noah and Joseph are never called "prophets" in the Tanakh but are considered so nevertheless by most Jews, Christians and Muslims. The latter seem to have a more generous criteria for prophets than Jews and Christians, however. In Islam almost all of the prominent figures in the Tanakh seem to be considered prophets and/or messengers. This includes Adam and Lot whom most Jews and Christians do not identify as such. See Appendix for a comparative list of prophets in Judeo-Christianity and Islam. For Muslims it is said that there were 124,000, most unknown.

Appendix

	2 Kings (uncertain)			Nahum
	1 Chronicles (Ezra)			Habakkuk
	2 Chronicles (Ezra)			Zephaniah
	Ezra (Ezra)			Haggai
	Nehemiah (Neh.)			Zechariah
	Esther (uncertain)			Malachi

In general, the five books attributed to Moses in column A are the oldest, *and* they cover the oldest time period from creation to the conquest of Canaan. One possible exception is the book of Job at the top of column C. Some scholars believe that Job is actually the oldest book in the Old Testament, but it is grouped with the wisdom literature because of its 'wisdom' genre rather than by its possible chronology. It doesn't purport to give any historical account of events at all, so it's timeless. The Jewish canon does this too in its own way.

Again, by saying that they're the 'oldest' I mean primarily that the period of history they purport to cover is the oldest epoch of history, I am not referring to the date of their composition necessarily. I realize there is controversy about their authorship and dating, but that is beside the point I am trying to make. Column B, then, is the grouping that purports to cover all the rest of Jewish history up through the last prophet, Malachi, including the Babylonian exile and after it. So all the writings in columns C, D and E fit within the timeframe of column B. If there were a special column for period of exile, Daniel and Ezekiel would go into it because they were prophets in Babylon/Persia; Esther, Haggai and Zechariah would be included in that grouping as well. Column C contains the 'writings' or "wisdom

Appendix

literature' that is also timeless in a sense because the historical timeline is not their concern. But unlike Job they still do have their places on it. The *Psalms*, as we have seen, is largely written by David in his own time, but not exclusively.

The Jewish Tanakh reflects the same historical chronology but the order and arrangement, or the groupings, of books is somewhat different than in Christian Bibles. When I say "Christian Bibles" I mean the collection of the Old and New Testaments together, the Hebrew and the Greek scriptures in their original languages. But they are both Jewish in the sense that they were all written by Jews. When I refer to the Hebrew scriptures or Jewish Tanakh I mean the Old Testament only, the collection that was written in Hebrew prior to the common era to which non-messianic Jews subscribe only.

Continue to peruse through the appendix to see several different arrangements of the Hebrew canon, i.e. the collection of books in the Tanakh. The one in Appendix 2 closely resembles the arrangement in the protestant Christian Bible but is not identical.

Appendix

Appendix 2

On the following page, this table of contents comes from a unique edition of the Bible called *The Scriptures.*[344] It is what I call an 'Hebraic' version of the whole Christian Bible. It contains the identical list of Old Testament (Tanakh) books found in protestant Bibles using their Hebrew transliterations. However, as you can see, the books are grouped together into their three Hebrew categories—Torah, Prophets, and Writings. On the next page it also contains the 27 books of the Greek New Testament, sometimes called the Christian Scriptures. Instead of using the standard English heading of 'New Testament' it calls them Kethubim Bet, or Writings (B) under the appropriate heading of **The Messianic Scriptures**. Back on the previous page note that the parallel heading is **The *Pre*-Messianic Scriptures**. I understand that to mean the scriptures before the arrival of the Messiah, which is true. But to be honest, in another important sense I don't think this is entirely accurate. ...Why?

It is indisputably true that the list of pre-messianic Hebrew writings were written entirely before the appearance of Messiah in almost everybody's view—Jews, Christians, and Muslims. However, there is a sense in which they are not really "pre-messianic" at all. Rather, Messiah appears prophetically throughout the Hebrew scriptures. He first seems to emerge rather cryptically in the third chapter of the very first book (Genesis 3:15) in which God himself speaks of him. I say "seems" because again, this example is cryptic and is disputed by traditional Jews. But it certainly refers to somebody special. He shows up more often, more clearly, and more dramatically later in the Tanakh. Jews and Christians agree on many examples, although the Jewish list is narrower.

It's true that Jews and Christians disagree about who the Messiah was and who he would be, and Jews tend to be more discriminating. But they certainly agree that he shows up in multiple passages and prominently takes the stage in Hebrew scripture.

---

[344] Institute for Scripture Research. https://isr-messianic.org/publications/the-scriptures

Appendix

BOOKS OF THE SCRIPTURES
TABLE OF CONTENTS
THE PRE-MESSIANIC SCRIPTURES

Torah – Teaching (commonly called *Law*)

Bookname (Alternate name)	Abbreviation	Page
Berĕshith (Genesis)	Ber.	1
Shemoth (Exodus)	Shem.	57
Wayyiqra (Leviticus)	Way.	104
Bemiḏbar (Numbers)	Bem.	137
Deḇarim (Deuteronomy)	Deḇ.	185

Neḇi'im – Prophets

Yehoshua (Joshua)	Yeh.	225
Shophetim (Judges, Rulers)	Shoph.	253
Shemu'ĕl Aleph (1 Samuel)	Shem. א	280
Shemu'ĕl Bĕt (2 Samuel)	Shem. ב	316
Melaḵim Aleph (1 Kings)	Mel. א	346
Melaḵim Bĕt (2 Kings)	Mel. ב	381
Yeshayahu (Isaiah)	Yesh.	414
Yirmeyahu (Jeremiah)	Yirm.	467
Yeḥezqĕl (Ezekiel)	Yeḥez.	528
Dani'ĕl (Daniel)	Dan.	583
Hoshĕa (Hosea)	Hosh.	600
Yo'ĕl (Joel)	Yo'ĕl	608
Amos	Amos	611
Oḇaḏyah (Obadiah)	Oḇaḏ.	617
Yonah (Jonah)	Yonah	618
Miḵah (Micah)	Miḵ.	620
Naḥum (Nahum)	Naḥ.	625
Ḥaḇaqquq (Habakkuk)	Ḥaḇ.	627
Tsephanyah (Zephaniah)	Tseph.	630
Ḥaggai (Haggai)	Ḥagg.	633
Zeḵaryah (Zechariah)	Zeḵ.	635
Mal'aḵi (Malachi)	Mal.	645

Kethuḇim Aleph – Writings

Tehillim (Psalms)	Teh.	648
Mishlĕ (Proverbs)	Mish.	730
Iyoḇ (Job)	Iyoḇ	759
Shir haShirim (Song of Songs)	Shir.	786

Bookname (Alternate name)	Abbreviation	Page
Ruth	Ruth	791
Ěkah (Lamentations)	Ěkah	795
Qoheleth (Ecclesiastes)	Qohel.	802
Estěr (Esther)	Est.	810
Ezra	Ezra	819
Neḥemyah (Nehemiah)	Neḥ.	830
Dibre haYamim Aleph (1 Chronicles)	Dibre א	846
Dibre haYamim Bět (2 Chronicles)	Dibre ב	878

THE MESSIANIC SCRIPTURES

Kethubim Bět – Writings

Mattithyahu (Matthew)	Mt.	919
Marqos (Mark)	Mq.	957
Luqas (Luke)	Lq.	981
Yoḥanan (John)	Yn.	1021
Ma'asei (Acts)	Ma.	1051
Romiyim (Romans)	Rom.	1090
Qorintiyim Aleph (1 Corinthians)	Qor. א	1106
Qorintiyim Bět (2 Corinthians)	Qor. ב	1121
Galatiyim (Galatians)	Gal.	1131
Eph'siyim (Ephesians)	Eph.	1137
Pilipiyim (Philippians)	Pilip.	1143
Qolasim (Colossians)	Qol.	1147
Tas'loniqim Aleph (1 Thessalonians)	Tas. א	1151
Tas'loniqim Bět (2 Thessalonians)	Tas. ב	1155
Timotiyos Aleph (1 Timothy)	Tim. א	1157
Timotiyos Bět (2 Timothy)	Tim. ב	1161
Titos (Titus)	Titos	1164
Pileymon (Philemon)	Piley.	1166
Ib'rim (Hebrews)	Ib'rim	1167
Ya'aqob (James)	Ya'aqob	1179
Kěpha Aleph (1 Peter)	Kěpha א	1183
Kěpha Bět (2 Peter)	Kěpha ב	1188
Yoḥanan Aleph (1 John)	Yn. א	1191
Yoḥanan Bět (2 John)	Yn. ב	1195
Yoḥanan Gimel (3 John)	Yn. ג	1196
Yehudah (Jude)	Yehud.	1197
Ḥazon (Revelation)	Ḥazon	1199

Appendix

Here is a Jewish list of passages from the Tanakh that purports to contain all of the messianic references that Jews accept.[345]

- *Isaiah* 2, 11, 42; 59:20
- *Jeremiah* 23, 30, 33; 48:47; 49:39
- *Ezekiel* 38:16
- *Hosea* 3:4-3:5
- *Micah* 4
- *Zephaniah* 3:9
- *Zechariah* 14:9
- *Daniel* 10:14

Another Jewish source included *Isaiah* 9:5, *Numbers* 24:17, *Daniel* 7:13, and *Zechariah* 9:7.[346] To my knowledge Christians agree with all of these. Another is *Deuteronomy* 18:15-20 that speaks of "a prophet like Moses". I don't think there is any dispute between Jews and Christians that this passage refers to the Messiah, only with Muslims who tend to believe it refers to Muhammad. But peering into the New Testament there is a clue: We can see the apparent Jewish anticipation of this Moses-like prophet when from the banks of the Jordan the people ask the prophet John the Baptizer pointedly, "Are you *the* Prophet?" (*Gospel of John* 1:21) ..."No," said he. John was *a* prophet, but not *the* prophet. Later in that chapter one of John's disciples said to another, "We have found him of whom Moses in the Law and also the prophets wrote..." (1:45)

The simple point is that I do not think the term "Pre-Messianic Scriptures" is entirely accurate since the Messiah Motif was 'living and active' throughout the Tanakh.

One last observation on this Hebraic table of contents is that its list of books conforms to the canon of the Old Testament in protestant Christian Bibles, not the Jewish Tanakh. Again, while the former contains 39 books, the latter contains only 24, and yet they both contain the same identical content. How is that possible, you ask? Because it

---

[345] www.jewfaq.org/mashiach.htm

[346] www.myjewishlearning.com/article/who-is-the-messiah/

Appendix

combines many of them. This table is interesting because it lists the Hebrew books with their Hebrew spellings and their meanings. They are grouped into their three divisions that partially conforms to the traditional Jewish canon which combines *1* and *2 Samuel, 1* and *2 Kings, 1* and *2 Chronicles, Ezra* and *Nehemiah*, and the minor prophets. But it shows only an incomplete list because it omits the *Chronicles*, the books of *Ruth, Job, Psalms, Ecclesiastes, Proverbs, Song of Solomon* (or *Song of Songs*), *Esther, Nehemiah, Ezra,* and *Daniel.*

Appendix

Appendix 3

For comparison, the table below shows most of the books of the protestant Old Testament (Tanakh), but not all, with their Hebrew names, transliterations, and meanings.

The Tanakh - Cross Reference Hebrew to English Book Names and Order

English Book	Hebrew	Transiteration	Translation
Group 1	תורה	torah	instructions
Genesis	בְּרֵאשִׁית	b're-sheet	beginning
Exodus	שְׁמוֹת	sh'mot	names
Leviticus	וַיִּקְרָא	vayikra	He called
Numbers	בְּמִדְבַּר	b'midbar	wilderness
Deuteronomy	דְּבָרִים	d'varim	words
Group 2a	נְבִיאִים	n'vi-im	prophets (earlier)
Joshua	יְהוֹשֻׁעַ	Y'hoshua	salvation
Judges	שׁוֹפְטִים	shofetim	judges
I/II Samuel	שְׁמוּאֵל	sh'muel	heard of God
I/II Kings	מְלָכִים	mal-khim	kings
Group 2b	נְבִיאִים	n'vi-im	prophets (later)
Isaiah	יְשַׁעְיָה(וּ)	y'sha'yah(u)	God has saved
Jeremiah	יִרְמְיָה(וּ)	yirmyah(u)	God will rise/be exalted
Ezekiel	יְחֶזְקֵאל	y'chez'kiel	God will strengthen
Hosea	הוֹשֵׁעַ	hoshea	deliverer
Joel	יוֹאֵל	yoel	God (is his) God
Amos	עָמוֹס	amos	burdensome
Obadiah	עֹבַדְיָה	ovad'ya	serving God
Jonah	יוֹנָה	yonah	dove, wine?
Micah	מִיכָה	michah	who is like God
Nahum	נַחוּם	nachum	sigh, to be sorry, pity, rue, repent, comfort
Habakuk	חֲבַקּוּק	chavakuk	embrace, clasp hands
Zephaniah	צְפַנְיָה	ts'fanyah	God has secreted (hidden, denied)
Haggai	חַגַּי	chagai	festive
Zachariah	זְכַרְיָה	z'char'ya	God has remembered
Malachi	מַלְאָכִי	malachi	ministrative, messenger

Appendix 4

Here all 39 books of the protestant Christian canon are listed in their Jewish arrangement. But the five books of the Torah come first, followed by by the Nevi'im, the prophets. Three of the books that

TaNaKh (תנייך)
The Hebrew Bible

Torah (תּוֹרָה) "Teaching"

Genesis (בְּרֵאשִׁית)
Exodus (שְׁמוֹת)
Leviticus (וַיִּקְרָא)
Numbers (בְּמִדְבַּר)
Deuteronomy (דְּבָרִים)

Nevi'im (נְבִיאִים) "Prophets"

The Former Prophets
Joshua (יְהוֹשֻׁעַ)
Judges (שֹׁפְטִים)
Samuel (שְׁמוּאֵל)
Kings (מְלָכִים)

The Latter Prophets
Isaiah (יְשַׁעְיָהוּ)
Jeremiah (יִרְמְיָהוּ)
Ezekiel (יְחֶזְקֵאל)

The 12 Minor Prophets
Hosea (הוֹשֵׁעַ)
Joel (יוֹאֵל)
Amos (עָמוֹס)
Obadiah (עֹבַדְיָה)
Jonah (יוֹנָה)
Micah (מִיכָה)
Nahum (נַחוּם)
Habakkuk (חֲבַקּוּק)
Zephaniah (צְפַנְיָה)
Haggai (חַגַּי)
Zechariah (זְכַרְיָה)
Malachi (מַלְאָכִי)

Ketuvim (כְּתוּבִים) "Writings"

Psalms (תְּהִלִּים)
Proverbs (מִשְׁלֵי)
Job (אִיּוֹב)
Song of Songs (שִׁיר הַשִּׁירִים)
Ruth (רוּת)
Lamentations (אֵיכָה)
Ecclesiastes (קֹהֶלֶת)
Esther (אֶסְתֵּר)
Daniel (דָּנִיֵּאל)
Ezra & Nehemiah (עֶזְרָא)
Chronicles (דִּבְרֵי הַיָּמִים)

Appendix

appear first in that category, however—*Joshua, Judges,* and *Kings*—are not generally thought of as books of 'prophets' by Christians, but rather divinely inspired scripture of the historical genre. In the book of *Joshua*, for example, Joshua himself is not considered a 'prophet' by either Jews or Christians, and there are no actual 'prophets' featured in it. But it makes perfect sense to list it right after *Deuteronomy* for reasons of chronology. At the end of *Deuteronomy* Moses dies, and Joshua was his chosen successor. Chronologically, it also makes sense to list Judges next even though it contains no prophets either, and *Samuel* after that. But Samuel *was* a prophet, as well as a priest. In fact he was the first prophet after Moses 300+ years later, and after the period of the judges (1350-1014 BC). The book of *Kings* comes next which introduces David when he was a lad, and tells the story of his divine selection as prophet-king. Together with the *Chronicles,* which is listed with the Writings, they also follow this chronology extending to around 586 BC. That's why in Christian Bibles these are all classified as historical books.

In fact, all the prophets from *Samuel* to *Jeremiah* are embedded within these narratives during this era, and their dates are fixed on its timeline. Aside from their respective writings, they each played their part on the historical plotline within its chronology. Some of them are recorded in *Samuel, Kings,* and *Chronicles,* and some are even double-recorded. But most of them, except a few such as Elijah and Elisha, still wrote their own books that take their independent places in the canon.

Now, count the books in this table. You will find that no matter how many times you count them they always come to 35. Why is that? It's because in the Hebrew/Jewish Bible, or Tanakh, the two books of *Samuel,* of *Kings,* and of *Chronicles* are all counted as one volume each, and *Ezra/Nehemiah* are counted as one volume only. So those 8 books in protestant Old Testaments are only 4 in the Hebrew Tanakh. Plus, the 12 minor prophets are counted as only one book. When you count them with this understanding you will come up with 24 every time. Also, you may note that the Jewish canon does not contain the 7 extra deutero-canonical (apocryphal) books as the

Catholic and Orthodox Bibles do. That's because the Jewish custodians of the Tanakh did not consider them to be divine revelation, or scripture. The decision to include them was made later, apparently by the Greek-speaking, or Hellenistic, Jews who translated the Tanakh into Greek around 132 BC.[347]

The main point of all this is that 1) Jewish and (protestant) Christian Bibles contain exactly the same content. As you can see, they have all the same books which are merely grouped and arranged somewhat differently. 2) Their arrangement generally follows the chronology of the actual historical timeline of the ancient millennia we now call BC, or BCE. This chronology matters a lot in the grand scope of things.

But what does all this have to do with the Messiah? Well, in one sense nothing. Since most representatives of all three religions agree that the actual Messiah did not emerge during that epoch, then it was entirely "pre-messianic." But in another sense, it has *everything* to do with him as a prophetic profile or *meta-motif* in Hebrew scripture. The multiple prophecies of the Messiah came forth as 'prophetic occurrences' by specific prophets at specific points on the historical timeline. This has implications for the possible candidates for who he could and would be, and whether anyone has ever emerged as *he*—the One who fulfilled the prophetic profile. Christians and Muslims say yes, while most Jews say no.

Appendix

Appendix 5

Some of the Hebrew Prophets in the historical eras in which they prophesied

	Kings of ...		Start of reign	Years since Solomon	Years of Reign	Prophets to ... / + OT Source		
	A.	B	C.	D.	E.	F	G.	H
	Judah	Israel				Prophets to Judah	Prophets to Israel	Biblical Source
A.	1. King David							1, 2 Samuel, 1 Kings
B.	2. King Solomon							1 Kings
C.	**Post-Davidic**	**Solomonic Era /**	**Divided**	**Kingdom**	-------	----------	----------	----------
---	Removed for	space						*See Appendix 2
M.		7. Ahab	874 BC	57	22		Elijah	1 and 2 Kings, 2 Chronicles
N.	4. Jehoshaphat		870 BC	61	25		Micaiah	1 and 2 Kings, 1, 2 Chronicles
O.		8. Ahaziah	853 BC	78	2		Elisha	1 and 2 Kings, 1, 2 Chronicles
---	Removed for	space						*See Appendix 2

Appendix

Y.	10. Uzziah (a.k.a. Azariah)		767 BC	164	52	Isaiah (unti Hezekiah)	2 Kings, 1, 2 Chronicles, **Book of Isaiah**[348]
---	**Removed for sake of space**						
KK.	16. Josiah		640 BC	291	31	Zephaniah, Jeremiah (into exile)	1 and 2 Kings, 1, 2 Chronicles, Books of **Jeremiah** and Zephaniah

Appendix

Appendix 6:

The Hebrew Kings and Prophets – A chronological timeline of the Hebrew kings and prophets starting with David and Solomon, and their scriptural sources.

	Kings of ...		Start of reign	Years since Solomon	Years of reign	Prophets to ... / + Source		
	Judah	Israel				Prophets to Judah	Prophet to Israel	Biblical Source
A.	1. King David							1, 2 Samuel, 1 Kings
B.	2. King Solomon							1 Kings
C.	Post-Davidic and	Solomonic Era /	Divided	Kingdom	--------	---------------	-----------	----------------------
D.	1. Rehoboam		931 BC	0	17			1 Kings, 2 Chronicles
E.		1. Jeroboam	931 BC	0	22		Abijah	1 Kings, 2 Chronicles
F.	2. Abijah		913 BC	18	3			1 Kings, 1, 2 Chronicles
G.	3. Asa		911 BC	20	41			1 Kings, 2 Chronicles
H.		2. Nadab	910 BC	21	2			1 Kings, 1 Chronicles
I.		3. Baasha	909 BC	22	24		Jehu	1 and 2 Kings, 2 Chronicles
J.		4. Elah	886 BC	45	2			1 and 2 Kings
K.		5. Zimri	885 BC	46	7 days			1 Kings, 1 Chronicles
L.		6. Omri	885 BC	46	12			1 and 2 Kings, 1, 2 Chronicles
M.		7. Ahab	874 BC	57	22		Elijah	1 and 2 Kings, 2 Chronicles
N.	4. Jehoshaphat		870 BC	61	25		Micaiah	1 and 2 Kings, 1, 2 Chronicles
O.		8. Ahaziah	853 BC	78	2		Elisha	1 and 2 Kings, 1, 2 Chronicles
P.		9. Joram	852 BC	79	12			2 Kings, 2 Chronicles
Q.	5. Jehoram		848 BC	83	8			1-2 Kings, 2 Chronicles
R.	6. Ahaziah		841 BC	90	1			1 and 2 Kings, 1, 2 Chronicles
S.		10. Jehu	841 BC	90	28			1 and 2 Kings, 1, 2 Chronicles
T.	7. Queen Athaliah		841 BC	90	6			2 Kings, 1, 2 Chronicles
U.	8. Joash		835 BC	96	40	Joel (guesswork)		1 and 2 Kings, 1, 2 Chronicles
V.		11. Jehoahaz	814 BC	117	17			2 Kings,

Appendix

							2 Chronicles
W.		12. Jehoash	798 BC	133	16		2 Kings
X.	9. Amaziah		796 BC	135	29	Jonah (to Nineveh, approx)	2 Kings, 1, 2 Chronicles
		13. Jeroboam II	782 BC	149	41	Amos and Hosea (until Hezekiah)	2 Kings, 2 Chronicles, Book of Amos
Y.	10. Uzziah (Azariah)		767 BC	164	52	Isaiah (until Hezekiah)	2 Kings, 1, 2 Chronicles, **Book of Isaiah**[1]
Z.		14. Zechariah	753 BC	178	6 mos.		2 Kings
AA.		15. Shallum	752 BC	179	1 mos.		2 Kings
BB.		16. Menahem	752 BC	179	10		2 Kings
CC.		17. Pekahiah	742 BC	189	2		2 Kings
DD.		18. Pekah	740 BC	191	20		2 Kings, 2 Chronicles, **Book of Isaiah**
EE.	11. Jotham		740 BC	191	16	Micah (until Hezekiah)	2 Kings, 1, 2 Chronicles, Books of Isaiah, Hosea, and Micah
FF.	12. Ahaz		732 BC	199	16	Micah	2 Kings, 1, 2 Chronicles, Books of Isaiah, Hosea, and Micah
GG.		19. Hoshea	732 BC	199	9	Micah	2 Kings
HH.	13. Hezekiah		716 BC	215	29	Micah	2 Kings, 1, 2 Chronicles, **Book of Isaiah**, Prov. 25:1
II.	14. Manasseh		687 BC	244	55		2 Kings, 1, 2 Chronicles
JJ.	15. Amon		642 BC	289	2	Nahum (to Nineveh, approx)	1 and 2 Kings, 1, 2 Chronicles, Book of Zephaniah
KK.	16. Josiah		640 BC	291	31	Zephaniah, Jeremiah (into exile)	1 and 2 Kings, 1, 2 Chronicles, Books of **Jeremiah** and Zephaniah
LL.	17. Jehoahaz		609 BC	322	3 mos.		2 Kings, 2 Chronicles
MM.	18. Jehoiakim		609 BC	322	11	Habakkuk (approx)	1 and 2 Chronicles, Books of **Jeremiah** and Daniel

---

[1] Note that Isaiah shows up in the timeline for the first time in relation to King Uzziah. His book of prophecy begins with, "…in the days of Uzziah, Jotham, Ahaz, and Hezekiah, kings of Judah." (Isaiah 1:1)

Appendix

NN.	19. Jehoiachin		597 BC	334	3 mos.			2 Kings, 2 Chronicles, Books of **Jeremiah** and **Ezekiel**
OO.	20. Zedekiah		597 BC	334	11			1 and 2 Kings, 1, 2 Chronicles, **Book of Jeremiah**
------	**End of the Kings**	--------------------	586 BC	-----------	--------	---------------	--------------	-----------------------
PP.	Babylonian Exile		592 BC	339		Ezekiel and Daniel		Books of Ezekiel and Daniel
QQ.	Uncertain		587 BC (maybe)	335		Obadiah (Edom)		Book of Obadiah
RR.	Babylonian Exile		520 BC	411		Haggai and Zechariah		Books of Haggai and Zechariah
SS.	(Esther) Persian Rule		478 BC	453				Book of Esther
TT.	(Ezra) End of Exile		458 BC	473				Book of Ezra
UU.	(Nehemiah)		445 BC	486				Book of Nehemiah
VV.	End of Exile		433 BC	498		Malachi		Book of Malachi

Appendix

Appendix 7

A Comparative Table of Prophets (Islamic)*

English Name *KJV Bible*	Hebrew Name *Jewish Bible*	Arabic Name *Holy Qur'an*
Adam	Adam	Adam
Enoch	Hanokh	Idries
Noah	Noah	Nūh
Lot	Lot	Lūt
Abraham	Abraham	Ibrahim
Ishmael	Yismael	Ismail
Isaac	Yizhaq	Ishaq
Jacob	Yaqob	Yaqūb
Joseph	Yosef	Yusuf
Job	Iyyob	Ayyūb
Ezekiel	Ezekiel	Dhul-Kifl
Moses	Mosha	Musa
Aaron	Aharōn	Harun
David	Dawid	Dawūd
Solomon	Salomoh	Sulayman
Elijah	Eliyahu	Ilyas
Elisha	Elisha	Al-Yasa
Jonah	Yona	Yunus
Zachariah	Zekeriya	Zakariyya
John "The Baptist"	Yohanan Yahya (Mandaic)	Yahya
Jesus	Yeshua Iesus (Greek)	Isa
Altogether Lovely *	Mahamad *	Muhammad
Comforter **	Paraklytos ** (Greek)	Ahmad

*This chart comes from an Islamic source. As such, not all the names in the left-hand column would be considered prophets in Judaism and Christianity (e.g. Adam, Lot, Ishmael, Isaac, Jacob, Aaron, and the last two entries). Still, it shows the Muslim perspective on these figures.

Appendix

Appendix 8
Additional explication of the time-elapse between the reported burial and resurrection of Jesus

"On What Day Was Jesus Crucified?" [349]

Jesus said in *Matthew* 12:40, "For as Jonah was three days and three nights in the belly of a huge fish, so the Son of Man will be three days and three nights in the heart of the earth." Those who argue for a Friday crucifixion say that there is still a valid way in which He could have been considered in the grave for three days. In the Jewish mind of the first century, a part of day was considered as a full day. Since Jesus was in the grave for part of Friday, all of Saturday, and part of Sunday—He could be considered to have been in the grave for three days. One of the principal arguments for Friday is found in *Mark* 15:42, which notes that Jesus was crucified "the day before the Sabbath." If that was the weekly Sabbath, i.e. Saturday, then that fact leads to a Friday crucifixion. Another argument for Friday says that verses such as *Matthew* 16:21 and *Luke* 9:22 teach that Jesus would rise on the third day; therefore, He would not need to be in the grave a full three days and nights. But while some translations use "on the third day" for these verses, not all do, and not everyone agrees that [this] is the best way to translate these verses. Furthermore, *Mark* 8:31 says that Jesus will be raised "after" three days.

The Thursday argument expands on the Friday view and argues mainly that there are too many events (some count as many as twenty) happening between Christ's burial and Sunday morning to occur from Friday evening to Sunday morning. Proponents of the Thursday view point out that this is especially a problem when the only full day between Friday and Sunday was Saturday, the Jewish Sabbath. An extra

---

[349] www.gotquestions.org/three-days.html

day or two eliminates that problem. The Thursday advocates could reason thus: suppose you haven't seen a friend since Monday evening. The next time you see him it is Thursday morning and you say, "I haven't seen you in three days" even though it had technically only been 60 hours (2.5 days). If Jesus was crucified on Thursday, this example shows how it could be considered three days.

The Wednesday opinion states that there were two Sabbaths that week. After the first one (the one that occurred on the evening of the crucifixion [*Mark* 15:42; *Luke* 23:52-54]), the women purchased spices—note that they made their purchase after the Sabbath (*Mark* 16:1). The Wednesday view holds that this "Sabbath" was the Passover (see *Leviticus* 16:29-31, 23:24-32, 39, where high holy days that are not necessarily the seventh day of the week are referred to as the Sabbath). The second Sabbath that week was the normal weekly Sabbath. Note that in *Luke* 23:56 the women who had purchased spices after the first Sabbath returned and prepared the spices, then "rested on the Sabbath." The argument states that they could not purchase the spices after the Sabbath, yet prepare those spices before the Sabbath—unless there were two Sabbaths. With the two-Sabbath view, if Christ was crucified on Thursday, then the high holy Sabbath (the Passover) would have begun Thursday at sundown and ended at Friday sundown—at the beginning of the weekly Sabbath or Saturday. Purchasing the spices after the first Sabbath (Passover) would have meant [that] they purchased them on Saturday and were breaking the Sabbath.

Therefore, according to the Wednesday viewpoint, the only explanation that does not violate the biblical account of the women and the spices and holds to a literal understanding of *Matthew* 12:40 is that Christ was crucified on Wednesday. The Sabbath that was a high holy day (Passover) occurred on Thursday, the women purchased spices (after that) on Friday and returned and prepared the spices on the same day, they rested on Saturday which was the weekly Sabbath, then brought the spices to the tomb early Sunday. Jesus was buried near sundown on Wednesday, which began Thursday in the Jewish calendar. Using a Jewish calendar, you have Thursday day (day one).

Appendix

Thursday night (night one), Friday day (day two), Friday night (night two), Saturday day (day three), Saturday night (night three). We do not know exactly what time He rose, but we do know that it was before sunrise on Sunday. He could have risen as early as just after sunset Saturday evening, which began the first day of the week to the Jews. The discovery of the empty tomb was made just at sunrise (*Mark* 16:2), before it was fully light (*John* 20:1).

A possible problem with the Wednesday view is that the disciples who walked with Jesus on the road to Emmaus did so on "the same day" of His resurrection (*Luke* 24:13). The disciples, who do not recognize Jesus, tell Him of Jesus' crucifixion (24:21) and say that "today is the third day since these things happened" (24:22). Wednesday to Sunday is four days. A possible explanation is that they may have been counting since Wednesday evening at Christ's burial, which begins the Jewish Thursday, and Thursday to Sunday could be counted as three days.

In the grand scheme of things, it is not all that important to know what day of the week Christ was crucified. If it were very important, then God's Word would have clearly communicated the day and timeframe. What is important is that He did die and that He physically, bodily rose from the dead. What is equally important is the reason He died—to take the punishment that all sinners deserve. *John* 3:16 and 3:36 both proclaim that putting your trust in Him results in eternal life! This is equally true whether He was crucified on a Wednesday, Thursday, or Friday.

Bibliography

Books

Akyol, Mustafa. 2017. *The Islamic Jesus: How the King of the Jews Became a Prophet of the Muslims. Amazon.* St. Martin's Press. https://www.amazon.com/Islamic-Jesus-Became-Prophet-Muslims-ebook/dp/B01IN98QH8.

Cahill, Thomas. 1998. *The Gifts of the Jews : How a Tribe of Desert Nomads Changed the Way Everyone Thinks and Feels.* New York: Nan A. Talese / Anchor Books.

Dunham, Kyle C. 2016. *The Pious Sage in Job: Eliphaz in the Context of Wisdom Theodicy.* Eugene, Oregon: Wipf & Stock Publishers, 2016.

Frei, Hans W. 1993. *Theology and Narrative: Selected Essays.* Edited by George Hunsinger and William Placher. Oxford University Press, 1993.

Glatzer, Nahum N. 2013. "The Book of Job and Its Interpreters." *Biblical Motifs*, edited by Alexander Altmann, Cambridge, MA and London, England: Harvard University Press, 2013, pp. 197-220.

Gregory the Great. 2014. *Moral Reflections on the Book of Job.* Collegeville, Minnesota: Liturgical Publications, 2014.

Hesselgrave, Ronald P. 2016. *I Know That My Redeemer Lives: Suffering and Redemption in the Book of Job.* Wipf and Stock Publishers, 2016.

Kassis, Hanna E. 1983. *A Concordance of the Quran.* Oakland: University of California Press, 1983.

Kapp, Jeremy. 2008. *Testament of Job (Revised English) | PDF | Book of Job | Satan.* Translated by M.R. James. *Scribd.* https://www.scribd.com/document/1251114/Testament-of-Job-Revised-English.

Lazarus-Yafeh, Hava. 1981. *Is There a Concept of Redemption in Islam. Brill.com.* https://brill.com/view/book/9789004378 605/ BP0000 05.xml.

Levering, Matthew, Piotr Roszak, and Jörgen Vijgen. 2020. *Reading Job with St. Thomas Aquinas.* Catholic University of America Press, 2020.

Bibliography

Mason, Mike. 2002. *The Gospel According to Job: An Honest Look At Pain and Doubt From the Life of One Who Lost Everything.* Wheaton, IL: Crossway Books, 2002.

McGrath, Alister. 2014. "[PDF] the Intellectual World of C. S. Lewis by Alister E. McGrath | Perlego." Www.perlego.com. 2014. https://www.perlego.com/book/1003261/the-intellectual-world-of-c-s-lewis-pdf.

Oswalt, John N. 2009. *The Bible among the Myths: Unique Revelation or Just Ancient Literature?* Zondervan Academic, 2009.

Talmon, Shemaryahu. 2013. *Literary Motifs and Patterns in the Hebrew Bible: Collected Essays.* Penn State Press, 2013.

Rahman, Fazlur. (1980) 2009. *Major Themes of the Qur'an.* 2nd Edition. Chicago, London: University of Chicago Press, 2009.

Rahman, Fazlur. (1980) 2009. "MAJOR THEMES of the QUR'ĀN." http:// www.geocities.ws/islamic_modernist/Major_Themes_of_the_Quran.pdf.

Schofield, Alison. 2008. *The Wilderness Motif in the Dead Sea Scrolls. Brill.com.* Brill. https://brill.com/view/book/edcoll/9789047432494/Bej.9789004164246.I-247_004.xml.

Wiesel, Elie. 1976. *Messengers of God: Biblical Portraits and Legends.* New York: Simon and Schuster, 1976.

Wiesel, Elie. 2002. *Conversations.* Edited by Robert Franciosi and Peggy Whitman Crenshaw. Jackson: University Press of Miss.

Williams, C.J. 2017. *The Shadow of Christ in the Book of Job.* Eugene, OR: Wipf and Stock Publishers, 2017.

Journals, Magazines, Theses

Burns, E.D. 2017. "Major Themes of the Qur'an." Review of *Major Themes of the Qur'an*, by Fazlur Rahman. 2009. *Trainingleadersinternational.org.* https://trainingleadersin ternational.org/jgc/82/major-themes-of-the-quran. February 2017.

Coleman, Steven. 2019. "Reading Jonah Backwards: Reconsidering a Prophet's Repentance." *Unio Cum Christo: International Journal of Reformed Theology and Life* 5 (1): 157–74.

Dennis, Sherry. 1978. "'SEHNSUCHT' and the ISLAND MOTIF in C.S. LEWIS' 'Out of the SILENT PLANET' and 'PERELANDRA.'" | Fau.digital.flvc.org." *Fau.digital.flvc .org.* Thesis, Florida Atlantic University Digital Library. http://fau.digital.flvc.org/islandora/object/fau%3A10739.

Bibliography

Estelle, Bryan. 2019. "Echoes of Exodus: Tracing a Biblical Motif." *Credo Magazine*, September 4, 2019. https://credomag.com/2019/09/.

Estelle, Bryan D. 2019. "Motifs and Old Testament Theology." *Unio Cum Christo: International Journal of Reformed Theology and Life* 5 (1): 27–44.

Galenieks, Erik. 2007. "Seeing God with or without the Body: Job 19:25-27." *Journal of Adventist Theological Society* 18 (1). https://digitalcommons.andrews.edu/cgi/viewcontent.cgi?article=1167&context=jats.

Gottlieb. Fred. 2019. "The Creation Theme in Genesis 1, Psalm 104 and Job 38-42." *Jewish Bible Quarterly*, March. https://jbqnew.jewishbible.org/index/books-of-the-bible/genesis/creation-theme-genesis-1-psalm-104-job-38-42/.

Hurst, L. D. 1999. "Did Qumran Expect Two Messiahs?" *Bulletin for Biblical Research* 9 (1): 157–80. https://doi.org/ 10.5325/bullbiblrese.9.1.0157.

Irwin, William A. "Job's Redeemer." *Journal of Biblical Literature* 81, no. 3 (1962): 217–29. https://doi.org/10.2307/32 64419.

Jackson, Wayne. n.d. "Job's Redeemer." Christian Courie. https://www.christiancourier.com/articles/24-jobs-redeemer.

Kaiser, Walter Jr. 2019. "The Canon of the Old Testament." *Unio Cum Christo: Journal of Reformed Theology and Life* 5 (1): 13–26.

Keulen, Emke Jelmer. 2007. "God-Talk in the Book of Job: A Biblical Theological and Systematic Theological Study into the Book of Job and Its Relevance for the Issue of Theodicy." *Research.rug.nl*. https://research.rug.nl/en/publications/god-talk-in-the-book-of-job-a-biblical-theological-and-systematic.

Parsons, Gregory. 1981. "Literary Genre: Literary Features of the Book of Job." *Bibliotheca Sacra* 138 (551): 213–39. https://faculty.gordon.edu/ hu/bi/ ted_hildebrandt/ote sources/18-job/text/articles/parsons-literaryjob-bs.pdf.

Sheriffs, Deryck. 2019. "Moving on with God: Key Motifs in Exodus 13–20." The Gospel Coalition. September 4, 2019. https://www.thegospelcoalition.org/themelios/article/moving-on-with-god-key-motifs-in-exodus-13-20/.

Talmon, Shemaryahu. 2008. Biblical Motifs, "The 'Desert Motif' in the Bible and in Qumran Literature," Harvard University Press, Cambridge 1996. *Center for Online Judaic Studies*, April. http://cojs.org/the_-desert_motif-

_in_the_bible_and_in_qumran_literature-_shemaryahu_talmon-_biblical_motifs-_harvard_university_press-_cambridge_1996/.
Young, Bruce. 2004. "Lewis on the Gospels as True Myth." *Inklings Forever* 4: Article 26. https://pillars.taylor.edu/cgi/viewcontent.cgi?article=1091&context=inklings_forever.
Nassrat, Silvy. 2015. "JOB as HIS OWN GŌʼĒL INTERPRETING JOB 19:25." *EVANGELICAL THEOLOGICAL SEMINARY in CAIRO*. https://www.academia.edu/40021 592/ JOB_AS_HIS_.
Nickel, Gordon. 2015. "The Gentle Answer to the Muslim Accusation of Biblical Falsification." PhD Thesis, Salmon Arm, BC, Canada. Bruton Gate.
Omar, Abdul Rashied. 1992. "A Mini-Thesis Submitted to the Department of Religious Studies, University of Cape Town, in Partial Fulfillment of the Requirements for the Degree Master of Arts." University of Cape Town. https://open.uct.ac.za/bitstream/ handle/11427/21780/thesis_hum_1992_omar_abdul_rashied.pdf?sequence=1.
Saleh, Walid A. 2016. "Narratives of Tampering in the Earliest Commentaries on the Qurʼān." *Al-Masāq* 28 (1): 101–4. https://doi.org/10.1080/09503110.2016.1152821.

Commentaries

Barnes. n.d. "Matthew 12:40 Commentaries: For Just as JONAH WAS THREE DAYS and THREE NIGHTS in the BELLY of the SEA MONSTER, so Will the Son of Man Be Three Days and Three Nights in the Heart of the Earth." Biblehub.com. Accessed July 6, 2022. https://biblehub.com/commentaries/matthew/12-40.htm.
Clarke, Adam. 1831. "Commentary on the Bible by Adam Clarke: Job: Job Chapter 19." Www.sacred-Texts.com. 1831. https://www.sacred-texts.com/bib/cmt/clarke/ job019.htm.
———. n.d. "Matthew 12:40 Commentaries: For Just as JONAH WAS THREE DAYS and THREE NIGHTS in the BELLY of the SEA MONSTER, so Will the Son of Man Be Three Days and Three Nights in the Heart of the Earth." Biblehub.com. https://biblehub.com/commentaries/matthew/12-40.htm.
Clarke, Barnes, Wesley. n.d. "Job 19:25 - For I Know That My Redeemer Liveth, and That He…" GodTube. Accessed June 1, 2022. https://www.godtube.com/bible/job/19-25.

Bibliography

HaChaim. n.d. "Numbers 24:17." Www.sefaria.org. https://www.sefaria.org/Numbers.24.17?lang= bi&with=Commentary&lang 2=en.

Lazarus-Yafeh, Hava. 2011. "Taḥrīf (a.)." *Encyclopaedia of Islam, 2nd Edition*. Editors P. Bearman, Th. Bianquis, C.E. Bosworth, E. van Donzel, W.P. Heinrichs. Brill Online. University Of Michigan-Ann Arbor. 09 May 2011 <http://0-www.brillonline. nl.wizard.umd.umich.edu/ subscriber/entry?entry=islam_SIM-7317>

Matthew, Henry. 1706. "Commentary on Job 19 by Matthew Henry." Blue Letter Bible. 1706. https://www.blueletterbible.org/Comm/mhc/Job/Job_019.cfm.

Poole, Matthew. n.d. "Matthew 12:40 Commentaries: For Just as JONAH WAS THREE DAYS and THREE NIGHTS in the BELLY of the SEA MONSTER, so Will the Son of Man Be Three Days and Three Nights in the Heart of the Earth." Biblehub.com. https://biblehub.com/ commentaries/matthew/12-40.htm.

Jamieson-Fausset-Brown Commentary: Job. 1871. Www.ccel.org. 1871. https://www.ccel.org/j/jfb/jfb/JFB18.htm#Chapter19.

Websites, Blogs, Videos

"Adonis." n.d. Wikipedia. https://wikipedia.org/wiki/Adonis.

Akbar, Waqar. 2016. "The Life of Muhammad: A Critique of Guillaume's English Translation." ICRAA.org. June 7, 2016. https://www.icraa.org/the-life-of-muhammad-a-critique-of-guillaumes-english-translation/.

Ala Maududi, Abul, and Ibn Kathir. "Surah Sad Ayat 44 (38:44 Quran) with Tafsir." n.d. My Islam. https://myislam.org/surah-sad-ayat-44/#:~:text=(38%3A 44)%20(and,turned%20to%20his%20 Lord).

"Alfred Guillaume." 2022. Wikipedia. April 19, 2022. https://en.wikipedia.org/wiki/Alfred_Guillaume.

"Authorship of the Epistle to the Hebrews." 2021. Wikipedia. December 30, 2021. https://wikipedia.org/wiki/Authorship_of_the_Epistle_to_the_Hebrews.

"Ayah Sad (the Letter Sad) 38:44." n.d. Www.islamawakened.com. http://www.islamawakened.com/quran/38/44/.

Bibliography

Batzig, Nicholas T. 2014. "Jonathan Edwards on David as a Type of Christ." Feeding on Christ. February 18, 2014. https:// feedingonchrist.org/jonathan-edwards-on-david-as-a-type-of-christ/.

Bell, William. 2019. "Job 19 25-27 out of My Flesh I Shall See God." All Things Fulfilled. July 6, 2019. https://www.allthingsfulfilled.com/job-19-25-27-out-of-my-flesh-i-shall-see-god/.

"Biblical Literature - Job." n.d. Encyclopedia Britannica. https://www.britannica.com/topic/biblical-literature/Job.

Ben-Dov, Jonathon. n.d. "Shemaryahu Talmon (1920–2010)." SBL – Society for Biblical Literature. https://www.sbl-site.org/publications/article.aspx?ArticleId=869.

"Biblical Motifs." n.d. TV Tropes. https://tvtropes.org/pmwiki/pmwiki.php/Main/BiblicalMotifs.

"Book of Job." n.d. Wikipedia. http://wikipedia.org/wiki/Book_of_Job.

Blumenthal, Yisroel. 2016. "My Redeemer Liveth – Job 19:25." 1000 Verses - a Project of Judaism Resources. January 13, 2016. https://judaismresources.net/2016/01/13/my-redeemer-liveth-job-1925/.

Cayce, Ken. n.d. "Job 19." Discover the Books of the Bible. https://www.bible-studys.org.

"Cinderella." 2022. Wikipedia. https://wikipedia.org/ wiki/Cinderella.

Crane, Gregory N., translation by Muhammad Marmaduke Pickthall, eds. 2019. "Qur'an - Perseus Digital Library." Tufts.edu. 2019. https:// www.perseus.tufts.edu.

Cresson, Walter. 2022. "David Proved to Be the Only True Messiah." Www.jewish-History.com. 2022. http://www.jewish-history.com/cresson/cresson05.html.

"David in Islam." 2022. Wikipedia. https://en.wikipedia.org/wiki/David_in_Islam#Narrative_in_the_Quran.

"Definition of Myth | Dictionary.com." n.d. Www.dictionary.com. https://dictionary.com/browse/myth.

Drazin, Michael. n.d. "Zechariah 9:9" the King Messiah - Source Book. Www.drazin.com. https: //www.drazin.com/indexb70b.html?9._The_King_Messiah.

"Dumuzid." n.d. Wikipedia. https://wikipedia.org/wiki/Dumuzid.

Elias, Abu Amina. 2016. "Hadith on Ayyub: Prophet Job Hates Arguments about Allah." Daily Hadith Online. February 4, 2016. https://abuaminaelias.com/dailyhadithonline/2016/02/04/ayyub-arguments-allah-dislike/.

Bibliography

"Fazlur Rahman Malik." 2022. Wikipedia. https://en.wikipedia.org/wiki/Fazlur_Rahman_Malik.

Gladwell, Mary Beth. n.d. "The Shepherd Motif in the Old and New Testament." Dwell Community Church." *Dwellcc.org* (blog). https://dwellcc.org/learning/essays/shepherd-motif-old-and-new-testament.

"The Greatest Prophets between Christianity and Islam: 9-Prophet Jacob." 2017. Islam for Christians. August 1, 2017. https://www.islamforchristians.com/greatest-prophets-christianity-islam-prophet-jacob/.

"Hadith." 2019. Wikipedia. Wikimedia Foundation. November 25, 2019. https://en.wikipedia.org/wiki/Hadith.

Hertzenberg, Stephanie. n.d. "What Is the Oldest Book in the Bible?" Www.beliefnet.com. http://beliefnet.com/faiths/christianity/what-is-the-oldest-book-in-the-bible.aspx.

"Ibn Hisham." Wikipedia. https://en.wikipedia.org/wiki/Ibn_Hisham.

"Ibn Ishaq." n.d. Wikipedia. https://en.wikipedia.org /wiki/Ibn_Ishaq.

"Ibn Kathir." n.d. Wikipedia. https://wikipedia.org/wiki/Ibn_Kathir.

"Isaiah." n.d. Wikipedia. http://wikipedia.org/wiki/ Isaiah.

"Job 19:25." n.d. Sefaria.org. https://www.sefaria.org/Job.19.26?ven= Tanakh:_The_Holy_Scriptures,_published_by_JPS.

"Job 19:26." n.d. Sefaria.org. https://www.sefaria.org/Job.19.26?ven= The_Rashi_Ketuvim_by_Rabbi_Shraga_Silverstein&vhe.

Jacobs, Louis. 2008. "Messiah." Jewish Virtual Library. https://www.jewishvirtuallibrary.org/messiah.

Ibn Kathir, Imād Ad-Din Ismāʿīl. n.d. "Stories of the Prophets." Translated by Muhammad Mustapha Geme'ah. https://islamguiden.com/ark iv/stories_of_the_prophets.pdf.

Lendering, Jona. 2001. "Messianic Motifs." Livius. https://www.livius.org/articles/religion/ messiah/messiah-8-other-titles/.

"Letter to the Hebrews | Summary, Authorship, & Facts | Britannica." n.d. Www.britannica.com. https://britannica.com/topic/Letter-to-the-Hebrews.

Link, Norbert. n.d. "How Are We to Understand Exodus 6:2-3? Church of the Eternal God." Www.eternalgod.org. https://www.eternal god.org/q-a-13026/.

"Meta." 2022. Wikipedia. June 23, 2022. https://wikipedia.org/wiki/Meta.

Bibliography

Malick, David. 2004. "An Introduction to the Book of Job | Bible.org." Bible.org. June 14, 2004. http://bible.org/article/introduction-book-job.

Mikhail, Labib. n.d. "The Spirit of Islam - Quran's Mistakes or Errors." The Spirit of Islam. https://www.thespiritofislam .com/bible-quran/15-quran-mistakes-or-errors.html.

McCracken, Randy. 2014. "Biblical Narrative: How Motifs Enrich a Story." Bible Study with Randy. September 30, 2014. https://www.biblestudywith randy.com/2014/09/biblical-narrative-use-motifs/.

Machen, Gresham. 2017. "The Divinity of the Messiah." Westminster Theological Seminary. March 7, 2017. https://faculty.wts.edu/posts/the-divinity-of-the-messiah/.

Miller, John Mark. 2014. "Job's Positive Message: The Creation Motif That Changes Everything." *The Artistic Christian* (blog). February 18, 2014. https://theartisticchristian.wordpress.com/2014/02/18/jobs-positive-message-the-creation-motif-that-changes-everything/.

"Myth | Definition, History, Examples, & Facts | Britannica." n.d. Www.britannica.com. https://britannica.com/topic/myth.

"One Thousand and One Nights." n.d. Wikipedia. https://wikipedia.org/wiki/One_Thousand_and_One_Nights.

Ostrow, Joann. 2014. "The Denver Post." The Denver Post. November 26, 2014. https://www.denverpost.com/2014/11/26/russell-brand-messiah-complex-a-crazy-brilliant-comedy-special/.

"Phoenix (Mythology)." n.d. Wikipedia. https://wikipedia.org/wiki/Phoenix_(mythology).

Ragnar. 2019. "Where Does 'Messiah' Come From?" Shalom from G-d - English. June 3, 2019. https://en.shalomfromg-d.net/2019/06/03/where-does-messiah-come-from.

Religion Wiki. n.d. "Tahrif." https://religion.fandom.com/wiki/Tahrif#cite_note-3.

Rich, Tracey R. 2011. "Judaism 101: Mashiach: The Messiah." Jewfaq.org. 2011. http://www.jewfaq.org/mashiach.htm.

"Shemaryahu Talmon." 2022. Wikipedia. February 6, 2022. https://en.wikipedia.org/wiki/Shemaryahu_Talmon.

Singer, Tovia. 2014. "Why Doesn't Judaism Have a King?" Where Is Our Messiah? | Outreach Judaism. April 28, 2014. https://outreachjudaism.org/why-doesnt-judaism-have-a-king/.

Bibliography

Smick, E.B. 1988. "(Job 19:25-26) Does This Passage Refer to the Concept of Resurrection?" Evidence Unseen. 1988. https://www.evidenceunseen.com/bible-difficulties-2/ot-difficulties/ezra-job/job-1925-26-does-this-passage-refer-to-the-concept-of-resurrection/.

"SparkNotes: Bible: The Old Testament: Job, Page 2." 2019. Sparknotes.com. 2019. https://www.sparknotes.com/lit/oldtestament/section11/page/2/.

Stacey, Aisha. 2009. "The Story of Prophet Job." IslamReligion.com. September 7, 2009. https://www.islamreligion.com/articles/2721/story-of-prophet-job/.

Sumner, Paul. n.d. "David, First Messiah." Hebrew-Streams. http://www.hebrew-streams.org/works/hebrew/david-mashiach.html.

"Sayings and Teachings of Prophet Muhammad (صلى الله عليه و سلم) – Sunnah - Job." n.d. https://sunnah.com/search?q=job.

"Surah As-Saffat 37:75-113 - towards Understanding the Quran - Quran Translation Commentary - Tafheem Ul Quran." n.d. Www.islamicstudies.info. https://www.islamicstudies.info/tafheem.php?sura=37&verse=99&to=113.

"Surat Yusuf [12:89-101] - the Noble Qur'an - القرآن الكريم." n.d. Legacy.quran.com. https://legacy.quran.com/12/89-101.

"Story of Ya'qub (Jacob), the - SunnahOnline.com." n.d. Sunnahonline.com. https://sunnahonline.com/library/stories-of-the-prophets/296-story-of-prophet-yaqub.

Telushkin, Joseph. 1991. "The Messiah." Jewish Virtual Library.org. 1991. https://www.jewishvirtuallibrary.org/the-messiah.

"The Scriptures." 2009. Institute for Scripture Research. 2009. https://isr-messianic.org/publications/the-scriptures.html.

Travers, Michael. 2008. "Literary Motifs." Bible.org. February 26, 2008. https://bible.org/seriespage/2-literary-motifs.

Walker, Kristi. 2019. "Who Was Job in the Bible?" Christianity.com. August 19, 2019. https://www.christianity.com/wiki/people/who-was-job-in-the-bible.html.

"What Are All the Myths and Stories Related to Phoenix?" n.d. Quora. https://quora.com/What-are-all-the-myths-and-stories-related-to-Phoenix.

"What Day Was Jesus Crucified?" n.d. GotQuestions.org. https://www.gotquestions.org/three-days.html.

Bibliography

Wiesel, Elie. 2015. "The Book of Job | 92nd Street Y Elie Wiesel Archive." Video. *92NY Plus*. https://www.youtube.com/watch?v=A2FMIc5HgjA.

Witherington, Ben. 2016. "Messiah/Christ." Apologetics. March 30, 2016. https://www.namb.net/apologetics-blog/messiah-christ/.

www.ingramcontent.com/pod-product-compliance
Lightning Source LLC
Chambersburg PA
CBHW050615300426
44112CB00012B/1511